MY FAMILY AND OTHER SAINTS

MY FAMILY AND OTHER SAINTS

KIRIN NARAYAN

The University of Chicago Press   ::   Chicago & London

Kirin Narayan is the author of *Storytellers, Saints, and Scoundrels*; *Mondays on the Dark Night of the Moon*; and the novel *Love, Stars, and All That*. A former Guggenheim fellow, she is professor of anthropology at the University of Wisconsin–Madison.

The University of Chicago Press, Chicago 60637
The University of Chicago Press, Ltd., London
© 2007 by Kirin Narayan
All rights reserved. Published 2007
Printed in the United States of America

16 15 14 13 12 11 10 09 08 07   1 2 3 4 5

ISBN-13: 978-0-226-56820-1   (cloth)
ISBN-10: 0-226-56820-2   (cloth)

Library of Congress Cataloging-in-Publication Data

Narayan, Kirin
　　My family and other saints / Kirin Narayan.
　　　　p.   cm.
　　ISBN-13: 978-0-226-56820-1 (cloth : alk. paper)
　　ISBN-10: 0-226-56820-2 (cloth : alk. paper)
　　1. Narayan, Kirin. 2. Women anthropologists—India—Bombay—Biography.
　3. Anthropology of religion—India—Bombay. 4. Family—India—Bombay.
　5. Hinduism and culture—India—Bombay. 6. Bombay (India)—Religious life and customs. 7. Bombay (India)—Social life and customs. I. Title.
　　GN21.N37A3   2007
　　306.850954'792092—dc22

　　　　　　　　　　　　　　　　　　　　　　　　　　2007022669

All photographs courtesy of the Contractor / Narayan family.

♾ The paper used in this publication meets the minimum requirements of the American National Standard for Information Sciences—Permanence of Paper for Printed Library Materials, ANSI Z39.48-1992.

With affection and gratitude
to my family, honorary family, and many dear friends
who helped make and remake these memories

Contents

The Hook

In 1969, when my big brother Rahoul was fifteen, he decided to drop out of school and go live with a guru. Our American mother Maw seemed to think that getting enlightened was a terrific plan. Paw, our Indian father, was less sure. Our relatives on Paw's side were baffled, but made sense of Rahoul's departure from home partly through the lenses of Hindu stories.

With his curly black hair and restless eyes, Rahoul had always experimented with turning limits into frontiers. He established my family's connection to gurus and ashrams just before a big wave of Western seekers curled, then splashed over India. As the 1960s gave way to the 1970s our beachside home in Bombay was flooded with young people from the United States, Europe, and Australia, and we rarely sat down to a meal alone. Paw called our guests "urugs"— which he pronounced *oo-roog*. This was a word of his own invention: guru spelled in mirror writing. At the reflecting edge between cultures, a guru's teaching ended and an urug's discipleship began.

"The urugs are coming, ah-ha, ah-ha," Paw chanted as more India-entranced Westerners set down their backpacks or orange satchels on our living room floor. I never knew if this chant was inspired by *The Russians Are Coming,* which showed in movie theaters downtown, or if he was spoofing an American song about an inmate in an insane asylum that he heard while switching channels on his shortwave radio.

The urugs were borne in by stronger currents than the Western beatniks, Peace Corps volunteers, students of Hindustani music, and hippies who had enjoyed our hospitality in the past. Maw had always loved the excitement of new people carrying fresh stories, and she exuberantly welcomed all these guests. She too found a guru, and called our visitors "seekers," "devotees," and "ashramites." I sometimes wondered if Paw invented the word "urug" partly to mock her.

Was Rahoul an urug too? He had never been to America, but as Muw's half-American teenage son he certainly identified with tuning in and dropping out; he grew his hair into a curly halo like Bob Dylan's and read the books by Aldous Huxley, Basho, Carl Jung, and others that crowded the built-in shelves through our house. At the same time Rahoul was also a son in Paw's Gujarati family, which claimed descent from Vishwakarma, the Divine Architect, and had produced a miracle-performing saint in recent memory. It seemed to me that Rahoul was inoculated against becoming an urug since his own quest wasn't across cultural difference. Gods, goddesses, and gurus had been part of the backdrop of our lives even before we began to pay close attention.

As a family, we were often gnawed by anxiety, a creeping unease that could jump up and send us chasing—helplessly, hopelessly—in inner circles. I recognized this presence slinking at the edge of our lives: in my father's vacant, melancholy stare even when he didn't smell fermented; in the rising tones and sweat pouring off my mother even when it wasn't summer. We all struggled to keep the shadow at bay, finding ways to lighten and brighten the world. We used words in funny combinations and delighted in the personalities of our pets. We walked on the beach soaking in the calm immensity of sea and sky. Together and alone, we lost ourselves in books, music, and art that melted fixed horizons. Paw went diving into the glinting amber of alcohol and sometimes emerged an unrecognizable person. Maw surrounded herself with distracting company and the swapping of stories. Then Rahoul brought the family both the silence of meditation and the cadences of Sanskrit chants as new techniques to tame what we learned to label "the monkey-mind." What we didn't yet know was how much we would need these taming tools to help us through life's harsh blows, like the sorrow of losing Rahoul too early.

I was a small and often bewildered observer when Rahoul started this new chapter in our family's search for ways to cope with the anxieties of being alive. I wanted our home to be "normal" and complained to Maw about our strange guests. When, as a ten-year-old, I first read My Family and Other Animals by Gerald Durrell, I was amazed to learn that books could feature eccentric families living at the crossroads of cultures and hosting lots of guests. Later on, when my family's spiritual aspirations and connections

Soda the cat communes with Kirin, 1968. Photograph by Didi Contractor.

seemed particularly embarrassing to me, I brandished my own spin-off title: "When I grow up," I fiercely warned my mother, "I'm going to write a book called *My Family and Other Saints* and put you in it."

In those days, I plotted to portray my family with the slapstick strokes that Gerald Durrell excelled at; casting us as essentially comic made the instability around me more bearable. But by the time I actually got around to writing this book, I had changed. I am now older than Maw, Paw, or any of my siblings were at the time that this story begins, and I see everyone's dilemmas from a different perspective. Revisiting the past, I've consulted inner images and echoes of conversations; also, I've looked at old writings, for even as a little girl I was in training as the self-appointed family ethnographer and folklorist. Still unsure when just being me, the perennially bratty youngest, might embarrass my living siblings, I mute their presence to focus more on Rahoul. Maw diagnoses my portrayal of everyone as a "'send-up' from a child's point of view." "Maybe you should make it even clearer," she diplomatically suggests in a recent e-mail, "that you are writing what *you as a child* remember?"

By now, I've had the chance to reflect for several decades on how my brother's quest changed everyone in the family, including me. The rhythms of our family life, the books we were reading, the people we knew—all took new directions. That even now I give some time each day to acknowledging an inner brightness derives directly from Rahoul, the unforgettably radiant, amused people he introduced us to, and the energetic Mother Goddesses who accompanied them.

In my outer life I also find echoes of the era of gurus and urugs. The 1960s and 1970s have passed, but words like "guru," "karma," and "yoga" have slid into the currency of global English. Meditation has gone mainstream as stress management. Living in Madison, Wisconsin, I buy various kinds of "Yogi Tea" with cosmic sayings on the tea bag ends. I attend a yoga class where my Belgian teacher sometimes plays recordings of Sanskrit chants pronounced by a new generation of urugs. Picking up the phone and encountering workers at Indian call centers who identify themselves as "Nancy" or "Brian," I recall the young Westerners who once passed through our home as "Bhagavan Das," "Saraswati," or even "Ramdas Cloud-over-Mountain."

Visiting India too, I see imprints of that earlier time. The press continues to discuss "Godmen," whose organizations now often span multiple countries, and the travelers from other lands, come in search of Hindu spirituality, now include partial insiders—the diasporic Indians. Occasionally Maw still receives letters addressing her as a holy mother, "Ma Dayananda." The Sixteenth Karmapa, a stately Tibetan teacher who brought a retinue of maroon-wearing lamas to breakfast at our house in 1973, has been reborn as the Seventeenth Karmapa, a handsome young man living in a monastery near Maw's home. ("We're old friends, I knew him in his last incarnation," she insisted by phone when trying to arrange a private audience, greatly amusing Ken, my New Jersey–born husband.)

For families like ours, shaped by migrations across regions and continents, stories are wonderfully portable, carrying weighty histories, places, and people with no excess luggage fees. I sometimes think of such stories as collections of beads. Key family stories are so highly polished through multiple retellings that handling them, we glimpse our own reflections in their facets. Joining the primordial images of early childhood memories, family stories are touchstones that reappear throughout our lives: not just in the performance of retellings, but also in half-glimpsed associations, motivations, anxieties, and dreams. Called on to make sense of ourselves in the world, we sort through these story-beads, choosing, restringing, emphasizing certain ancestors and episodes over others. Retelling these stories, we reshape them too. Though I try to precisely evoke the voices of other family storytellers, my writing inevitably recasts the tales: highlighting some angles, smoothing others.

I've strung this set of stories from the first stirrings of my brother Rahoul's restless urge to leave our family home; that thread runs through the incidents that follow, for the immediate or distant presence of different gurus shaped our precarious family life even when Rahoul wasn't around. The challenge for me has been to add story-beads both through the forward motion of action and the backward loop of explanation. I bring in family stories to understand why Rahoul's birth had been so important for my parents' marriage; cross-generational expectations for sons, and particularly eldest sons; our family precedents in piety; our artisan caste tales, rooted in mythology. Gripping the thread of spiritual quests that led us, an Indian-American family in India, to follow Rahoul toward new adventures and insights, I hold back—for now—from other stories that might be strung around the theme of artistic questing in Maw's German and American ancestry.

"So, why are you calling this a *me-moir*?" Ken asks when I sit him down to read pages, still warm from the printer, in which my version of events often mixes with the voices of others in my family: "It's a *we-moir*." Like me, Ken is a cultural anthropologist and folklorist, familiar with theories of how shared stories shape self-understanding and social life. I laughed when Ken first coined the term *we-moir* for shared stories and laugh again at its playful audacity each time I use it. There really is a "me" here—both the skinny, searching little girl in Bombay who made it through the difficult times narrated in this book, and the grown-up who contains and narrates her. But I don't mean this book to be just about me; I'm trying to portray my immediate, extended, and honorary family living at the crossroads between India and America through a time when spirituality directed a fair amount of traffic. This is why I move beyond "me," threading beads of family stories in my attempt to encircle our "we."

Gods' Eyes

Even before he left home at fifteen to become enlightened, my brother Rahoul had been making sculptures with gods' eyes. He bought eyes in many sizes from the Gods' Eye Shop in the Bhuleshwar temple bazaar of central Bombay. Back from the sweaty trip to town, he stood in the breezy living room of our seaside home, unfolded packets of searing pink tissue paper, and spilled eyes onto his palm. I raised my chin for a better look. Pitch-black irises gazed up blankly from moist-looking whites, a hint of lifelike pink staining each corner.

"All the better to see you with . . ." chanted Rahoul he turned the eyes on me.

"Don't!" I objected, pulling back fast.

The largest eyes spanned Rahoul's palm; he looked down, considering, and the eyes considered him back. The tiniest eyes clustered like shiny seeds in the hollow of his hand. Usually, such unblinking eyes looked out from gods and goddesses in temples or in household *pujas*. Eyes staring from the creases of my brother's palm were too weird for me. I was intrigued and also scared.

Rahoul didn't intend these eyes for actual gods, but for the Rahoul-beings he made from odds and ends he found washed up on the beach. He gathered scrap wood, shells, bones, and rusty tin cans. He glued, hammered, or welded combinations of these materials to create his beings, and then he gave them character with gods'

« Rahoul-being. Photograph by Stella Snead.

eyes. One Rahoul-being was just a cross-eyed, puzzled face with eyes of different sizes on either side of the nose-knob of a sea-bleached animal bone. Another was a huge wood head ending in a hook, big eyes looking with surprise down its long nose, joined by a small armless torso to giant feet. Yet another, made of tin, had oversize eyes glaring with fierce dignity from between fanning metal ears, arms extended as though in blessing. A female Rahoul-being contemplated the world sweetly, her eyes tilted downward at the edges of her flattened condensed-milk-can face, her hands clasped over the long lilac gown of another, painted can. Of all these beings, she appealed to me the most, but all the same I protected my own dolls from seeing her.

Rahoul was my big brother, with a six-year head start on life. Even when he baffled me, I usually assumed I would someday grow into understanding his actions. The gods' eyes watching from multiple angles in our home reminded me how, since I was the tiniest child, I had yearned for a connection to forces hidden within the visible world. I had examined the frames of mirrors looking for a way through; watched my dolls' mouths in hopes of conversation; checked on the progress of a fairy chrysalis stuck to the underside of a cane chair before someone else, seeing it as a glob of red Kissan jam, wiped it away. I loved reading partly for the ways that it made the realities around me crumble and grow indistinct; I loved holding a pencil close to the point to write my way into story-worlds. I vaguely understood that Rahoul was reaching for something I couldn't yet see. Though I frankly preferred art with symmetry, happy colors, and straw-haired heroines, my brothers had all teased me so much for liking *The Sound of Music* that I now hid my opinions. I listened in and watched everyone else's reactions to the Rahoul-beings without saying anything myself.

Maw, our mother, was thrilled by the Rahoul-beings. She borrowed one for a Bombay party scene in a Merchant-Ivory film, *The Guru*, for which she was arranging sets. Our father, Paw, raised his eyebrows, twisted one corner of his mouth, and went back to his room. Our grandmother Ba, who periodically enjoyed personal meetings with gods and goddesses, was at first startled when she came to visit and saw gods' eyes on a Rahoul-being, but because her adored eldest grandson was responsible, she just laughed. Various guests streaming through our house studied the sculptures, exclaiming over Rahoul's genius. Even our next-door neighbor, the British surrealist painter-turned-photographer Stella Snead, came across the driveway to take a look.

"They're rathuh *good*, aren't they?" Stella airily pronounced, snorting down her nose with a laugh.

"Remember when he was nine and writing haiku?" Maw asked.

"Don't, Maw," said Rahoul.

Stella went back to get her camera and snapped portraits of each being. A few weeks later, I came home from school and found her prints lying out on our living room table. I leafed through them, awed that my teenage brother had inspired a grown-up's art, especially a grown-up as grand and formidable as Stella. In addition to the series of portraits, Stella had made a black-and-white collage. The Rahoul-beings gathered in a mountainous landscape around a lake, where they all peered, puzzled, over reflections that didn't quite match.

Later, I wondered: had handling all those gods' eyes inspired Rahoul to leave home?

: : :

Eyes were, for us, a source of family groupings. For years, grown-up visitors had observed that our Indian-American looks fell into two matched brother-sister pairs. Our sister Maya, the oldest, and brother Deven, the third child, were supposed to look alike because of their hazel "Western" eyes; second-born Rahoul and I, the youngest, were similar because of our darker "Indian" eyes. (Tashi, our adopted brother, who was around Deven's age, had always looked Tibetan.)

As a teenager, Rahoul's eyes were still deep-set and intent, fixing on an object as if he could see into it and through it at the same time. Otherwise, he had become unfamiliar, as though viewed in a mirror that stretched and warped his features. He had grown tall, with an oversize head, narrow hunching shoulders, bony elbows, erupting skin, and a nose that the rest of his face had yet to catch up with.

Sometimes, Rahoul brought up our old pairing to torment me.

"Just a few more years and your nose will be just like mine," he said one afternoon when I appeared by his side to watch him make art. He sat at his desk in the room that had been Maya's before she left for college. With a Rahoul-being looking on, he experimented with drawing while never lifting his pen from the paper. He bent forward, left elbow jutting awkwardly above his hand, as he outlined figures jumbling, tumbling, and overlapping in big, heaped patterns.

"Never!" I objected. I could never be sure when anyone in the family was making things up to tease me, the gullible youngest. Still, looking at the shiny end of his nose, my hand crept to my face.

"And then your nose will grow even longer. Why do you think we used to call you Baby Elephant?"

I had thought this affectionate title came from a recognition of my special relationship to the royal family of Babar. "That's not true!" I said.

"You'll also grow curly hair all over your legs," Rahoul went on in a matter-of-fact voice. He stuck out a leg, bare below the knee. "Look how hairy my legs are?"

"Don't!"

"Anyway, you don't have to worry that no one will marry you, because your horoscope says you'll have seven husbands."

"It does not!"

"And you know what? You'll always be my beautiful baby sister."

I was not used to being described as pretty, let alone beautiful. Our American grandmother, Nani, had worried aloud that I looked like my Indian grandfather. Maw always said that my big sister Maya was the beauty, while I was sharp. But there was a big step between having stern or sharp features and becoming a freak! Would I really grow up into some sort of Rahoul-being with an elephant trunk and poodlelike leg hair, surrounded by seven equally weird husbands?

"Don't tease me!" I ordered.

But Rahoul was smiling so brightly that I couldn't help smiling too.

Rahoul had reminded me so often of the skills I had learned from him that I could list them inside my own head.

"Hey Baby, I taught you to walk!" he said, and I remembered a faraway time when I had faced him, my hands raised to his, resting my small feet on top of his bigger ones as he walked backward taking me forward, or forward so that I walked backward.

"I taught you to fly!" he said, reminding me how he and Maya had hauled me up by my then-chubby hands to speed along the beach, their feet leaving tracks in the sand but not mine.

"I taught you mirror writing!" he claimed. I immediately pictured Maw's low dressing room table and Rahoul holding up an EMIT / TIME magazine soon after I'd learned to read. *"All spies can read in mirrors,"* Rahoul had instructed. *"You have to learn how to watch so people never know it."*

I carefully watched my family and everyone coming and going through the house, never entirely sure who I was spying for.

Juhu houses, 1959. On the left is Nani's house, on the right, Stella's.
Photograph by Stella Snead.

: : :

We lived beside Juhu Beach, in the northern suburbs of Bombay, inside a long, fenced stretch of coconut grove that contained three houses: my parents' house, our American grandmother Nani's house, and Stella's house. The land had been leased to us with the understanding that once or twice a year a swarm of bare-chested, bare-legged men would fling their arms and legs around the trees and climb straight up to harvest smooth green coconuts. Maw had designed the low, whitewashed houses to accommodate the trees. Set into our porches were squares of earth from which coconut trunks rose up, through the roof.

Paw remembered childhood outings by ferry to Juhu's stretches of beach. But by 1959, when our houses were built, Juhu was connected to downtown Bombay by roads and bridges, and Paw could drive to his architecture and engineering office in the old Fort area almost two hours away. Through the 1960s, Juhu remained partly a fishing village; in the mornings fishermen still brought in their boats laden with flopping silvery nets. Juhu was already becoming famous for people associated with the Hindi film industry. Between our house and the beach stretched a grand mansion rented by the film star Meena Kumari, and saying "behind Meena Kumari" made it easy to direct a taxi from town. On the other side of Stella's house was the home of a screenwriter named Abrar Alvi; down the road, Kaifi Azmi wrote Urdu poems that were adapted as film songs, and his daughter Shabana would one day be a movie star. Beyond them the actor Prithviraj Kapoor, who we knew as Papaji, had his weekend home and theater.

Paw loved playing with language, and the names he tossed could stick. When he and Maw were poor students with a baby living in a trailer under the Flatiron mountains in Boulder, Colorado, he had called for her, in a hill-billy twang, "Hey Ma-a-aw!"—to which she answered, "Hey Paw!" My big sister Maya picked up these titles and passed them on to the rest of us, born later in India. As the child born last, into family traditions that were already set, I found that having a "Maw" and a "Paw" was awkward to explain when everyone else's parents were Mummy and Daddy, Mama and Papa, Ma and Baba, or Ammi and Abba. The only other Maw and Paw I'd heard of were in Bob Dylan's song about Maggie's farm, and they didn't seem like the sort of people who lived in Juhu.

Maw often told the story of how I was born because of their move to Bombay from Nasik, where she and Paw had lived with his family for eight years. Her mother, Alice Fish Kinzinger, whom we called Nani, had retired from her job teaching art in Taos, New Mexico and decided to move to Bombay too. She arrived with seventeen steamer trunks and a request: "I haven't had a chance to enjoy any of the grandchildren. Have another for me." One of those trunks was filled with clothes for a baby girl; Maw said I was lucky to fit the plan.

By the time I was born, Maw had grown bored with the company of small children and, as she said, the endless repetition of instructions like "No, the other foot." She had just turned thirty-one and was keen to pur-sue her own interests. She had never finished college in America, but she painted canvases and designed everything from buildings to furniture to fabrics. When His Highness of Udaipur came to consult Paw about struc-tural engineering for transforming his ancestral Lake Palace into a tourist hotel, Maw persuaded the suave king to employ her as decorator and to do the place up in a traditional Rajasthani aesthetic. Throughout the early 1960s, she often traveled to Udaipur for long stretches, leaving me in Nani's care.

Nani was my doting, almost constant companion. I had lived with her across the driveway from the main house. She taught me to read and write when I was barely three: first printing, and later the looped script of her childhood schoolhouse in Grand Rapids, Michigan. As I grew bigger, she

Maw, Paw, and kids, 1962. Standing: Maya. Seated, from left: Deven,
Paw, Kirin, Tashi, Maw, Rahoul. Photographer unknown.

sewed not just my clothes but also tiny matching outfits for my dolls. But by 1967, Nani could no longer stand the heat, the bugs, the chaos that encircled her daughter's life. She moved back to New Mexico, taking Maya to college.

With Nani gone, my existence had lost substance. Without her constant protection, something scary happened to me that I didn't have words for, only fears that would tighten into a banging heart and stinging throat. I ran mysterious fevers and was absent from school so often that when classmates assembled a crossword using our names, the entry for which mine was the clue (six letters, ending in Y) was not "brainy" (as I had hoped) or even "skinny" (as I'd feared) but "sickly." Sickly! I cringed at the shaky

Weekend party, Juhu, mid-1960s. Photographer unknown.

weakness of that word. I often looked away from the thin girl who watched me in the dressing room mirror, her dark eyes rimmed with dark circles. Observing other people was easier than looking too hard into myself. That was one reason I hovered around Rahoul and the many visitors who came through our house.

Since we lived by the beach and near the airport, our home was a perfect place for city friends wanting to escape to the seaside and cosmopolitan travelers moving between destinations. On weekends, parties swelled out of the divans in the living room into butterfly chairs or cane *modas* under the pipal tree in the garden. There newspaper editors, musicians, physicists, documentary filmmakers, and other Indians from downtown Bombay mixed easily with the Westerners associated with universities, news agencies, consulates, and the Peace Corps. Stories swirled around us in multiple languages and accents.

I'd learned early that if grown-ups thought a child was occupied, they would talk as freely as if she wasn't there. So as grown-ups swapped accounts of events experienced, observed, and imagined, I kept myself busy. I hopped between squares of pale gray stone on the living room floor or knelt over tiny flowers growing in the grass. I stroked the vibrating under-sides of cats' chins, turned pages of books, colored in gowns of princesses, folded origami. My eyes were studiously lowered, but my ears fanned out like a baby elephant's.

Maw especially loved talking about wildly unconventional, creative, and surprising people, which is probably why she told more stories about Rahoul than about the rest of us. She enjoyed remembering how in 1963, Rahoul had come in from a walk calling, *"Hey Maw! Guess what I found on the beach!"*

Maw looked up expecting shells or driftwood or maybe even a stray puppy. Instead, she saw two shaggy British beatniks with backpacks. Rahoul gestured backward. "They are poets!" he said. At that point, he was a poet too, writing haiku. To them, he grandly offered, "You can pitch your tent in our garden."

These poet-beatniks, it turned out, were precursors of the hippies, and again, Rahoul was partly responsible for bringing them to us.

:::

In 1968, Maw's friend Marilyn Silverstone received an assignment from a French magazine to cover the hippies finding their way to India. Marilyn was an American photographer for the Magnum agency, and in 1960 she had done a photo essay about Maw called "East-West Wife" for *Coronet* magazine. Marilyn usually lived in Delhi, but she thought that Maw could help her locate hippies. So she traveled to Bombay, bringing along a British hippie to serve as a decoy. Maw was off in Udaipur for the week, and Paw was away in Nasik. Nani and Maya—who usually stood in as parents—had left for America. So it was Rahoul who received Marilyn and the hippie called Broderick.

Broderick must have been in his early twenties, and to me he looked like a glamorous version of George Harrison, my favorite Beatle, crossed with Jesus Christ: dark brown locks parted in the middle, well-fitting white cotton *kurta* and pajama, and an extra-long wooden *mala* that hung beyond his waist. Sitting on the beach watching sunsets with Rahoul, Broderick shared stories about his spiritual adventures with gurus in Rishikesh, far to the north, where the Beatles had recently visited the Maharishi. I squatted nearby building a drip sand castle with a moat, the wind blowing strands of their words from my grasp.

Broderick and Rahoul reasoned that if the beautiful people and freaks in America crowded around Ravi Shankar, hippies in Bombay would be drawn

Broderick and Rahoul on the beach, Juhu, 1968.
Photograph by Didi Contractor.

to a free Hindustani music concert. Rahoul phoned up our family friend, the musician Pandit Ram Narayan, who agreed to play his bowed *sarangi* in our garden. (Though he shared part of Paw's name and often visited us, Ram Narayan was not a blood relative but a ritual *"rakhi* brother" of Maw's.) With the date set, Marilyn and Broderick went downtown to the area around the Salvation Army and American Express, spreading the word of a Happening among any hippies they could find.

Maw was back by the afternoon that hippies began streaming in from the driveway and the back gate. I put down *Gulliver's Travels* and came out to observe. Pandit Ram Narayan's bow drew out shimmering palaces of emotion among the pipal branches, the coconut palms, the white clouds drifting high above. The hippies wore amazing getups: tie-dye, velvet, and crocheted outfits, with bits and pieces of Indian clothes. They sat on cushions and mats spread out over our lawn, rolling their heads to the music and passing around joints. Marilyn wandered among them, focusing her lenses.

Rahoul looked on. When the concert was over, servants brought out a big buffet supper. A few hippies asked if they might "crash" for the night—the mats and cushions were spread out, after all—and, still flushed with excitement, Maw agreed.

This was the moment our home became a Groovy Pad. From the Happening onward, young foreigners with lots of untidy hair began appearing at our open doors, asking for Maw on their migrations between Kathmandu and Goa. They camped out on our porch or in the living room for a few nights, a few weeks, sometimes a few months. We hosted American draft dodgers, German stained-glass makers, French women who had traveled overland. Sometimes people showed up who couldn't even remember who had sent them. One couple had been robbed and assaulted in their Volkswagen bus but had been left with a piece of paper bearing Maw's name and address; they camped in our backyard, becoming honorary family, and Maw helped them find jobs—teaching art at our school and serving as Hindi movie extras—until they were able to travel onward.

"My address is passed all along the hash trail," Maw observed with satisfaction.

: : :

But it wasn't just the gods' eyes and the hippies that lured Rahoul to leave home. I later realized that Rehana Ma, the first mystic I remember meeting, had a role in this too.

We children came to know Rehana Ma in the winter of 1968, when Maw decided to leave Paw and took us all to Delhi. Maw said she could no longer handle Paw's drinking and our constant worry over money; Delhi, she thought, would be a good place for her to find interior decorating jobs. None of us children wanted to go to Delhi, and Rahoul in particular was furious about being yanked away from working on his sculptures and drawings. But Maw was adamant that we should at least travel as far as Delhi and then decide what to do next.

We had piled into our old gray Ambassador car along with Maw and a driver, taking a rambling route north, with stops to stay with relatives and friends and to visit monuments. In Delhi, we crammed into the various guest rooms of Maw's friends. But just as Maw was starting to make contacts for possible jobs and schools, she was needed in Bombay. She left us younger children in Rahoul's care: me, who had just turned nine, Deven, who was thirteen, and Tashi, who was also probably a recent teenager. No one was sure of Tashi's exact age. The dentist had said he was probably around five when he joined us, but other details had been lost when the Chinese invaded Tibet and his family fled to India.

Delhi cold was colder than anything we had known before; the air was smokier, the city flatter and more spread out. Days passed, and I felt as though we had wandered into a dream where everything was both too bright and too faded, and we ourselves had lost our outlines. In the mornings, Rahoul insisted that we dress warmly in sweaters, then took us down to the Yamuna River, where a fringe of wilderness still stretched out beyond new rows of cement houses. He brought along binoculars so we could scan the water for migrating winter birds or half-burned corpses that had floated downstream from cremation grounds. After lunch, we ventured further: to the zoo, where a chimpanzee smoked the lit cigarettes that laughing visitors threw toward him; the National Museum, where Rahoul herded us through echoing galleries; or the bat-scented monuments in Delhi parks, where we clambered up and down narrow stairs. Most often, by late afternoon, we dropped in to visit Maw's friend Rehana Ma.

"Rehana Ma is a mystic," Maw had explained before she left for Bombay. "She's from a famous Muslim family. She lived in Gandhi's ashram when she was a young woman, and now she's also a Hindu."

"What's a mystic?" I asked. I knew the word "mystery" and was intrigued.

"A person who talks to God," Maw said.

Rehana Ma lived in a house that also contained an exhibition of objects that Gandhiji had once used. In the big echoing front room, we viewed a spinning wheel that Gandhiji had rotated to make cotton thread, a copy of the *Bhagavad Gita* he had thumbed through, and his bottle-cap spectacles.

"Anyone who puts on those glasses sees through Gandhiji's eyes and starts acting nonviolent," Rahoul announced.

"Really?" I asked, wide-eyed.

"Yeah, right!" said Deven.

Tashi offered to find a way into the case so we could make off with the glasses, but Rahoul shepherded us onward, down the corridor to Rehana Ma's room.

To me, Rehana Ma was mysterious as an old brick well so deep that it turned the sky into a silver coin. Her room was dim and close, with drawn curtains, closed shutters, and an aromatic smell that might have been oranges, camphor, or cloves. White patches of leukoderma mottled her face. She wore a knit scarf wrapped around her head and knotted under her chin.

She seemed to be wearing a sweater and a sari, but it was hard to be sure since a shawl concealed her torso and her legs were hidden under blankets. She was not sick, as far as I could tell, though she never seemed to leave her bed. I wondered if, as a mystic, she needed to stay put so she could enjoy conversations with her favorite god, Krishna. Other families in Delhi, busy with their routines, didn't really see us, it seemed, but she, staying put in the twilight, saw not just our displaced present, but our past and future.

"Come, child." Rehana Ma received us one by one from her bed, grasping our hands as we stepped forward. Rahoul said that she could read character from the way your hand draped around hers. I felt her goodwill and acceptance, but still, when we touched, I was careful to keep my mind on good thoughts.

We children settled on chairs and stools around her, Rahoul usually taking the lead in the conversations. I darted looks at the framed picture by her bed, where a blue-skinned, long-haired Krishna looked on. I hoped I might catch his lips in motion.

"You brothers and sisters have karma together," Rehana Ma said one afternoon, the whites of her eyes glinting in the semidarkness of the room. "This is why you were born sharing the same parents. You all have been connected over many lifetimes, being born as a group again and again. Sometimes you died together. Just one or two lives ago, you were all together in a building when it collapsed."

She closed her eyes, consulting the inner vision. I imagined the crash of beams, the floor caving in: the shock of an instantaneous ending instead of the slow, draining departure from life as we knew it in Bombay. I felt a pang for the girl who had fallen asleep to the sounds of waves and sea winds; she too seemed to belong in some other life, and I didn't yet know whether I should mourn her.

Rehana Ma unexpectedly smiled to herself, then opened her eyes and beamed at us.

"Another person in the group hasn't as yet joined," she announced, voice filled with gladness. "You will meet up later!"

I sat up straighter. Wasn't it about time that I stopped being the youngest and had someone with whom I could be the authority for a change: someone I could teach to walk, fly, and read in mirrors? A few years earlier, when I had delicately brought up the possibility of a baby sister, Maw had said sharply, "It's never going to happen." But Rehana Ma, I thought, knew more than Maw when it came to the future. The only problem was the verb she used: what did she mean by "meet up"?

Another afternoon, Rahoul said, "Rehana Ma, I need a guru. I'd like to take off for the Himalayas. Places like Hardwar and Rishikesh aren't that far from here, right?"

Rehana Ma turned her gaze behind her lids. We waited, suspended in the peaceful time-outside of time of her presence. Then her lids fluttered open. She looked around, finding us. "Why go to Himalayas?" she asked. "First you go back to Bombay."

My heart turned into a big, pink blossom of hope. So, she had seen that we wouldn't remain like ghosts at the margins of friends' families in Delhi. And truly, Maw returned soon after, her voice sounding unnaturally bright and American after her absence. She told us that she had worked things out with Paw. He had agreed to see a psychiatrist and to stop drinking, and we were going home to Juhu.

But already, Rahoul's plans for leaving home to find a guru had begun to unfold.

::::

We had missed the beginning of the school term. Our high-strung, cross-eyed cat Whisky had disappeared, though his brother Soda was still a stolid purring presence. Some of our toys were missing too. The house smelled strange, as though other people had been living there.

Maw was energetically reclaiming the space by changing things around. She often moved high cupboards and unfolded wooden screens to split or shrink rooms. Now she moved the big bed into what used to be a guest room off the back veranda, making this Paw's room. She lined up separate beds along the walls of the room they had once shared, and I joined her there. Maw also arranged for Tashi to go to a Tibetan boarding school in northern India. His older Tibetan sister had studied at the same boarding school, then moved to Switzerland, where his younger brother had been adopted as an orphaned infant; their older brother was still at the school and Maw hoped that he would be a good influence on our Tashi. For years, Tashi had seemed unable to stop himself from being willfully bad—cutting up Paw's shoes for slingshot "catties," smoking *bidis* in the servants' quarters, throwing ink bombs from the school balcony, and other things that I found too scary to talk about.

I was glad to be back in school. Rahoul, though, had always done most of his learning on his own. After our trip, he began to openly rebel. He carried a sandalwood *mala* to school and rolled the beads in his pocket when classes were boring. He told us that he stretched out on the floor in the corpse pose for meditation during recess. He didn't turn in homework, flunked tests, and talked more about leaving school to become enlightened. Rahoul's teacher called Maw in after the class took IQ tests and his high scores contradicted his low grades.

"What's the point of it all?" Rahoul shrugged his bony shoulders at Maw. "If you don't know the meaning of life, how are grades and degrees going to help you? At school, everything is 'Learn page 113 by heart because it has the answer.' It's this indirect, secondhand experience. I don't want lots of numbers, formulas, and facts clotting up my brain. I want to learn to use my mind. I want to *be* for a change."

I looked up from rows of fractions, waiting for Maw to defend school, but she said emphatically, "I know *just* how you feel."

So Rahoul wrote to Rehana Ma, asking again where in the Himalayas he could find a guru. She wrote back, "What is the need of Himalayas? One of the greatest gurus in India today lives in Ganeshpuri, just outside Bombay. His name is Swami Muktananda."

"What an *amazing* coincidence," Maw said, rereading the letter. "Can you believe we were already there?"

It turned out that when Pandit Ram Narayan had given a concert for Swami Muktananda's sixtieth birthday celebration on the full moon of May the previous year, Maw and Rahoul had tagged along. Maw brought out an orange Agfa box of black-and-white photographs she had taken at the event. I hung around as she and Rahoul sorted through the prints of a wiry man with piercing dark eyes, a short beard, knit cap, dark glasses, and cloth hanging loosely around his shoulders. I was especially struck by a photograph that showed him resting in a chair, his feet stretched out atop a huge pile of coconuts brought as offerings by disciples.

Rahoul studied the pictures intently. "I guess I'm headed to Ganeshpuri," he said.

"At least finish the term," Maw coaxed.

Paw was mostly off in Nasik, selling yet another piece of land from the properties that his father had assembled. He spent some weekends in the misty green hills of Khandala with his friends Mulk, Shirin, and especially Dolly. When he was around, he sat reading or listening to Hindustani classical music in his room. He was staying away from his bottles but seemed too tired and subdued to pay much attention to Rahoul's plans.

Maw, though, was excited. "Rahoul is renouncing the world," she announced to her friends. "He's leaving home. He's going to find a guru so he can get enlightened."

"Oh, *not* the guru with the sunglasses!" sniffed our neighbor Stella, when she heard the news. She looked down her shapely nose, pursing her lips. "I've already met *that* one."

Apparently, in 1962, in the misty era before I could remember, a New York painter friend of Stella's, Sam Spanier, had visited Juhu and taken her to Ganeshpuri. Stella had asked her cook Zachariah to pack a picnic of roast chicken, and she and Sam ate this under a tree near the vegetarian ashram before proceeding inside. Sam had just returned from a visit to his own guru, a French woman known as the Mother, who lived in southern India. Meeting Sam, Swami Muktananda said through a translator, "I can see you have already found inner sweetness." Stella thought this sort of conversation was absurd, and she insisted that they leave. "For a guru to wear sunglasses!" Stella had complained, turning up her nose at Sam's suggestion that maybe the guru saw too much light.

Now, years later, Stella was still fixated on the sunglasses. "He wasn't even out in the sun," Stella said. "I never trust anyone who wears sunglasses indoors, and I'm absolutely *not* into gurus."

Rahoul put sunglasses on his big-eyed, big-footed being and set it on the hood of Stella's white Ambassador.

"*Oh Ra-hooul!*" said Stella, snorting with laughter. She brought out her camera for a photograph.

:: :

"Remember how Maw always says that Stella's my godmother because she was there when I was born?" Rahoul asked as we walked on the beach. The sea blew in evening coolness after the day's humid heat. We moved from scattering pale brown sand under our bare feet to where our toes sank into darker sand still moist from the withdrawing tide. The stretch of the wet sand reached out, reflecting sky, to where the gray blue ocean rushed and receded, rimmed in white. Dobeyboy, our Doberman who had been raised by cats, ran in wide circles, digging soggy tracks around us.

"Um-hmm," I nodded.

As I knew well from family stories, Stella was about twenty years older than Maw, a friend of both Maw and Nani's from the artists' colony in Taos. When Maw moved with Paw to India, Nani had followed a year or so later to bring her home, and Stella came along. Nani wasn't able to dislodge Maw, and Stella stayed on. Stella was waiting in the next room when Rahoul was born at home, and so she became his godmother. Later, when Maw and

Paw were building a house in Juhu and Nani decided to build beside them, Stella opted for a third, fancier house with an air-conditioned darkroom.

By the time I knew Stella, she was in her midfifties: slim, perpetually tanned, and with a shock of white curls. Her tailored clothes were often in searing colors like lime green, which enhanced the vivid green of her eyes, and she wore gold leather *chappals* to set off the hot pink of her toenails. Stella claimed that she didn't like children, so we mostly spied on her through the big screen of crimson bougainvillea that cascaded between her and Nani's houses. Rahoul though, had always been the exception to Stella's not-liking-children rule.

"See, the year before I was born, Stella traveled overland from England to Nasik," Rahoul said. "On the way, the bus stopped in Afghanistan. She got out to climb to the top of the head of this giant standing Buddha and to take photographs. She met a chief and fell in love, so she lived with him for a while. But you know how Stella is really independent, so she left. Then she arrived in India and found out she was going to have a baby. That was me. Since Stella doesn't like children, she gave me to Maw."

"No!" I objected, thrown into confusion. I had heard about many of Stella's "lovuhs'; Maw relished quoting Stella's breathy pronouncement, *"I've always prefuhed to be a mistress rathuh than a wife."* I assumed that being a mistress made a man into a kind of pet; wasn't I, after all, part-mistress of Dobeyboy, sending him to the ground with the command "sit," causing him to leap over the coffee table with the word "walk"? But I had never heard of Stella's being either a mistress or the wife of any chief.

"Haven't you ever wondered why I look Afghani?" Rahoul pressed.

"Never."

"Where have you been, Baby?! You have to learn to wonder about how things look, you have to start digging under the surface. See, now that I'm leaving home, the truth is coming out. Stella is writing to the chief so I can go back to my father in the Hindu Kush mountains."

Was it because I was the baby that I had so far been protected from this truth? If Rahoul really wasn't the special eldest son, then how did this rearrange everything I had taken for granted about my family?

"Really?" I ventured.

"Really!"

But Rahoul's eyes crinkled, a smile signaling mischief played over his face. Beside us, the sun was sinking, growing long and orange as it touched the horizon over the sea. The waves made a crunching, sighing sound as they rushed and withdrew. Dobeyboy dropped a piece of driftwood before us as an invitation to throw.

"I'm leaving home soon, Baby," said Rahoul, looking down at me, taking hold of my smaller hand. "Are you coming?"

"I have to go to school," I said.

:::

In May, Maw accompanied Rahoul to the Ganeshpuri ashram so, as Rahoul put it, they could "scope out the joint." Maw returned home alone. Nani's rooms were already rented to an American ex–Peace Corps couple, and Maw now rented out Rahoul's room to a lean Indian painter of mysteriously lovely and almost uniformly black canvases, who usually lived in Switzerland.

Maw visited Rahoul whenever she could get away from the jobs she picked up as a freelance interior decorator for rich people in downtown Bombay. Every week or two, she would bring back a bulletin on his spiritual progress. "Rahoul is getting up at 3:30 to meditate," Maw reported to friends. "He's seeing a blue point of light between his eyes—it's called the *neel bindu,* the blue pearl, and it's the light of consciousness. He does a lot of *seva* in the ashram: you know, garden work, serving food, standing behind Babaji to hold the garlands that people offer. I think he's learning so much more than he ever would in a classroom."

Swami Muktananda, it turned out, was "Babaji" to his disciples. Soon Maw also began referring to Babaji as "my *Gurudev,*" or guru-god. "The root for 'god'—*dev*—is *divya,* or shining," Maw reported. "I tell you, his skin shines!"

"Babaji's the real thing." Maw told everyone. "All through my years in India, I've been reading *The Gospel of Sri Ramakrishna* and wondering if I'd ever have a chance to meet a live saint. Babaji has the same message as the classic Hindu scriptures: you know, that the divine Self is inside you for you to meditate on and recognize. But Babaji says it all in this wonderfully earthy Hindi, with a great sense of humor."

Maw regularly brought home more photographs of Babaji, especially close-ups of his face. At first the photographs crowded into the *puja* alcove in Maw's dressing room. Then they spilled onto the bulletin board above her desk and out into the living room, where many of our guests eyed them warily. I sensed that Maw's semiabstract paintings of women with nets in the ocean or coconut palms twirling in the wind were regarded by most of

Swami Muktananda (Babaji), with Rahoul and Paw in the background, 1969.
Photograph by Didi Contractor.

our friends as more appropriate wall decoration than photographs of staring saints.

"But Didi, aren't those godmen guru-baba types all charlatans and
rogues?" an occasional downtown Bombay friend would ask her. To them,
gurus were part of a backward, traditional religiosity best left behind if you
were a cosmopolitan intellectual. "Really, you can't be so idealistic."

"He's the real thing," Maw insisted.

The hippies were more encouraging. "Far out," they said. But when they
heard of the ashram's separate dormitories for men and women they didn't
usually take up Maw's invitation to visit with her.

The ashram people who occasionally showed up at our house, though,
were attuned to Maw's new vocabulary and décor. Maw referred to these
ashram friends as her *guru-bhai* and *guru-bahen*—brothers and sisters through
the guru; they gave Maw rides and asked her help with the things she was
good at, like designing. The Indian disciples who visited the ashram from
Bombay were often businesspeople, film stars, and politicians, who seemed
reassured by a guru's blessings. In 1969, very few Westerners came through

the ashram, but those who did usually stayed with us when traveling to or from Ganeshpuri or recuperating from illness.

Paw seemed to treat the ashram as an enthusiasm that he could best tolerate by ignoring, but he did go to Ganeshpuri to visit Rahoul on Guru Purnima, the full moon honoring gurus. The picture that Maw brought home showed Babaji gesturing impishly, Rahoul looking on from behind with amusement, and Paw seeming distinctly uncomfortable with a set chin.

: : :

One drizzly day at the end of the monsoon, Maw took Deven and me with her to the ashram. By this time, Rahoul had moved from Ganeshpuri to a different ashram, on a mountaintop near Nasik, run by one of Babaji's older disciples. Maw's own connection to the Ganeshpuri ashram, though, was undisturbed.

Paw gave us the use of the car and driver. Deven and I skipped school to ride with Maw through Bombay's suburbs, across the Thana creek and then through flooded rice fields. We entered through a front gate adjoining the road, and suddenly Maw was animatedly greeting everyone she met as if they were old friends. We trailed after her into a small hall fragrant with incense. Orange carpets were folded in strips over the linoleum, making long low seats around a single oversize orange chair.

Maw pointed Deven to the men's side, and she talked for a minute with a thin man whom she introduced as a professor and Babaji's translator into English. Then she and I sat cross-legged on the women's side. Maw had said that weekends and holidays were crowded, but on this weekday morning the hall stretched spaciously beyond a cluster of ten or fifteen people.

I pressed my knee against Maw's and looked around. Sparrows were hopping in and out through open windows, and the call of other birds was louder than in Bombay. I could feel that this was a peaceful place, but I was surprised by the décor. As the daughter of two painters, Maw had very particular tastes. Only feelings so strong that they lifted her out of herself could have allowed her to overlook the blaring synthetic tangerine and saffron colors. At home, she would have unfolded lengths of vegetable-dyed hand-printed cloth and banished the big plastic clock and overstuffed chair.

The walls, though, were lined with huge photographs of the sort that Maw now favored, including many of a holy man with a big belly wearing just a loincloth.

"That's Bhagavan Nityananda, Babaji's guru," said Maw in my ear. "He left his body in 1961."

"Bhagavan" meant God. Together, the photographs of him from different angles gave me the sense of a live, three-dimensional presence. The weighty intensity of Bhagavan Nityananda's round face, flared nose, and unblinking eyes gave me the feeling that he was looking into me.

I tried to think of something else, something firm and graspable like a school assignment, but my heart was racing. What would happen now when a live guru with gods' eyes saw straight inside me, saw everything about me and my family that I was ashamed of and tried to hide? With Rehana Ma in her cavelike room, the possibility of being looked into hadn't seemed scary at all, but this setting was so much grander, both more formal and more mysterious.

People scrambled to their feet as Babaji strode in, a blur of orange clothes. He wore his trademark orange knit cap and sunglasses. An orange cloth was tied around his waist, falling to his knees, and another length of cloth hung loosely around his shoulders, revealing a *mala* of brown *rudraksha* beads on his bare chest. He settled briskly into his chair, cross-legged, and looked around. As Maw had said, he really did shine: with his own high energy and also, it seemed, from the focus of everyone's attention.

Maw joined others to bow, dropping to her knees and pressing her forehead to the floor. Deven and I hung back, palms joined in greeting, uncertain what was expected of us. I looked down, eyes fixed on Maw's hand-loom sari-wrapped bottom.

"Rahoul's little brother and little sister," announced Maw in Hindi when her bottom was no longer the topmost part of her and she stood tall beside me.

Babaji examined us through his sunglasses. My breath was heavy with worry, and I tried to think good thoughts.

"*Bade dant aur bade kan,*" Babaji said to Maw, speaking Hindi in a strong, resonant voice. "Big teeth and big ears. Those are good signs. Very good."

I peered from the corner of my eye toward Deven. The guru liked our big teeth? Our big ears? If Babaji's presence had not been so awe-inspiring, I would have giggled with relief. But Deven was still calmly evaluating Babaji and would not catch my eye. Babaji was already talking to other visitors.

A harmonium was brought out, and slim chanting books were passed around. The small group began chanting. I stared at the Sanskrit words, too disoriented to follow. Maw, though, happily blasted along without even looking at the text. She had always said that she was tone deaf and couldn't sing, but in this group her voice emerged from so deep inside her front-tying sari blouse that I couldn't help remembering the opera singer Bianca Castafiore from the *Tintin* comics we exchanged at school.

Eyeing my mother sideways over the edge of my chanting book, I was baffled: did I really know her? I sensed that it wasn't just Rahoul but also Maw who wanted to see the world through gods' eyes.

As Maw's daughter and Rahoul's sister, was I also supposed to focus on this goal? I tried to figure out how I could fit in going to school and getting enlightened at the same time. As the group rose, I decided: maybe later, maybe when I was a teenager.

Maw shepherded us out through a courtyard and toward another building. "Big teeth and big ears are the marks of yogis," Maw explained, clearly pleased by our review. "It's like long arms with elbows below the waist, which all my children have."

We entered a shadowy hall smelling of grated coconuts and savory spices. Everyone sat on rows of sacking. Servers rushed up and down the lines, flipping down leaf plates, clanking metal glasses, pouring water. I looked around, half expecting to see my biggest brother. But once again, as Rahoul walked backward, his feet guided me forward into spaces he had left behind.

Crazy Saints

The ashram on a mountaintop where Rahoul now lived was just a few hours away from Nasik, our other home. The Nasik house, which Paw's father Sethji had built, was where our grandmother Ba, our widowed aunt Kaki, and four playmate cousins lived. Paw had first brought Maw here, and still claimed a wing where he sometimes stayed for long stretches. When Maw sent Deven and me up to Nasik to join Paw and the others for a long weekend, I wondered if we might visit Rahoul.

Much of what I knew about gods, goddesses, gurus, and *sadhus* I had learned from my grandmother Ba, but she did not seem to approve of Rahoul's going off to get to know them better.

"Rahoulia is a *chakram*," Ba decreed to Paw in his downstairs room. She lifted a slender arm, and twirled an index finger round and round by her temple. Blue tattoos marching up Ba's forearms flashed as she demonstrated how a *chakram* giddily circled without a sense of its own center. Paw laughed from his armchair, then turned back to All India radio, where a male singer explored the inner spaces of a raga. After a while, Ba went upstairs.

Ba was expert at mocking people through nicknames. She gave out titles like *potio* ("belly"), *tonio* ("shorty"), *genda* ("rhinoceros"), and even *bhens* ("water buffalo"). Ba also warped names, usually adding a hard "di" at the end of women's names and an "ia" at the

« Paw's family, early 1940s. Standing, from left: Narayan, Chanda, Bhanu. Seated, from left: Shantilal, Ramji Keshavji (Sethji), Kamla-bai Ramji (Ba), Manorama. Photographer unknown.

:: 31

end of men's. Ba's servant Madhav, for example—still a *"chokra,"* or boy in baggy shorts, at forty—had spent decades smiling forebearingly as Ba belittled him as "Madhia" in her commands. Saying "Rahoulia," Ba was stressing that she didn't like her grandson's going off to one ashram after another.

I knew well that Rahoul was the special eldest grandson whose birth defied an astrologer's predictions that Paw's father would not see the male line carried onward. I could see that everyone expected a son—and especially an eldest one—to finish school or whatever other training he had embarked on, submit to an engagement with the right girl from the caste (as Paw once did), marry the girl (as Paw did not, choosing Maw instead), make money through one of the caste professions, all associated with building (engineering, in Paw's case), and produce more sons. Setting off for an ashram, Rahoul had derailed this plan.

Running through the four wings of the house as we cousins played hide-and-seek, I overheard other fragments of conversation. Crouching in the "gallery" filled with ironed clothes and sewing materials in my cousins' part of the house, I overheard Kaki talking to her visiting sister as they sat on the floor of their sitting room, cleaning and chopping vegetables. "How does a family look when a boy goes off like this?" Kaki asked in Gujarati. "What will this mean for my children's marriages?"

Quickly, I crept out of range, hunching my way toward the open door to Ba's back balcony. I peeked in through the vertical bars on the window to her sitting room.

"Is Rahoul's mother telling him to do this?" asked someone in the group of visiting relatives enjoying an audience with Ba. They sat drinking tea on the gray vinyl sofas that could let out farting sounds for the unsuspecting. Everyone poured tea from their cups into their saucers, balancing the filled saucers in both hands and blowing ripples over the brown surface between sips.

I should have been used to seeming strange to Paw's relatives, and yet I yearned to fit in. Sometimes I wanted to pretend that I wasn't associated at all with the tall foreign woman who wore her hand-woven saris just a little too high, showing her ankles; whose unruly hair was never plastered down with enough oil; who uninhibitedly shared her strong opinions. I knew that though I too was a member of Paw's caste, with a claim to our shared stories, because of my American mother I would always be a little different, looking on rather than fully belonging.

: : :

"We are the sons of Vishwakarma," our relatives often said. Even women said it, for we all traced descent to Vishwakarma, the Divine Architect, through his sons who were craftsmen and artisans. We called him Bapa, or father, and we worshipped his daughter Randhal Ma as an important caste goddess.

I knew Vishwakarma Bapa through colorful prints that I saw in *pujas* and on the walls of relatives' homes. He appeared as a wise old man with a full white beard, a gold crown, and four arms. He held a manuscript—probably a book on building—in his lower right hand and a measuring tape in his upper right hand. His upper left hand grasped a ruler and his lower left hand held a water pot. Building tools circled in a big halo around his shoulders: wrenches, pliers, weights, T squares, and so on. Usually, a few sons stood around him, palms joined, and his vehicle, a white swan, rested nearby. From what I had heard, Vishwakarma Bapa had designed the Sun's chariot for travels through the sky; he had crafted the weapons of the gods; and he had built all the important temples, palaces, and cities in mythology, even Ravana's golden Lanka.

Maw sometimes said that Rahoul had arrived in her belly accompanied by a dream in which men with gold hoops in their ears and a big white bird appeared—she thought it was a peacock, or maybe a swan. When she woke up she knew she had conceived a son for the lineage.

Paw said that our caste, the Gujar Sutars, had long, long ago come from the area between the Black and Caspian seas and then migrated through India, going wherever kings called them to build temples. I didn't know how much Paw had pieced together through his own reading and how much he was echoing what the *bhat*, our caste genealogist, recited from his thick, handwritten manuscripts.

"We built the Kailash temple at Ellora," Paw liked to say. "We are allowed to put on our own sacred threads in Ellora, since we are both artisans and Brahmans. We built the Somnath temple, where an image of Shiva was suspended above the ground through the power of magnets, and if you pulled a rope 1,008 bells rang. We built the Sun Temple of Modhera, where the sun rises on each equinox to shine on the image inside."

Around the eleventh century, Paw said, our ancestors had stopped building in stone and working with kings. Instead, they became village carpenters in the arid expanses of Kutch. Almost as though it might diminish him personally, Paw didn't like to tell the story of why the period of building

grand monuments had ended. But we children heard it from our other relatives, particularly our uncle Sukhlal-phua, who was married to Paw's sister.

"A king of the Solanki dynasty, Sidhraj Jaisingh, had invited our ancestors
to build a temple in honor of Shiva in his fierce Rudra form," Sukhlal-phua
explained, "This king was arrogant, and wanted to be remembered for having built the most impressive of all temples. At the time that the opening
pujas were being done for the temple, he cut off the right hand of every
man in our caste. So our ancestors took a vow. 'People who work in stone
will never be happy,' they said. 'From now on we won't work in stone anymore. We will become carpenters.' The king gave them land in Kutch, and
that was where we settled."

But then, Sukhlal-phua went on to say, the Rudra temple was struck by
lightning, and knocked down by earthquakes: "Now just one pillar remains,
a single, beautifully carved pillar lying on its side in the dust."

This story haunted me, and whenever we went to caste "functions"—
engagements, weddings, and other celebrations where hordes of relatives
gathered—I felt the sad knowledge that everyone present was the descen-
dant of a family that had lived through the pain and humiliation of its men
losing their hands and their work. Our genealogist the *bhat* said, "You people
carry intelligence in your hands."

As Gujar Sutars, we traced links to different villages in Kutch, in western India, where our ancestors had settled and our family deities still lived.
Though I'd never been to Kutch myself, and Paw had never lived there either, if anyone asked me where I was from, I could readily give the name of
"our" village: Bhorara, near the city of Bhuj. Paw's father, Ramji Keshavji,
who later became known as Sethji, had left Bhorara as a twelve-year-old
in the 1870s to find work as a carpenter in his older brother's workshop in
Bombay. From the late nineteenth century onward, droughts and plagues
in Kutch had combined with new forms of building work related to British
settlement to pull many Gujar Sutars to cities like Bombay or Karachi. Still,
everyone in the *gol,* or "marriage circle," maintained their connection to
the Kutch villages, and in-marriage meant that most people were related in
multiple ways.

By marrying an American, Paw had slashed at the caste fabric woven
between families through the giving and receiving of daughters. Enough
years had passed that Maw was now accepted, but in the big round tent of
caste connection, she and her children still stood out like a jagged tear sewn
up with clumsy stitches of the wrong color. At caste functions, groups of
women fell silent as Maw neared, her extra-fair children trailing after.

Rahoul's behavior, I feared, was turning into another bright strand of story that called attention to our difference.

∷∷

Whenever our grandmother Ba saw me after an interval, she stared in a strange way. Other adults might exclaim about how *big* I had grown, how *thin* I had become, or how Maw had cut my hair *too short* for ribbons, but seeing me, Ba usually became solemn.

"*His eyes,*" she pointed. "*His ears. Exactly his chin.*"

She didn't touch, and she didn't smile. She was referring to her husband, Sethji, about forty years her senior, who had died nine and a half months before I was born. I felt the old man's features creep across my face, like a shadow reflected in glass. I stood up straighter, sensing that this resemblance could win me more respect than little girls usually commanded.

Some of Paw's other relatives still joked about how, as a bald baby, I had looked just like the old man before he died at ninety-six. Was it possible, they wondered, that the stern head of the family had come back to keep an eye on everyone? Women especially burst into laughter when they floated this theory. I recognized that they loved rolling around the thought, like a hard sweet in a cheek, that Sethji—the great champion of sons and grandsons—might have ended up as a girl. Even Maw, who mostly told the story of how Nani had requested that I be born, sometimes talked about how the last time she had seen Sethji on his sick bed, he had held her hands, looking into her eyes through heavy glasses, and she felt his "wordless plea for a new form" and her own inner response that she preferred another daughter.

I often stared at Sethji's large framed portraits, which still watched over the Nasik house. Downstairs, above the armchair where Paw often sat reading, Sethji was a young man, with high round cheeks, heavy brows, a thick black mustache, high collar, and maroon turban. Upstairs, in an oval frame on the gray blue wall of Ba's sitting room, his turban was still maroon but his mustache was gray, and he stared out sternly with the same deep-set eyes that Paw, Rahoul, and I later shared. Separated from Sethji by a rectangular blue wooden clock, eighteen-year-old Ba looked out from a matching oval frame. She had dreamily vacant, wide-set eyes, fair skin, and a single blue dot tattooed into the dimple on her chin. Her shiny black hair was mostly hidden by her sari's heavy gold border. She was pregnant with Paw.

I had heard enough stories to know that as a new bride, the odds had been stacked against Ba: a husband old enough to be her grandfather, specters of his three wives already dead, two stepsons born of different mothers before her own birth. Sethji apparently had a frighteningly strong Mars in his horoscope, and everyone knew that this was disastrous for spouses. Sethji's third wife, just before Ba, had been a beloved cousin, and he had paid a fine to the caste elders for marrying a relation considered too close even for the in-marrying marriage circle. Before that marriage produced children, she had died too. Decades later, we still heard whispers about how she had gone up in flames while cooking, and how sad and ill Sethji had been afterward.

Ba could have been cowed by this situation, but no! "Cow" was not the right word, for headstrong Ba came from a small village called Untadi, "female camel"—a village not in Kutch, but in Kathiawar, the adjoining region from which Kutchi Gujar Sutars sometimes took brides. Her name had been Kadvi-ben, "Bitter Sister," since she was born at a bitter time when her entire village was camping out in the Gir forest during an outbreak of plague. Like many other brides who received new names in their husband's home, after marrying Sethji Ba became Kamla-bai, "Lotus Woman."

Kamla, of course, was a name for Lakshmi, goddess of good fortune, with whom Ba enjoyed a special relationship. *I was born just as Surya Narayan, the Sun, rose in the forest,* Ba told us. *My father's luck changed after my birth.* Her father, Hirji Velji, had been a carpenter who specialized in bullock-cart wheels. Ba had crossed a big divide from being a village girl to a city matron when she married the prosperous, much older Sethji, but all the same, she insisted: "He made most of his money after I came." Ba saw herself as on such familiar terms with Lakshmi that she even specified what sort of pose Lakshmi should be in when worshipped. "You must always keep an image of Lakshmi *sitting* in her lotus," Ba instructed. "If you worship her *standing,* she might just wander off." Ba also said that Lakshmi appeared in her dreams as a little girl with her palms brimming with gems, saying that she was buried near an abandoned well in our fields. "Dig me out!" she instructed, and for years Ba had been looking for the right holy man to help extract the treasure.

Ba sometimes twisted her agile leg to show off a sole, using a finger to trace intersecting lines between the ball of her foot and the high instep.

"See? It's a lotus. It's the lucky mark that helped your grandfather."

Even if you didn't see the lotus, you would never dare contradict Ba. Her Mars, Ba said, was *even stronger* than Sethji's, which was why his stars couldn't kill her. Her luck-granting presence had helped him recover from his bad health in the early years of their marriage, brought him new properties, and made his business flourish. And because of her, the gray-haired man had fathered seven additional children.

But of those seven children, only three were alive in 1970. The first boy, who never received a name, had died at birth. This made our father Narayan the eldest. Less than two years after Narayan, his sister Chanda was born, an adoring audience for his pranks. After a gap of a few years, another son, Shantilal, arrived. He had been a dedicated cricket player and never went to college, managing the farm and properties instead. He married an orphaned girl of Ba's choice—our Kaki—to produce our four Nasik cousin-playmates before he tragically tumbled down the wooden stairs and died in 1965. After Shantilal, a girl said to look just like Ba had joined in the family; her name was Bhanu, and she was smart, slim, and also headstrong like Ba. Struck by typhoid when she was ten, she had insisted on getting up to play too soon and had died of a relapse. Tribhuvan, a boy, emerged next from Ba's womb. He had crippled limbs, and Ba declared him to be a great saint with just a little bodily karma left who needed to spend his time immobile and meditating in a pious household. He was never able to talk or walk, and he had died in the same sweep of typhoid that carried off Bhanu. Finally, Ba's youngest, Manorama or Manu, arrived when Sethji was in his midseventies. She grew into a pretty, bored girl whose discontent Ba took no responsibility for, saying she had taken after Sethji's sister. (Ba had never met this sister but claimed to know enough about her to deflect blame.)

By the time I knew Ba, she was in her late fifties, straight-backed and slender, with a vigorous and sometimes nasal voice. When she spoke, she always sounded as though she were issuing decrees. With us grandchildren she used a rough Hindi mixed with Gujarati spoken with the accent of her Kathiawar village: *"Hui ja,"* she'd say ("Go to sleep") instead of *"So ja."* (The reason she spoke mostly Hindi rather than Gujarati or any of its dialects was Maw. As Maw told the story, when she first moved to Nasik, her new in-laws had collapsed in helpless laughter whenever she tried to speak Gujarati. *"Doesn't she sound like a Parsi?"* they cried, holding their stomachs, for Parsis, who had in the eighth century migrated from Persia, spoke Gujarati in a distinctive way. In self-defense, Maw stopped using Gujarati altogether and declared Hindi—the national language of newly independent India— the household lingua franca to be used with her children.) Ba didn't know any Hindi at first, but she was not one to be deterred from releasing the full force of her personality on an unfamiliar language. Ba's Hindi—like Maw's—ran along with no regard for the polite forms of verbs, for singular and plural, or even for the gender of things, people, or herself the speaker, all the while forcefully communicating her intentions.

Fiercely erect, with her widow's white sari covering her gray hair, Ba now ruled over everything that went on in the two stories and four wings of Ramji Mistry Bungalow. Facing the main road, she presided over the garden full of rare flowering trees that Sethji had assembled from across India. Facing inward, she reigned over the courtyard, with a well at one end where neighbors lined up twice a day to draw water with a creak and a clang. Our well water was locally famous for being sweet, and then too, because of those seven children born to an old man, people murmured about the water's special properties.

Standing out on the upstairs balcony beside her apartments, Ba issued tart comments about the comings and goings at the well, or else she talked to Manik-bai, her water buffalo, who was tied under the jackfruit tree by the well.

"Manik-bai," Ba crooned, "*Khem che?* How are you, Manik-bai?"

"BAAWWWW," bellowed Manik-bai in return. She lifted the stiff black curls between her horns and flapped her long lashes toward Ba.

"*Majha ma chhe, na?* Having a good time, aren't you?"

"BAAWWWW."

"*Pani jyoech?* Want some water?"

"BAAWWWW!"

Ba understood Manik-bai. She yelled for a servant to serve Manik-bai a bucket of freshly drawn water cooled in the depths of the well.

Every year or two, Ba arranged Manik-bai's "marriage" to a handsome male buffalo, and for a while a hairy calf joined Manik-bai at the well. Ba also arranged for a barber to come in once a month to shave unladylike hair off Manik-bai's gray skin. In the summers, Ba hired a small boy to splash Manik-bai with water through the sun-baked afternoons, then lead her out for a stroll when the day cooled down and flocks of parrots settled in the trees. According to Ba, a cow or a buffalo would only produce healthy milk if she was not bored and got out to exercise and enjoy the sights. Ba took personal credit for the big foaming, creamy tubs of milk that Manik-bai produced—another mark of household abundance linked to Lakshmi.

∶∶∶

As evening shadows gathered around the trees, Ba sat out on a garden swing as big as a bed. We grandchildren piled on beside her, some seated and facing the house, others standing, holding the swing's chains as though they were the cords of sails and we were taking off for the sea. Ba pushed against the ground with her feet, rocking us back and forth as she gazed up into the *gul-mohur* tree that had been planted sixteen years earlier in honor of Rahoul's birth.

"*Khimji Bhagat apne Bapa ka akela chhokra hota,*" Ba began. "Khimji Bhagat was his father's only son. His son, Keshavji, too was an only son, with four sisters. Keshavji had three boys: Govindji Bapa, Devramji Bapa, and Ramji, your grandfather."

As Ba pronounced the numbers, she held up fingers. Blue tattoo dots patterned in little diamonds flashed along the the back of her hands and up her slender forearms.

"Khimji Bhagat was a tremendous devotee," Ba said, flinging up a palm, fingers splayed out for emphasis. Then she began to sway, strumming at an imaginary instrument. "He played the *tambura* and people collected around him to sing God's name. When he was young, his father sent him to guard the fields. They grew millet—*javar* and *bajra*. He was supposed to keep cows away, but he called over the cowherds and the cows. He said, 'Let the cows eat today,' and the cows ate until the crop was all finished. His father was furious, but Khimji Bhagat said, 'You will get at least twice that amount of grain.'"

Rocking back and forth in the rhythm set by Ba's feet, we understood that it was a great thing to feed cows. Ba was a tremendous proponent of the sacredness of cows. She regularly bought grass outside temples for cows to snack on; she gave donations to cow old-age homes; she sprinkled cow urine when she wanted to purify the atmosphere; and she sometimes raised a doe-eyed cow or two in the shed set back from the well.

"The next year there was a drought," Ba continued. "Even then, the millet in our fields sprouted. It sprouted three times—people ate, animals ate, the birds ate, and the insects ate. No one else in the village had a crop that year, but because of our fields, they ate.

"Then Khimji Bhagat said to his family, 'Take this, it's for all of you. Now let me go free, so I can sing to God.' He sang *bhajans* praising Ram. His guru was Ramananda Swami, who lived in Kandagra, the place in Kutch where our *kul-devata,* our family deities, live too.

"Khimji Bhagat didn't just *sing* to God, he actually *met* God," Ba asserted. She looked through her black-framed glasses to those of us on one side of the swing, then those of us on the other. Her voice lowered. "He saw God, and he received God's blessings! Through his life, he never hoarded anything just for his own family. As many *sadhus* as came to him were fed.

He was a *siddh purush*—a perfected man. I know this because if you pray to him, 'Oh Bapa, have compassion,' whatever you want comes to pass."

Ba bent her head ceremonially, palms joined at her forehead. The swing moved with the rhythms of lapping water. Parrots clamored from the tall trees, and the sawmill across the way fell silent. We sat quietly, awed, as shadows settled over the garden and the crickets started up.

"Rahoul is becoming a devotee too," Ba said.

: : :

Going indoors, we children made off for the mattress storage room. This room was upstairs in Ba's wing of the house, set between the open area where the coal-burning brass *bomba* produced hot water and the food storage room lined with enormous glass jars of yellow and red pickles, shining brass containers of spices, and bulging sacks of grains. The mattress storage room was dominated by two built-in trunks about four feet high, with hinges opening upward. When Ba's older sister Maushi came to visit, she stayed in this room and spent hours on top of the trunks beside the vertical bars of the window, embroidering scenes from blue-skinned Krishna's life in bright colors. Devji-bhai, our neighbor and tailor, sometimes set up his black sewing machine in this room to sew new clothes for the family. But when neither Maushi nor Devji-bhai were around, we children made this room one of our headquarters for games.

Ba worshipped a gold-framed, painted photograph of Khimji Bhagat in her *puja* but we knew that the original black-and-white photograph was hidden at the bottom of the built-in trunks. We shut the parallel doors of the room so as to be undetected by grown-ups, for we knew from past experience that we could be scolded for playing with precious old photographs. One of the boys jumped in among the musty cotton smells of the trunk and began to burrow under the rolled-up striped mattresses and pillows stained with hair oil. The rest of us held the lid up, peering in. Soon enough, a big sheaf of photographs mounted on gray or off-white cardboard surfaced. We settled cross-legged on the floor around them.

Most of these photographs recorded buildings and monuments constructed by our grandfather Sethji across Bombay. When Sethji arrived in Bombay, the port city was booming; the Manchester mills' demand for Indian cotton had surged with the halt in American cotton production during the Civil War. Though Sethji started out as a poor boy planing wood by hand for just a few pennies a day, he saved, made connections, and taught himself English. Within a few years, he had progressed from carpentry to become a contractor for British projects to expand Bombay. He had constructed water pipes, drainage systems, and some of the city's bridges. He had built the Lovegrove Sewage Station at Worli, the water fountain in a Matunga park, and many buildings besides. In his will, he left a special provision to build a clock tower for the Swami Narayan temple in Dadar.

We flipped through pictures of these structures, which were not particularly interesting since most didn't include people. Finally, we found the fading black-and-white photograph we were looking for. Confident that Paw was too detached from the household rules to scold us, we decided to see if he might add anything interesting to Ba's story. One cousin went ahead to make sure the path was clear. Then we wrapped a soft shawl around the picture to smuggle it downstairs.

We hunched, trying to keep out of sight of the kitchen across the courtyard, where our aunt and her sister would be preparing dinner. We crept past the open door of Ba's sitting room; luckily she was hidden in her bedroom lighting evening lamps for her gods. The stairs made impossibly loud thumps and creaks as we went down them, but we knew that Vasu-kaka, whose iron bed was under the stairs, would be in the phase of day when he developed red eyes and the tendency to giggle over everything. (Vasu-kaka was a neighbor my uncle's age who had come to spend the night some twenty years ago but had never departed. He now helped out with managing the farm.) Vasu-kaka was asleep, snoring lightly with the newspaper on his chest as we passed by.

The lights were all on in Paw's apartment. In the outer room, one of Stella's paintings of surreal cloud creatures dancing around a New Mexico mesa faced a painting by Maw of a woman in a sari carrying a brass pot on her shoulder. In the inner room, Paw sat reading in his armchair with his big wooden radio tuned to a Sibelius symphony from the BBC. He wore his usual at-home wear: a tubular-sewn and folded cotton *lungi* around his waist, and a sleeveless undershirt. Because this was Nasik and a little cooler than Bombay, he had slipped on a bush shirt for the evening but left it unbuttoned. His delicate bare ankles and high arched feet lay crossed, resting atop his leather *chappals*. His days often passed like this, alone reading, with occasional visitors dropping by to ask after his health or for his help—which mostly involved money. Evenings were when he drew groups of men.

"Hey Paw, look what we found!" we announced.

Paw set down the paperback by Jorge Luis Borges, his current favorite writer.

"Hullo everyone," he greeted us, looking up over the glasses that, since turning forty, he had started wearing when he read. He smiled as all six of us streamed into the room. "So it's the full *Bacche Log* Brigade. What have you brought?"

We handed him the photograph with its cardboard backing.

"Oh yes," Paw said, raising his high cheekbones, sunken cheeks, and dimpled chin so he could look through the bottom part of the glasses. "Our saintly ancestor Khimji Bhagat. That was taken by a traveling photographer who came to Bhorara long ago, sometime in the 1880s, I think. Khimji Bhagat and his group sang *bhajans* together. They were intoxicated by music."

Khimji Bhagat sat on a small mat spread on the ground, his bare feet close together and knees splayed to either side, surrounded by five friends. He wore a white turban that slanted down from right to left over his forehead, a cloth over his left shoulder, a long-sleeved *kurta* tied in the front, a *dhoti* of fine white cotton wrapped around his legs. Three white *puja* marks slanted up his forehead, and a long necklace of wood holy beads hung down below the bulb of the one-stringed *ektara* that he strummed while singing. He was old. His cheeks hung slack and dented, and his forehead was wrinkled. The expression in his eyes was hard to read: he seemed solemn, disoriented by the presence of a camera.

Paw handed us back the photograph. He reached down to his ankle to slap at a mosquito. "Off to better reincarnation!" he said. My eyes traveled toward his ankle to note just how squishy and thirsty the mosquito had been before being freed from this particular life form. Beside Paw's leg, at the shadowed inside edge of the shelf unit holding the radio, I saw a small, flat bottle with a black metal top.

My heart somersaulted. Was Paw drinking again?

There had been times when Maw assured people that he was "on the wagon," which to me evoked the shuddering, jolting bullock cart we still used on our farm. But whatever wagon Paw was on, I knew that bottles could start appearing in strange places. I had most often seen them in the bathroom: squeezed between piles of shirts, stashed behind the murder mysteries and popular anthropology paperbacks, camouflaged by stacks of molding *National Geographic* magazines, lurking presences before they returned to the place of honor at his side.

This bottle seemed to announce that we would soon return to Delhi. I stepped to the other side of the armchair to make it disappear. Maybe the bottle had been sitting there for a while, I reasoned; maybe it would be gone by tomorrow. I decided I wouldn't say anything to Deven.

When we returned upstairs, Ba was spreading out cards for solitaire on the Formica coffee table in her sitting room, the transistor radio beside her playing devotional music. She didn't notice us round the corner to return the smuggled photograph to its place under the mattresses, but Kaki, seeing the light go on from across the courtyard, called for my cousins. We disbanded, and I crept past Ba, into her bedroom. I wanted another look at our ancestor.

The main household *puja* room was near the kitchen, and a Brahman arrived to worship and chant each day. Ba's bedroom contained her own *puja* and always smelled like a temple with the scents of ghee lamps, sandalwood *agarbatti,* and jasmine flowers. A range of gods and goddesses looked down from large posters framed with rows of tiny bulbs that I associated with Christmas trees. Oil lamps flickered from the floor in front of Ba's *puja* cupboard, which was lined with shelves bearing more gods, goddesses, and holy people. Among them, Khimji Bhagat looked out, minus his musical companions, enlarged and touched up with color. He had a dusky brown complexion; a square of yellow-edged maroon cloth had been painted lovingly under him, while a low white balustrade and two bushes of stylized white flowers had been added in the background. Located in Ba's *puja,* he seemed to have gods' eyes: fully accepting of human weakness.

Ba's *puja* also contained a photograph of Sethji's guru, Yogi Bapa, whose beaming round face with white stubble on the scalp and cheeks was familiar to me though I had never met him. One of Sethji's early wives had introduced Sethji to the Swami Narayan sect, and he had developed a close bond with Yogi Bapa even before Yogi Bapa became the sect's head guru. Because of this affectionate association, Yogi Bapa had personally named Sethji's newborn son Narayan. This name honored Lord Vishnu, preserver of the universe, for the long episodes in which he slept on his serpent Shesh Nag in the cosmic waters between creations: *nar-ayana,* "lying on water."

Sethji had been a staunch patron of the Swami Narayan *sadhus,* their temples, and their monasteries. These *sadhus* were so strictly celibate that they were not allowed to look at women. When they visited the Nasik house—which they often did in Sethji's time—all the women in the family were required to hide. In addition to these orange-robed Swami Narayan *sadhus,* Sethji gave donations and alms to other pious *sadhus,* worthy Brahmans, and the Muslim fakir who for many years had visited the Nasik house each morning.

Ba too paid her respects to all *sadhus* she encountered, but the ones she seemed to like best were those she could interact with and who acknowledged her divine connections. She was especially looking for a *sadhu* with

"Khimji Bhagat didn't just sing to God, he actually met God." Painted photograph of Khimji Bhagat from Ba's *puja* cupboard. Photograph by Rahoul Contractor.

the power to help her excavate the massive treasure she was convinced lay hidden in our fields: the gold ornaments, coins, and bags of gems that Lakshmi had revealed to her in dreams. Often in the late afternoons, Ba would take off with the car and driver for an audience with any special *sadhus* who happened to be in town. "Gods rarely show their true forms. They come in the form of a *sadhu,*" Ba liked to say.

Ba also enjoyed housing *sadhus* in the rooms near the cowshed during periods when these weren't rented. Sometimes she ushered us children in to greet her latest *sadhus* and receive *prasad* of crunchy sweet *kadi-sakar* sugar crystals in our right hands. Once a *sadhu* taught us all—even the girls—how to recite the sacred Gayatri mantra. An older male relative who was visiting had objected, saying that it wasn't right for girls to know such a powerful mantra, though we couldn't erase it. Another *sadhu* decided to teach us yoga, and Ba looked on approvingly as her swarm of grandchildren posed feet up in shoulder stands. Yet another *sadhu* gave each of us a sandalwood *mala* with the kind instructions to hold tight, saying God's names, if we were ever scared at night.

Maw loved telling the story of a *sadhu* who, in the 1950s, had received room, board, and a charge account from Ba for an alchemy project. Ba was so enchanted by the thought of homemade gold that she didn't object to the mounting expenses for ritual supplies through the year. "By now you could have bought so much more gold for the money you're spending!" Paw had teased. In the end, Ba got a thumbnail of her personally manufactured gold leaf, which she hoarded in her bedroom cupboard amid spiritual books and pilgrimage paraphernalia. She called this cupboard her *tresooory*—a physical counterpart to her treasury of tales.

Most *sadhus* were men, but Ba also cultivated a *sadhvi*—a small stern woman with graying hair piled like a snake on top of her head, whom she called Mataji. Mataji sometimes came to stay a few days with Ba, parking her large iron trident in the corner. She and Ba sat up late into the night swapping tales of gods and powerful holy people they had encountered.

"I wish I had been born a man," I once heard Mataji tell Ba. "Ignorant people don't like a woman living alone and they harass her."

"I'll drop you off in the car," Ba offered. "Just show me who's troubling you and I'll let them know what will happen to them if they continue!"

Even as Ba looked to *sadhus* and *sadhvis* for blessings, it seemed, she also saw herself as their patron and protector. The question now was: would Rahoul become a *sadhu* living away from us, or like Khimji Bhagat would he return home and remain partly attached to his family, a devotee?

: : :

After dinner, for which we sat on inch-high rectangular wooden *patlas* with steel *thalis* set before us, we children went off to the mattress storage room to play some more. Our favorite evening game was "Kikeri-kee"—a kind of hide-and-seek in the dark adapted from a book that Nani had once given me for Christmas: *What Katy Did*. When the 8:30 p.m. siren, the *"bonga,"* blared from the distant mill, we knew that our aunt Kaki would soon call for us to drink Manik-bai's milk flavored with Bournevita, then go to bed, and so we emerged from our game. Kaki, though, was still deep in conversation with her visiting sister. From downstairs, we heard one of Paw's visitors singing Marathi *bhajans* out of tune, and we considered creeping into the garden shadows to spy through the window. The man's voice sounded dangerously drunken, and I was relieved when we settled on an alternate plan.

Instead, we drifted into Ba's sitting room. In the evenings, Ba often played a few rounds of cards with Devji-bhai, the tailor. Devji-bhai was a slight, fine-boned man with black eyebrows, thick white hair, and a round black cap. He lived with his mother in rooms near the cowshed, beyond the well. When Ba wanted a card companion, he was easy to summon.

Ba sat cross-legged on her gray vinyl sofa, and Devji-bhai occupied a low stool opposite her. The green spiral of mosquito coil burned in one corner, mingling with the scent of sandalwood incense from Ba's *puja*. From Devji-bhai came his trademark aroma of snuff. Some of us children settled around Ba on the sofa or matching armchairs, lowering ourselves carefully so as not to release the embarrassing sounds we associated with this furniture. Others of us gathered on the low divans covered with coarse pink material, with matching pink bolsters.

Ba was telling Devji-bhai about a *sadhu* she had originally met in 1944 when *sadhus* from all over India had camped in our fields. They had been visiting Nasik for the river bath called the Kumbha Mela, and Sethji had invited them to stay: hundreds and hundreds of holy men from all kinds of sects. Ba described a *sadhu* named Godhadia Baba. We called rag-stuffed comforters *godhadis*, and Godhadia sounded suspiciously like Rahoulia. I was puzzled by the name until Ba explained:

"Godhadia Baba, you know, liked to collect rags that lay around the bazaar, knot them together, and bind them on his head in a big turban. 'I'm Krishna,' he said. He looked like a crazy person. He carried a framed picture of Ram on his chest, hanging from a string. Sometimes he'd put on ankle-bells, and then he'd start singing Mira *bhajans* and dance. 'Radha is crazy, Mira is crazy,' he'd sing. He was a crazy one himself."

Ba set down her cards and raised her tattooed wrists on either side of her, bobbing in her seat and turning her head from side to side, as though singing to Krishna like Godhadia Baba and before him, Mira-bai, the ecstatically devoted queen of Mewar. My cousin Yeshu started to shake with the giggles beside me, and I elbowed her to stop before I too was swept up in a flood of laughter. If Ba set to scolding, we might lose the thread of her story.

"Was he old?" asked Devji-bhai, looking up from his cards and discreetly inserting snuff in a nostril. Above his head, the oval portraits of Ba and Sethji looked on, and the pendulum of the blue wooden wall clock wagged the minutes between them.

Ba smiled, remembering. "He was about eighty years old. His head was shaved. His face was full of light. He had no wrinkles. He dressed like a madman because he didn't want people to bother him. After I met him, I asked him to come eat at our house.

"'*Pagli*,' he said, 'You fool, what will you feed me?'

"'I'm not a fool,' I said. 'I'll be very happy if a great soul like you takes food in my house.'

"'Will you feed me *chappan bhog*?'

"'Yes.'

"'Will you eat with me?'

"'Definitely.'

"I understood what *chappan bhog* was, a dish made from wheat and ghee and sugar. I went home and asked our *maharaj* to cook some up, along with *dal*, rice, vegetables, and everything else."

Already, I could see that a *sadhu* who dared to call Ba a fool then asked that she, a woman, should ignore hierarchy and eat beside him, was truly as eccentric as his rags and frame-necklace getup promised.

Ba continued, "When Godhadhia Baba arrived at the house, he sat down before my gods. He danced in front of them for a little while, singing '*more to Giridhar Gopal*.' Then the food came from the kitchen and I brought him into this room to eat." She gestured at the gray blue walls and furniture around her.

"He said, 'I want to wash your feet first.'

"'But I want to wash yours,' I said. Then I said, 'If you don't let me wash yours, I won't let you eat.'

"'And I won't eat if I don't wash yours.'

"So I had to let him do it. He washed the big toe of my left foot with milk and water, and then he applied some *kumkum* and rice too. He folded his hands."

Ba folded her hands too, a pleased half-smile on her face. Since you were only supposed to touch the feet of people older and more important than you, Godhadia Baba's insistence underlined her own specialness, even if he was a little crazy.

"Then I washed his feet," Ba continued. "I sipped a little of the water. After this, I told him to eat.

"'You little fool, where's your *thali?*' he asked.

"'I'll eat afterward,' I said.

"'No, you have to eat with me.'

"So then a *thali* of food was brought for me too. I ate beside him, and he gave me food from his own *thali*.

"When we had eaten, I brought out money and said, 'Take this offering.'

"'What do you have?' he asked. 'I already have everything inside me.' He rubbed his chest, and just like that, a hundred-rupee note came into his hand."

Ba sat up very straight, circling her closed fingers around her breasts with her sari end hanging forward, Gujarati-style. Then she dramatically thrust her hand out with the imaginary note as though offering it to Devji-bhai.

"One hundred rupees!" marveled Devji-bhai.

"I said, 'Baba, I don't want money. Give me your blessings that we may always be happy. We are not hungry for money in this house. Put this back wherever you got it from!'

"So he gave me a one rupee note instead. I have this note locked up in my treasury.

"This is what happened. Do you understand?" Ba confronted all the grandchildren gaping on either side of her. "This was Godhadia Baba! He wandered like a fool so people wouldn't latch onto him and follow him around. Actually, he was perfectly sane.

"When I brought other women for audience, he'd ask, 'Why do you bring these *randis,* these prostitutes, with you? Can't you come alone?' These were respectable ladies, and they were insulted. Who likes being called a prostitute? After that, I went by myself."

"Prostitutes!" echoed Devji-bhai, laughing. The boys hunched toward their knees, embarrassed. I was not sure what the word meant, but I knew it was dirty, not one to be casually spoken. I had already made the mistake of calling Maw's American filmmaker friend Mira a "streetwalker"—when I had meant to loftily dismiss some opinion of hers as "pedestrian." I was mortified when Mira cried, "Didi, do you know what this dreadful child just said?" and then was embarrassed afresh when I had to admit I didn't really know what the word meant.

"Where is Godhadia Baba now?" one of us asked.

Ba was still smiling to herself, twiddling with slim fingers at her toes.

"He's dead now," she said. "He's become a god."

I understood that saintly people—whether relatives, gurus, or traveling *sadhus*—connected you with a world of strange and marvelous possibility. They were allowed to wear framed pictures around their necks if they chose, to disregard parents' orders, to ignore respectability. If Rahoul was in training to be a saint, and maybe a god too, Ba seemed to be granting him license to act as crazy as he pleased.

The Seven-Horned Mountain

When the gray Ambassador drove in under the portico, we children came rushing. Our aunt Chanda-phui emerged, skinny as a teenager, glasses glinting over her broad cheekbones as she beamed. "How are my *rani-betis,* my queen daughters?" Chanda-phui stroked the heads of us girl cousins in turn. She patted the boy's shoulders. "How are my *chhokre-log,* the boys?" She looked around. "Has Rahoul come?"

Paw appeared on his ground-floor balcony and immediately began bantering in Gujarati with his younger sister. Ba yelled at the servants not to drop anything as they thumped up and down the stairs carrying in Chanda-phui's bags, parcels, and steel containers. We children trailed after Chanda-phui as she made her way to Ba's rooms and washed her feet, as she always did after a journey. Then she settled down on the cool tile floor in the small dressing room next to Ba's bedroom and began unpacking her bags. Paw undertook one of his rare visits upstairs and stood nearby, still punning and teasing.

I watched Paw's happy animation with relief. If anyone could distract him from the spell of the bottles, it would be Chanda-phui, his devoted fan. They were less than a year and a half apart, and as far as I could tell, Paw had always reveled in her company. I remembered occasions when Ba bragged that she had produced so much milk that Paw and Chanda-phui had suckled together, and even then there was milk to spare! (Maw's response, which she aired in private to her own children, was, "I think it's really strange that Narayan and

Chanda remember nursing at the same time. If Ba breastfed Narayan until he was five, I don't see why she's proud of it.")

Chanda-phui arriving was like Christmas and Divali at the same time. Cross-legged on the floor, she zipped open her bags to bring out new clothes: the finest handkerchiefs for Paw, a shawl for Ba, shirts and shorts for the boys, audaciously bright satin tops and skirts embroidered with silver ribbon and mirror work for the girls (a far cry from Maw's determinedly handspun, handloom, vegetable-dyed, block-printed aesthetic). Though her husband, Sukhlal-phua, couldn't leave his work as a refrigeration engineer to accompany her, he had sent fat bundles of his favorite cast-off comics (which Maw scorned): assorted *Classics,* as well as *Archie, Richie Rich, Flintstones, Phantom, Incredible Hulk,* and especially *Superman.* Chanda-phui also brought tubs of *nasta,* various savory snacks glistening with oil: wriggles of fine *sev* and thicker, softer *ghatia* made from chickpea flour, flattened rice *poha, batata chivda* (slivered potatoes), crispy sheets of wheat *khakra*—all of which Maw labeled junk food. Gathering us children around her, in a circle on the floor, Chanda-phui began dispensing treats.

Paw withdrew to his armchair downstairs to enjoy his own plate of treats. Soon enough, Chanda-phui followed him with us children in tow, our games temporarily suspended. She carried her Chinese steel nail clippers, a fine-toothed plastic comb, cotton wool, and a bottle of the coconut hair oil that Ba boiled up with herbs each winter. Laying out her grooming tools out on the table beside Paw's radio, Chanda-phui blithely ignored the tall beer bottle that had appeared, sweating onto the wood.

I didn't want to look at the bottle either, so I fixed my vision on Chanda-phui. With her broad face, Chanda-phui looked so much like the portraits of Sethji that it was a mystery to me why she and I—his other copy—didn't strongly resemble each other. As though monitoring any hint of similarity, Maw often pointed to Chanda-phui's rapid-fire nasal clang as the sort of "disputative Gujarati voice" I should be careful to suppress, as it was likely latent in my genetic makeup.

Chanda-phui draped her skinny body with saris worn Gujarati-style, pulled forward over the right shoulder. Ever since her younger brother Shantilal—our cousins' father—had died a few years earlier, she wore saris in only the most muted of colors and with the tiniest of patterns. Her shoulder wings poked out through the back of her fitted, crisply ironed sari blouse, and her graying, well-oiled hair was pulled tightly into a bun anchored with both hairpins and a hairnet. As a well-off Gujarati married woman, she displayed the usual flowerlike diamond studs in her ears, a diamond glittering from one nostril, a *mangal sutra* with gold and black beads, and several gold bangles, but it all seemed more like a uniform than dressing up.

Chanda-phui had worn glasses since she was a young woman, and had an intriguing way of momentarily rolling her eyes up into her head, lids fluttering behind the lenses, when she thought hard about something. For years, she had clipped and chewed at *supari*—hard brown betel nuts. All that vigorous chewing had developed her jaw muscles so much that they seemed permanently clenched and bulging. Yet when she smiled, she beamed sweetness.

Chanda-phui pulled a bobby pin from her netted bun and wrapped cotton around it. "Your Paw produces little stones in his ears," Chanda-phui announced, preparing to angle the curved end into his ear. She always knew who in the family had moist earwax and whose earwax was dried up and hard.

"My *ghungru* bells," said Paw, laughing with his sister. He quickly adapted a *bhajan* that described Mira dancing before Krishna with *ghungru* bells around her ankles, singing, "*kan ghunghru re* . . . , bells in my ears."

Chanda-phui gurgled appreciatively. With the flair of a magician, she brandished the dark solidity of Paw's earwax. Then she unscrewed the small, flat bottle of hair oil, which looked suspiciously like it might once have contained whisky.

"What does Rahoul eat in that ashram?" Chanda-phui asked, pouring the shiny green liquid into her creased palm.

Paw shrugged his bare shoulders. "All ashrams serve food. I haven't heard that they live on grass."

"But nice snacks?" Chanda-phui pressed, transferring the contents of her palm to the top of Paw's head.

"Since when do people go to ashrams for snacks?" Paw asked.

"Let's go tomorrow to receive the blessings of the Goddess on the mountain and take Rahoul and all the ashram children good things to eat," Chanda-phui urged, working her fingers through Paw's scalp.

Paw made no comment. His head was bent forward, his eyes squeezed tightly shut, almost as though he were in pain. Chanda-phui continued briskly, using the tips of her joined fingers to massage his scalp.

"It's not so far away," Chanda-phui murmured, letting go of his head. She wiped her hands on the handkerchief tucked at her waist and looked around for the nail clippers.

Paw leaned over and refilled his glass. I watched, heart sinking as the white line of foam rose. He took a long sip but didn't say anything.

After a while, as Chanda-phui squatted on the floor, intent on trimming his toenails, Paw said, "Go see what he's eating. Take my car and driver."

Family outings had never, in my memory, interested Paw.

: : :

We all knew that Paw's marrying Maw had caused Chanda-phui terrible hardship. I was still piecing together the story, never sure if there were more chapters hidden within awkward silences. Rahoul's birth might have eased difficulties for Maw, but it hadn't helped Chanda-phui.

One part of the story clung to a silver tray that Ba displayed with other commemorative gifts in the glass-fronted cupboard in her sitting room. Sethji had received this tray in 1932 at the opening of the school he built, which was also named for him: the Ramji Keshavji Kutchi Gujar Sutar School in Karachi—now part of Pakistan. By the early twentieth century, Sethji had become an established leader of the caste community in Bombay; building this school, he also laid a claim for status in the branch of the community settled in Karachi.

Ratansibhai Gundecha was a correspondingly big man among the Gujar Sutars in Karachi. Ratansibhai had been born on an island outside Karachi, yet, like Sethji, he actively retained his connections to his Kutch village and family deities. He had worked as an engineer for the railroad and later established an ice factory with several branches in the province of Sind.

At the opening ceremonies of the Ramji Keshavji Kutchi Gujar Sutar School, an elderly woman relative suggested that the two illustrious families join up. Ratansibhai had a son, Sukhlal, born in 1925; Sethji had a daughter, Chanda, born in 1929. The fathers agreed, and so, at the age of two and a half, Chanda was promised in marriage.

Sethji might build schools to educate other people's sons and daughters, but when it came to his own daughter, he feared that too much education might make her unmarriageable. He withdrew her from the Gujarati-language girls' school in Nasik after she'd studied just five years, while arranging for her older brother Narayan (who was not yet Paw) to continue with an English-language education that could only make him a more desirable groom. When Chanda turned fifteen, Sethji put on a huge wedding in the Nasik house. In one photograph, fifty or so important males of the caste pose around the groom, with Sethji and Ratansibhai at the fore; in another, all the important women and girls pose around shy, sunken-shouldered

Chanda while Ba glares at the photographer. In that photograph is a thin, long-faced girl from Rajkot, to whom, at that time, Narayan was engaged. In the front row, among the children, sits his new brother-in-law's round-faced younger sister Sarla.

After the wedding, Narayan let his preference for plump women be known, declaring the Rajkot girl "so skinny that she looked sick," and the engagement was called off. Sethji and Ratansibhai then decided to further cement their ties by planning a marriage between Narayan and Sarla.In 1947, when handsome Narayan set off for America to earn an engineering degree, he was safely engaged to fourteen-year-old Sarla. Everyone expected that he would return to marry her. Instead, he wrote from Boulder saying he was marrying an American girl, Didi Kinzinger. He sent home pictures of her in a sari.

As Maw told the story, Ba did not take easily to being crossed. She refused to break off the earlier engagement when Paw informed the family of his courthouse wedding, and still wouldn't break it when Paw sent pictures of the first grandchild: a girl with hospital bracelets around her thin wrists and tufts of black hair. Even when Maw and Maya came to live in Nasik, the engagement to Sarla stood. Ba brought in an astrologer, who warned that baby Maya would be a liability. She'd have buckteeth and glasses and would end up a spinster, he said; it would be better if this marriage were immediately dissolved.

If Ba disapproved, so did Nani. In 1952 she took leave from her job teaching art in Taos and, accompanied by Stella and another friend, traveled by ship to India. A year of living with an extended, largely uneducated family in a house without plumbing was enough, Nani reckoned; she planned to bring her only daughter and grandchild safely home with her to Taos.

In each dismissing the other's cherished child, Ba and Nani might have ended up in open warfare, even if they shared the goal of breaking up the marriage. But hospitality is a great Indian virtue, and so, when Nani and her friends arrived in Nasik, Ba welcomed them. Ba could not speak English, and Nani's teach-yourself-Hindustani books mostly contained sample sentences intended for servants ("Serve the food!" "Why is there not more starch in this collar?"), but they managed to communicate politely with others translating.

Ba took Nani and her friends along with her to a wedding feast in town. Maw was feeling queasy and stayed home. Someone at the wedding teased Ba in Gujarati, "You said you'd get rid of your daughter-in-law, and now her mother and her friends have moved in too!" If there was one thing Ba would not tolerate, it was being mocked. She spewed fiery curses, saying she would soon be rid of the whole troupe of no-good foreign women.

A helpful woman who had been translating pleasantries and explanations at the feast took it upon herself to also translate Ba's tirade into English. Nani was enraged. She came back to the house and announced that they should all leave for Taos immediately. Maw was upset and told Paw—who was upset that anyone would be upset with his mother.

In the midst of this turbulence, Maw found she was pregnant again, and that decided matters for the moment. Ba decided to give Maw another chance. Nani went back to Taos with one friend, while Stella stayed on, traveling around India to take photographs and returning regularly to the Nasik house for nude sunbathing in private corners of the big garden. Paw's fiancée Sarla continued to live at home with Chanda-phui, awaiting news of Maw's eviction.

Rahoul was born in July 1953, and instantly Maw's status shifted. Stella, who was present in the next room of the Nasik house, described how Paw threw open the double doors, rushing out with *"a Nijinsky leap, shouting, 'It's a boy, it's a boy.'"* Maw had produced the first grandson! Sethji was in his late eighties, but Maw's fertility had defied the astrologers' predictions that he would not see the male lineage continued. Ba fed Maw almonds, cooked her special sweet dishes to bolster her strength, and arranged for women to massage her with healing oils. Three years after Maw and Paw married, a tiny boy with steady black eyes and black hair finally prompted Sethji and Ba to break off the engagement with Sarla. Maw finally received the silk saris, heavy gold bangles, and flowered diamond ear studs usually presented to a Gujarati daughter-in-law. Maw said that what she really wanted was a refrigerator, and she received one instead of more gold and saris.

Chanda-phui's in-laws were already upset when Maw appeared. Then, to make matters worse, Chanda-phui produced no children. Sukhlal-phua was the only son among three sisters: for the lineage to be carried forward, she would need to bear a son. At one point, Chanda-phui's mother-in-law instructed her to stop serving morning tea. "It's unlucky to see the face of a barren woman first thing in the day," she said.

Ba sometimes pointed out that none of Sethji's sisters had borne children either, and blamed a distant ancestor for offending a snake, causing a curse to cling to women of the male lineage. Still, any curses, she said, could be undone by the right blessings. She remained constantly on the lookout for powerful holy men, and she hired learned Brahmans to chant and underline passages about conception in the *Atharva Veda,* which she then locked up in her treasury. Ba seemed to be confidently preparing for the day when she would tell a triumphant story of how, through her own special spiritual connections, she had produced a miracle grandson.

Paw's ex-fiancée Sarla married someone else, but she remained our relative. We sometimes saw her at weddings staged in the caste hall in the Bombay suburb of Matunga. She fascinated me. I could not stop staring at the way she parted her hair over to the side, or the sari that was brighter than anything Maw ever wore. I sometimes tried to imagine who I would be if half my self had come from her. Would we still be the same souls regrouping across lifetimes, as Rehana Ma described? I found myself grateful to Rahoul for being born, clearing the way for Deven and me to follow.

And yet I could never see Chanda-phui without knowing how much our existence had cost her.

:::

We set out to visit Rahoul early in the morning, while women still stood lined up with pots and buckets in front of our well and the top of the jackfruit tree glittered in the morning sun. Ba had stated that she would not ride with any boys, who were likely to stir up a storm of naughtiness, so the boys, all around the same age, piled into one Ambassador car along with the Nepali servant and a driver. In the other car, Ba presided from the front seat, beside Mani Driver. Chanda-phui, my two girl cousins, and I crammed into the back, along with squat round water bottles, stacked stainless-steel tiffin containers, tubs of snacks, and boxes of milk sweets.

We started through the cool morning past the fields that had once belonged to Sethji. In the 1950s, during the era of land reforms, the fields had been confiscated by the government (*"sala gor-ment,"* Ba cursed) and now lay fallow. We drove past the wayside shrine to the buffalo god Mhasoba, past the edge of town, past camping goatherders and small villages. Taller mountains in irregular volcanic formations opened out across the horizon.

"That goddess Saptashring Devi has appeared to me," announced Ba. She turned to make sure she had commanded our attention, then waved grandly toward the windshield.

"Many years ago we went for *darshan* on the mountain," Ba began. "Just like we're going today. When we climbed down the mountain, it was almost seven in the evening and had gotten dark. We reached the car and sat inside. The driver started the car. Then we saw something in the evening light. It was a tiger walking toward us.

"'Stop the car!' I told that driver. He was a Brahman driver. He was scared, but he listened to me. He stopped the car and he turned off the engine. Then the tiger came close to us! The tiger rubbed against the car door on my side. I joined my palms. We had gone to see the Devi, and the tiger she rides had come to us. I understood that the Devi had appeared to bless us." Ba joined her palms, bending forward toward the Goddess, whom we neared with every mile.

"And then what happened?" I blurted from the back seat. The tiger sounded like a big, affectionate cat to me; I almost could hear purrs as he nudged the car.

Once Ba had delivered a punch line, she had little interest in narrating further. "What do you think happened?" she countered. "The tiger left and we drove home. We were blessed, understand?"

We continued whipping past fields, past villages where goats and children played in the dirt. Stray dogs charged out to race barking beside the car until they fell behind, wagging their tails. I pressed my nose against the car window and recalled what Rahoul had told us about his life on the mountain during his visits home.

While still at Ganeshpuri, Rahoul had met the *sadhu* who drew him to the mountaintop; this *sadhu*, Swami Prakashananda, had for many years been a disciple of Babaji's and still visited Ganeshpuri for big celebrations like Guru Purnima, the full moon honoring gurus. Swami Prakashananda had his own ashram too: a small establishment dedicated mostly to housing and feeding small boys from impoverished families in the area so that they could attend a nearby school. Rahoul had liked Swami Prakashananda's genial zaniness and also his advice that *"if you want to change the world, start with children. With adults it's too late."* Rahoul had decided to go help out at that much smaller ashram.

I was already struck by a *sadhu* who devoted himself to children, and everything else Rahoul said about Swami Prakashananda sounded intriguing too. "Man, he's far out!" Rahoul had laughed. "He calls himself *agrambagram*—topsy-turvy. He's really into cooking and feeding people, and he invents recipes from whatever offerings people bring. He constantly tells these parables and stories from mythology in a funky mixture of Hindi and Marathi and I guess Kannada or Tulu or whatever. But since he chews tobacco, *he shounds like jis.*"

Swami Prakashananda's ashram was on Saptashring Gadh, the "Seven Horned Fort," a mountain plateau sacred to the Goddess. Rahoul described this mountain almost as though it were a giant person. "From the bus, you

see the mountain rising like a fort, with almost vertical battlements," Rahoul said. "Other mountains stand to the right of Saptashring Gadh in an
almost perfect line, as though they're bowing. About halfway up, you see a
strip of green, like a belt—that's the plateau with the town of Saptashring.
The mountain continues up with cliffs at one side. The temple to the Saptashring Devi is halfway up the cliff."

Rahoul described this Goddess as having emerged from the face of the
cliff with eighteen arms, one hand cupped by her ear, when a sage sang her
praises from the opposite mountain. Her name was officially Saptashring
Nivasini Devi, the Goddess Who Dwells in the Seven-Horned Mountain.
Rahoul told us that Swami Prakashananda said that she was a form of
Lakshmi, goddess of good fortune. Since she was standing on a turtle, he
said that she also represented the *kundalini* energy, coiled at the base of
everyone's spine, that can be made to travel upward through spiritual practice. She presided over the mountain, making for all kinds of mysteries and
miracles. One man who lived at the ashram had opened his eyes during
meditation in an underground cave to find a woman watching him, but
when he looked more closely, she disappeared. Sometimes the sound of a
tiger's breath filled the room. One story in particular had caught my imagination, inspiring me to make it my own through a retelling for my friend
Fatty Rasha on the school bus the next day:

Everyone's been talking about this little kid who fell off the cliff. This woman didn't have any children for ages. She made a vow to Saptashring Devi,
and a son was born. She was so happy and busy with the baby that she for-
got to bring him back and properly offer thanks. The boy fell sick again and
again until she realized her mistake. She brought him to the temple and
decided to do a special puja at the cliff's edge. While she was making offerings, the little boy wandered off and jumped. He must have fallen hundreds
and hundreds of feet. His mother went crazy with grief, and people had to
stop her from throwing herself off too.

Then a few days later, the boy was found, absolutely unharmed, wandering around in the villages below. He was too small to tell the full story,
but he said that his mother lived on the mountain. When he was brought
up to the plateau, someone sent a message to the parents who had lost
their son. They came and found he was their own boy. People say this
was the Devi's grace, reminding the family that the boy wasn't really theirs,
but hers.

We had entered a landscape of fields and occasional villages, the mountains rising up like titans. When Ba pointed out the mountain to which we
were headed, I could see how those nearby really did, as Rahoul said, seem
to be offering their respects. We parked at the base of the fortresslike mountain. The other car had already arrived. A few village men squatting nearby
stepped forward and offered to carry Ba up in a chair, which offended her.
"What do you know of the meaning of 'old,' you donkeys?" she inquired.
"My grandmother had a straight back and all her teeth in her mouth until
she was 110 years old! Go carry some fat merchant's wife, but let me climb
by myself!"

We started climbing, following a rough trail of compacted earth and
rock. Grass grew around the edges of the trail. The boys went ahead,
scrambling up embankments to bypass the path's looping curves. As we
climbed higher, the air cooled and thinned, the sky stretched blue across the
far horizon, and the fields below assembled into a patchwork of pale greens
and dusky browns.

"All kinds of holy people and saints live in special places like these two
mountains," Ba announced. She lowered her voice, as though someone
might overhear though the path around us was empty. "Some saints are
hidden in caves, meditating for hundreds of years at a time. Some become
invisible, because they don't want to be bothered by people wanting their
blessings. You can smell them if they're passing by. It's the smell of *dhoop,*
the finest sweet smoke."

I looked around, lifting my nose. The bright light and tingling chill in the
shadows really did seem to hold mysterious, hidden dimensions.

Finally we arrived on a broad plateau. At the western edge, a sweep of
tall cliffs loomed. Ba and Chanda-phui joined their palms together as they
sighted the temple protruding from the cliff. "As soon as we've met Rahoul,
we'll go visit the Goddess," they promised.

We made our way through the small bazaar, where shops displayed wares
for pilgrims: coconuts, bundles of green glass bangles, hillocks of sacred red
kumkum, hanging green saris interspersed between marigold garlands. At
the ashram, we learned that Swami Prakashananda had taken Rahoul down
the mountain for supplies. "Don't worry," the lanky man who was in charge
assured us in Marathi, "They'll be back by evening. Sit, have some tea. Then
you can go for *darshan.*"

He led us into a dim front room; if there was electricity, there was no
power just then. From somewhere nearby, we could hear a chorus of
children's voices reciting what sounded like lessons. As my eyes adjusted,

I recognized pictures of Babaji from Ganeshpuri, and his guru, Bhagavan Nityananda, a visible reminder that Swami Prakashanda belonged to the same *parampara,* or lineage of gurus and disciples, spreading out like a big family.

:::

Saptashring Nivasini Devi stared down at us, beyond us, and upward with giant goddess eyes as we crowded into her shrine. Her intense black pupils were rimmed with round white irises, and she had bow-shaped black brows. She was the color of coral, with black beauty marks on her chin and cheeks; a giant red sun adorned the center of her forehead. She wore a sari the deep green of mango trees in full leaf, bordered with hibiscus red. Her silver crown carried the sun, the moon, and many stars. Matching silver boots with etched toes encased her huge feet. Eighteen arms fanned around her body in a coral circle: every hand except the one nearest her left ear held a different weapon or holy object. The empty hand was cupped beside her ear, and her head tipped slightly toward it.

Bells clanged, incense burned, oil-lamps flickered, the *pujaris* busily accepted and distributed flowers, coconuts, packages of white sugar balls. I watched closely to see what Ba and Chanda-phui were doing, then followed suit, scrambling down on my knees to touch my forehead and fingers to the cool stone floor. Then I too joined my palms. Near us, a woman's head flew in circles; *ahe-ahe,* she panted, black hair whipping like snakes around her, members of her family gathering close in case she fell.

"The Goddess has come into her body," Chanda-phui explained in a whisper.

As a team of cousins, we were usually unabashed gigglers when adults made a spectacle of themselves. But watching this woman, we were wide-eyed, silent. If the Goddess's fierce energy had found its way through that woman's body, could it grip any one of us?

I thought of the goddess I knew best, Pallas Athene, met through my old habit of reading whatever Deven was reading—in this case, the illustrated retellings of the *Iliad* and *Odyssey* provided by Nani. With her dark curls, powerful shoulders, draped dress cinched at the waist, sandals that tied up the ankle, and skill at rescuing Odysseus from the most fearsome difficulties, gray-eyed Athene had always been a wonderfully reassuring goddess. But she had been contained within the pages of a book, not to mention a distant time and place; this raw energy pulsing through a person right in front of me was unsettling.

We retreated, unusually quiet, down the steep stone steps back to the ashram to wait for Rahoul.

The cliff cast a deep afternoon shadow as a middle-aged *sadhu* wearing faded ocher robes came in through the ashram gate. Rahoul and a few other teenage boys followed with gunnysacks and bulging bags slung over their shoulders.

Rahoul looked like a different person. He was wearing an old T-shirt with a coarse white *lungi* wrapped around his waist, leaving his calves bare. His usual curly mop was shorn close to the skull. But when he burst into a smile, ears jutting wider from his close-cropped head, I saw that he was still my brother. We gathered around Rahoul as he explained who we were to the *sadhu,* his new teacher, Swami Prakashananda.

"*Jai Jagadamba! Amba Mata ki jai!*" Swami Prakashananda rumbled blessings, smiling with uneven tobacco-stained teeth. "Victory to the Mother of the Universe! Victory to the Mother!" His face was framed with soft, furry gray hair and a beard, and he looked us over with the bright eyes of an intrigued child. His eyelashes, I noticed were unusually long and thick, clustering into spikes. One faded and crumpled ocher cloth was tied around his belly and another hung loosely forward from his shoulders. The thought that I should worry about him looking into my darkness darted off, vanishing into the steady sunshine of his apparent happiness to see us.

I watched Ba and Chanda-phui to see how they greeted this *sadhu*. Would they just join palms in a *namaste,* and if they bowed, how far down would they go? They bent forward from the waist, extending their fingers to his toes, and we children lined up to follow suit. "*Jai Jagadamba! Amba Mata ki jai!*" Swami Prakashananda repeated for each person.

When my turn came to bow, I was flushed and awkward. I dipped my fingers downward but didn't really touch his feet. Then I stepped back, almost stumbling, certain everyone, including the swami, had noticed that I didn't do it right.

But all Swami Prakashananda said was "*Ao, Kirin Mataji.*"

Respected Mother Kirin! I burst into a big-toothed smile. Rahoul was right, this old Swami was a little crazy. But when he greeted my younger girl cousins they were each a Mataji too.

"*Rahoul ka bap nahin aya?*" Swami Prakashananda asked. "So Rahoul's father didn't come? Is he well?"

"He wanted to come, but he has to work," Chanda-phui said, covering for Paw.

A few other visitors, who seemed to be local peasants, pressed in behind us to touch Swami Prakashananda's toes. Standing up, they turned and bent before Rahoul's feet—after all, he too was dressed almost like a *sadhu*. Rahoul tried to step aside, objecting *"Naka!"* and gesturing with his palms. I looked on, dumbfounded, afraid to meet my cousin Yeshu's eyes. I didn't want her to laugh. So now Rahoul was granting blessings too?

"I tell people not to do it," Rahoul said in English, embarrassed.

The other visitors trooped off. Swami Prakashananda looked at the lengthening shadow of the cliff spreading coolness around us. "Why don't you all stay the night?" he asked. "It will be dark soon."

"No, Baba . . ." Ba and Chanda-phui made polite excuses. Chanda-phui brought out her tubs of snacks and boxes of sweets to leave for Rahoul and the ashram children.

"You must at least eat something before you start down the mountain," Swami Prakashananda said, starting into a kitchen with a low roof and walls blackened with smoke. We sat on long strips of sackcloth in the outer hall and caught up with Rahoul. When Swami Prakashananda returned, he flipped hot, greasy pancakelike *malpuas* onto metal plates for each of us. Then he sat on the floor nearby to watch us eat, fingers slick and sweetness searing our tongues.

"*Khoob khao,* eat lots," he instructed, voice soft and slurring from the wad of tobacco in one cheek "You'll need energy to get down the mountain. The body needs petrol. See, the *atman,* the Self, lives in the body, but it's not the body. But because the body is the seat of the Self, you should look after the body—your own body and others' bodies too. To feed people is a kind of worship."

"In our family, we always feed holy men and Brahmans," Ba said grandly.

"Not just *sadhus* and Brahmans, Mataji," Swami Prakashananda responded. "The Goddess is in everyone, all beings, even animals."

Without our suggesting it, Swami Prakashananda offered us our prize. "Why don't you take our Rahoul home with you for a few days?" he said. "He works too hard here. Will you go, Rahoul?"

Rahoul nodded.

It was that easy, prying Rahoul loose. The swami's relaxed farewell made it seem there was no big divide between life in ashrams and life in households. I reflected that maybe, like Khimji Bhagat, Rahoul could be as holy as he wanted but live at home. But imagining Rahoul back in Nasik made me want to turn away, as though shutting a book. When Rahoul noticed the reappearance of Paw's bottle, he would probably say something and it would all become real, known to Maw too.

As we gathered by the ashram gate, preparing for our long walk downhill, Ba poked at Chanda-phui, pressing her forward.

"Babaji, my daughter has no children," she said. "Bless her with a son."

Chanda-phui bent her graying head low. Her face was so impassive it seemed almost as if she couldn't bear to be present and had temporarily vacated her body. It was painful to watch her and think of the many times Ba and others must have made her bow for blessings. We all knew that sons were special, but why did sweet, kind Chanda-phui again and again have to present herself as a failure in need of help?

"May the goddess Bhagavati bring you good fortune," Swami Prakashananda said, and reached out a hand to Chanda-phui's head for a moment. "Pray to Her. She is compassionate."

He picked something from the dust, holding it up. "We're all like pieces of metal lying at the side of the road," he said. "What use is a scrap of metal? It's just junk, isn't it? But when a craftsman pounds at it, he can make something valuable, like a watch or a flashlight. In the same way, we are hammered by fate. When we don't immediately get what we want, or when we lose what we have, the Mother is pounding at our understanding, making us wise. We are being changed from useless bits of junk to something that can be of use to others."

"*Amba Mata ki jai!*" he called out from the gate as we led Rahoul away through the lengthening shadows, racing the sun to descend the mountain before tigers began to roam.

"How's it going, Baby?" Rahoul took hold of my hand and swung it high. Knowing he would soon witness the activities around Paw's armchair—that we would all be hammered by Paw's promise coming undone—I swallowed hard before I could find bright words.

Blind Blue Heavens, Pure Blue Light

Back in Juhu, the school term proceeded without Rahoul. Maw seemed to know that Paw was drinking again. I heard her confide to friends that Paw had "gotten sloshed" at the party celebrating the opening of the Merchant-Ivory film *The Guru,* for which she had arranged some sets. She sounded so upset that I waited, worried, for her to mention Delhi.

One evening I settled after supper into my favorite reading corner in the living room. Maw had made me this special corner by sliding together two of Nani's steamer trunks; covering them with pads, a block-printed spread, and cushions; and hooking up a bulb behind a sheet of handmade paper hung at an angle. I found this corner a perfect place to hover, in case the grown-up conversation proved juicier than the latest book from the school library.

When the phone rang out its double-trills, I dashed, thinking it might be Fatty Rasha asking about some aspect of our homework. "5717-double-4?" shrieked a woman operator. "International trunk call is coming from U.S.A., madam."

"Hey Maw!" I yelled. "America on the line!"

We received international calls very rarely; the last one I could remember had been almost two years earlier, in the era when Rahoul was working with gods' eyes. Maw and Paw had been away for a rare weekend together in Khandala, and since Rahoul was in charge, he picked up the phone. He had been mysteriously quiet about why anyone would telephone from America, and he didn't say why he began trying so frantically to reach Maw and Paw. Days later, I learned that the phone call had brought the news of Nani's death. I had taken this in numbly, not understanding how this word applied to my adored grandmother, who had already left me behind.

Now Maw clutched the heavy black receiver. Standing nearby, I could smell the panic rising off her. "Oh no! Oh no, really?" she shouted. "Oh no. This is terrible news. Where is she right now? Oh no. It's hard to know if I can do it. Well, I don't know, but I can try."

When Maw set down the phone, she sat still for a minute, drenched in sweat. Everyone else in the house had anxiously gathered; even Dobeyboy pressed against Maw's knees in a responsibly protective head-in-the air pose. Paw, though, was still off with his friend Dolly for the evening. "That was Marilyn Hirsch in New York," Maw said. "Maya's ill and needs an operation. I'm going to have to go."

Tickets abroad were so expensive in rupees that in the nineteen years she had lived in India Maw had never traveled back to America. But with this crisis, Paw managed to produce funds for an air ticket within a few days, and Rahoul was summoned home to run the household. I was used to Maw's traveling for decorating assignments. Rahoul had looked after the rest of us often before. All the same, the open-ended uncertainty of Maw's departure, and Maya's unnamed illness, made me feel as though I were being sucked downward, off a cliff, to a patchwork of unknown land.

: : :

Rahoul reoccupied his room in Nani's house and started wearing jeans again. He filled his room with books that fit his new interests; some he found on the shelves in the main house, some he bought at the downtown Strand Bookstore: Jung's *Memories, Dreams, Reflections*, Herrigel's *Zen in the Art of Archery*, Merton's *The Seven Storey Mountain*, Shah's *The Way of the Sufi*, Wilhelm's translation from Chinese of *The Secret of the Golden Flower*, Swami Prabhavananda's translation from Sanskrit of the *Upanishads*. I flipped through the pages, looking for stories of children or animals.

Unlike Maw, who so enjoyed her guru's presence through photographs, Rahoul put up no photographs of Swami Prakashananda. "Prakashananda Baba says that the guru is a principle, not any particular person," Rahoul told us. "He says: every step you take, find a guru in it."

Rahoul reported the different ways to meditate that Swami Prakashananda had taught him. "Not just mantras and watching your breath and

the usual sort of thing. He also tells me to listen to silence. He says you
can tune into the inner *nada,* you know, this inner hum—I can't describe
it—this thick sound of silence, like a swarm of bees or the inside of a big
conch: that's the sound behind all sound, he says. And then sometimes he
sends me out to lie on my back and look at the sky when the sun isn't overhead. After a while, if you keep looking, you see all these little sparks of
light flying around. Just watch the sky, he says, it's filled with the blue light
of consciousness."

I tried to tune in to the inner honeybees but became restless to hear them
say something; I went out to the Juhu garden and looked at the sky but only
saw the shifting patterns of pipal leaves and long swirls of coconut fronds.
I wondered if you had to be in a holy place or near a holy person to hear
and see the magical things Rahoul described. Just as Rahoul's stories made
Swami Prakashananda vivid to me, so I could see that the company of gurus had made these other, hidden realities become real for Rahoul.

Paw set off for Nasik to finalize the land sales that had funded the hugely
expensive air ticket, leaving Rahoul in charge. On school days, Rahoul set
several alarm clocks to trill in different rooms so that Deven and I would
wake up in time to catch the school bus. Tashi was back from boarding
school for his own long winter vacation, but Rahoul woke him up too. For
breakfast, Rahoul made us Maw-style German pancakes served with *gur pak,*
or jaggery syrup; unlike Maw, he sometimes stirred a few drops of green
food coloring into the batter. He made lists, kept accounts, and instructed
all the servants: Ramu, the cook from Karnataka; Chitti, the all-purpose
houseboy from Andhra Pradesh; Aji, the old woman who arrived twice a
day from the Juhu fishermen's village to squat, hissing, as she scrubbed at
dishes; the *bai* whose husband was the next-door *mali,* who showed up in
the late afternoon to thump at our buckets of clothes; and Moti, who came
from the sweeper's colony down the road with a stiff broom to scour the
toilets each morning. (Since Mani Driver, from Kerala, answered only to
Paw, Rahoul did not need to instruct him.) Sitting out on the porch near
the driveway, Rahoul counted the clothes when they were sent out in a
chaotic bundle to the *dhobi,* and counted them again when they returned
in crisply ironed piles. When stray guests showed up, Rahoul brought out
clean sheets and towels and sat them down for conversation. But without
Maw our house was less interesting, and guests didn't linger.

Maw had asked various friends and relatives to come stay and help out.
Two British friends of Maw's, Davina and Georgina, joined Rahoul to play
house. They were both in their early twenties, just a few years older than

Rahoul. They helped Rahoul reorganize the kitchen shelves and threw out what they dismissed as ridiculously small amounts of Kashmir saffron and Japanese ajinomoto; they cooked stews and called us to stop reading or playing, and to come to the dinner table while the food was still hot.

Beautiful, swollen-lipped Davina meditated often. She gave me a copy of *Old Possum's Book of Practical Cats,* which I immediately loved, both for the cat characters and because it made me feel very sophisticated to be reading T. S. Eliot. This book became my new resource for elocution contests over the next few years, endlessly puzzling society-lady judges who were more used to Wordsworth or Tennyson. It also started a new trend in household cat names. Until then, Paw had usually named our cats. Manuela, multi-colored mother of many batches of kittens, commemorated a "catty" ex-girlfriend in America; Whisky and Soda, part-Siamese brothers handed over by a departing consulate worker honored another duo favored by Paw; orange and white Meow-ji, found wandering in the neighborhood, was named for her shrill kitten voice. Now, with Eliot in hand, Deven and I assigned tongue-twisting names to our succeeding cats: orange Mungojerry, black and white Bombelarina, and so on.

Georgina told witty stories about everything from British girls' boarding schools to the hippie scene at Majorca, periodically laughing with the staccato of a machine gun that felled all of us in her audience into shared laughter. I was mesmerized by her crisp use of language and awed that her mother wrote detective stories. I confessed to her that I wrote too, and her encouragement gave me a new commitment to writing a few pages every day on the adventures of Princess Snow Rose.

Davina and Georgina made Maw's absence seem like an exciting party in a foreign film. All too soon, though, they moved on.

: : :

Deven and I came home from school one afternoon and found Rahoul cross-legged on the floor, peering into one of the low, modular cupboards that Maw periodically moved around to rearrange the living room.

"White ants," Rahoul said grimly. "We're going to have to save all the family photographs."

Cockroaches of many sizes scattered as he pulled out albums, envelopes, and plastic bags. Ant tracks stained brown veins along the inside of the cupboard. Deven, Tashi, Chitti, Ramu, and I all began to help, sorting through the pictures to make sure they weren't harmed.

Rahoul flicked a cloth over the three leather-bound family albums, quickly checking for ant markings on the black pages separated by yellowed, creased leaves of tissue paper. The albums recorded the years before my birth, and as always when I saw them, I was torn. Part of me wanted to study the pictures closely, absorbing all the images and accompanying stories as if I'd been there too. Another part of me felt left out, even a little hurt. Why, by the time I was born, had Maw and Paw run out of energy to document family life?

Pictures that included me weren't in albums at all but jumbled up in manila envelopes and plastic bags. I spotted a plastic bag with black-and-white pictures from the years that I lived next door with Nani and took it over to the coffee table to straighten. Nani beamed as she held me up as a one-year-old, Rahoul looking on, hands on his hips, behind her; Nani's hand curled around my chubby fingers as she taught me how to write; Nani admired a painting on the child's easel as I gestured with my brush. I arranged the pictures so they all faced the same way, viewing that confident, adored little girl as though across a stony ravine.

"Hey guys, guess what I found," Rahoul called from the floor. "It's Maw and Paw's wedding certificate."

Deven, Tashi, and I gathered around him to look at the signatures. "Look, they got married at a courthouse in Colorado, not in Taos," Rahoul said. "Nani wasn't even a witness. Hey! We have to start celebrating this properly."

I couldn't remember our parents ever having celebrated a wedding anniversary. I studied the date—January 21, 1950—trying to place it among the family birthdays. I counted out months on my fingers, starting from the pinky of the left hand: *February, March, April* . . . right up to Maya's birthday in September. I kept coming up with eight months. I had only the haziest idea of the facts of life, but I knew that nine was a crucial number. I couldn't understand it; maybe for this kind of calculation you had to count January as the first finger.

"And look at this!" Rahoul said, "It's Maw and Paw arriving at the Bombay airport."

They were young, thin, and unsmiling, clearly worn out by their long flight. Under the thick flower garlands of welcome, Paw wore a gray suit, Maw a pale short-sleeved dress and high heels, the sheen of stockings glinting on her calves. I remembered Maw telling how Nani had insisted that Maw carry a hat and gloves on the trip to prove to the hostile in-laws that she was from a respectable family, but by the end of the trip, Maw was wearing neither hat nor gloves. Paw's elderly father stood stern beside them, his

dark turban adding to his authority and his bottle-cap glasses reflecting back
the photographer's flash. Surrounding them were other grim men from the
caste, possibly a few of the same elders who a year earlier had offered to
travel to the United States and forcibly bring Paw back before he married
the upstart American. Manu-phui, Paw's youngest sister, was the only other
female in the photograph, a little girl looking overwhelmed. Baby Maya
was nowhere to be seen; I remembered Maw saying that Chanda-phui had
given her the warmest welcome, taking charge of her new niece. Probably
they had wandered off beyond the frame of the photograph.

How did that pretty, dazed girl with the defiantly set chin turn into
the mother I knew? We had just seen her off and, again, an airport photographer had documented the occasion. In this picture, she stood alone,
her body wrapped in a printed, dark silk sari. She was heavier, softer, with
deeper lines joining the edges of her nostrils to the ends of her lips. Even
without Paw at her side, she had dressed for this big trip with all the formality of a Hindu married woman: a jet-beaded *mangal sutra* she herself had
designed around her neck, diamond flowers in her ears, a vermilion spot of
kumkum on her forehead. I worried for my mother: just as Paw's relatives
may not have fully appreciated the stockings, high heels, hat, and gloves,
would the faraway Americans now understand the sari?

:::

Sometimes Rahoul left us for a few hours to ride the train downtown. He
went to huge public lectures by the philosopher J. Krishnamurti, who had
long ago been discovered as a messiah by Theosophists and whose books on
education Rahoul admired. He also visited a Polish Jewish man called Mau-
rice Frydman, who had lived in India for many years. Frydman took him
to meet a "householder guru" called Nisargatta Maharaj, a *bidi* seller who
received small groups, teaching in Marathi. Rahoul also took to dropping
in at the apartment building near the downtown overpass where Acharya
Rajneesh, a professor who had become a guru, gave articulate talks with
references to Zen Buddhism.

Mostly, though, Rahoul devoted himself to the house. Having dusted off
the phonograph records that Maw and Paw had brought from America, he
systematically played his way through them. Leadbelly's deep voice called
out through the house, Wanda Landowska struck precise notes on the harpsichord, *Carmina Burana* gathered its mesmerizing force. But then, as if continuing his quest to find himself, Rahoul turned to a nearly constant sound
track of Bob Dylan.

"Dylan is a prophet, man," Rahoul said, balancing records by their edges as he changed them. I observed that Rahoul's curly hair was once again growing out to resemble the thin young man on the album covers.

I sat beside the record player in the living room, folding origami cranes, lilies, and boxes and trying to puzzle out the stories contained in particular Dylan songs. Maggie had her farm, and what sounded like a "Paw" and a "Maw," but why was everyone in that family so strange? Was "It's All Over Now, Baby Blue" a warning to the blue baby Krishna that his wicked uncle King Kamsa was sending demons to kill him? Was the Tambourine Man a wandering performer like those who sang for donations on the sands of Juhu Beach?

When Fatty Rasha came over on weekends, we listened eagerly to Dylan's rousing warnings about how everybody could get pelted with rocks, no matter what they did. We waited for Bob Dylan to shout out the shocking F-word, and then we rushed off to giggle.

Rahoul was amused that we requested this song so often. "You know what 'get stoned' means, right?" he asked me, then explained.

"Really?"

"Where have you been, Baby?"

Yes, pot had been appearing in our house for a few years. I had observed hippies bring out special stashes wrapped in tin foil and plastic, fondly remembering Kabul or Kathmandu. Then too, I'd heard Maw explain to the hippies how marijuana could be bought at the government shop in the Juhu village on the road beyond the church and bus terminal. An American professor friend on a research trip had confided that he'd like to know what exactly his long-haired students were so enthused about, and Maw sent a servant out to "score." I had gone to bed but I'd heard the event told and retold with such proud amusement by Maw that I almost felt I had seen that professor take off his tie, fold up his glasses, and lie back against the bolsters in the living room, smoke billowing from his nostrils.

Another afternoon, Deven and I came home from school to find Rahoul defrosting the refrigerator. He pulled a foil-wrapped package from the melting ice. "Hey guys, Maw's left us some cake," he said.

We thought this must be Grandma Wilde's cinnamon cake, a recipe that Nani had passed on from her own grandmother, a distant cousin of Oscar Wilde. But Rahoul tasted a corner—"Brownies!" he announced.

Maw didn't usually bake with chocolate, and anyway, I only liked sweet milk chocolate so I said I didn't want any. The three boys shared the treat with their friends, who had just arrived to play from the Juhu Christian fishing village. Then they all raced down to the beach with a football, and I settled down at the coffee table with old *National Geographic* magazines spread around me, meticulously copying illustrations for a social studies assignment on world religions.

I had written out the four noble truths of Buddhism in bamboolike writing and traced a calm Japanese Buddha when Rahoul rushed in, sweaty and laughing. "Oh man," he said, panting. "We were playing football without a ball."

Rahoul went across the driveway to consult with the ex–Peace Corps couple who currently rented half of Nani's house and who used our refrigerator for their milk and eggs. He came back laughing even harder. "Guess what! That was their hash cake."

"Really?"

"Really!"

Rahoul seemed happy enough, so I calmly continued to write out the Lord's Prayer in Gothic lettering. Rahoul set a temperamental early Dylan album playing, then sat down near me at the table, writing in his notebook in a continuous rush of words:

> *I saw—I said.*
> *Universe unlimited burst,*
> *Blind blue heavens*
> *Pure blue light.*
>
> > *Heaven within the head*
> > *Dome of crystal light*
> > *Mind was just present*
> > *trembling as I did fall*
> > *Up and low, heaved, blown around,*
> > *spiraling flying*
> > *saucer sound,*
> > *thrown stricken to the ground. . . .*

Decades later, when this notebook came into my hands, I thought that Rahoul might be describing a mystical experience brought on by Swami Prakashananda's exercise of staring into the vastness of sky: blind blue heavens, pure blue light. Then I saw the title, "On a hash cake trip," and remembered being ten: tumbling, blown around, Rahoul standing in as my mother.

:::

Paw returned from Nasik, bringing Ba with him. When Maw was around, Ba didn't usually stay for long, but now she settled in for a holiday by the beach, and Chanda-phui joined us too.

Even in her own room in Nasik, Ba had the habit of filling her cupboards with spiritual paraphernalia, including books. Her clothes—white saris, white *cholis,* white petticoats, and gray shawls—remained in khaki-covered suitcases that she slid under her bed with its mosquito-net frame. Now she stored the same suitcases under a less grand bed in our house. She had also brought a briefcase-size piece of luggage, filled with her traveling gods in little steel frames, that served as a *puja* when the lid was folded back.

"When you sit at your *puja,* praying calmly, the gods arrive smiling." Ba announced as she sat on the floor, rearranging her gods. "They come just for a second. It's not like they're going to lounge around for an hour or two [*ek-be calock*]." Ba popped open her tubular box of *agarbatti,* and poked a few sticks into a small silver holder. She turned to look over her shoulder to where we grandchildren were watching her settle in. "I've met God often," she reminded us, holding a match under the sticks until smoke swirled. She circled the sticks and settled them into the thimble-size silver traveling holder. Then she joined her palms.

Ba walked dedicatedly up and down the beach in the early morning, and again in the evenings, white sari fluttering in the wind, eyes fixed on the sand. In the last few years, with big hotels and apartment buildings going up, there were fewer shells on the beach, but Ba was looking for cowries. "When cowries are lying in the sand with their teeth up, as though they're smiling, it's especially lucky," Ba instructed. She went on to describe how, when our caste goddess Randhal Ma was invited to pujas, two coconuts were each given clay faces with two cowries for eyes and a third for a smiling mouth. I darted around Ba, eager for lucky cowries that would protect my sister and bring my mother home.

Chanda-phui filled the house with brass containers and plastic tubs of savory *nasta.* She made daily trips to the bazaar to supplement this stock, returning with packages wrapped in oil-stained newspaper, and carrying snacks like triangular potato-stuffed *samosas* or spicy sweet *kachoris* aflame with chili. Maw always warned about the stomach infestations we might pick up from these roadside snacks, and Paw joked that we would need a round of Flagyl treatment to rout out parasites—a familiar story that he called "Amoebaba and the Forty Pills." Chanda-phui, though, trusted the bazaar, and her enthusiasm lured us on. *"Garam-a-garam!"* she called, laughing as she settled cross-legged on the floor to unwrap packages, "Hot-hot. Come eat while it's still hot!"

Chanda-phui dusted and bustled, and took over counting clothes for the *dhobi*. I watched her rearrange Maw's *puja* alcove, face-high in the bedroom cupboard, to highlight the Swami Narayan figures over the Swami Muktananda photographs. Chanda-phui demoted Ramu—our South Indian cook of unknown caste and so-so cooking skill—to being a regular house servant and she brought in a proper Gujarati Brahman *maharaj* from the Byculla apartment. This thin, nervous man wrapped a lightweight *dhoti* around his legs and stripped to the waist whenever he entered the kitchen to stir up sugar-tinted Gujarati food. For my tender stomach, he set aside bland versions of his red-flecked dishes.

Chanda-phui herself couldn't eat much. After all her years of nervously gnashing at sliced betel nuts, her teeth were little more than stubs. She had made a series of appointments with a dentist for the time she was in Bombay. Sukhlal-phua was busy with his refrigeration business in Ahmedabad, and so she was escorted across town to her dental sessions by one of his cousins: Mulji-bhai, a mild, kind man. Waiting patiently in our living room as Chanda-phui changed her sari in preparation for going out, he sometimes told us stories in a very soft voice about our Gujar Sutar ancestors.

Ba, as always, used any opportunity to tell stories of her own privileged encounters with gods, goddesses, and holy people. "When I was a girl, I went to the jungle to cut grass for the cow," she informed us as she sat beside a kerosene stove where she was stirring *mohantal*, her favorite winter sweet, in a big vessel with rings at each end. "An ancient man was sitting under a tree filled with fragrant *champa* flowers. His elbow was resting on a stick. His face was filled with light." Ba set her flat steel implement down, and Chanda-phui took over the stirring. A rich, brown scent of ghee, *dals*, and sugar filled the porch.

Ba impersonated the old man, drawing her back straight, raising her elbow. Then she waved her fingers inward, motioning her imaginary young self forward. *"'Ao beti,'* he said. 'Come forward, daughter.'"

Ba dropped her shoulders and joined her palms, speaking in a thin girl's voice. "'Baba, is there some way I can serve you?' I asked. 'Would you like to drink water?' 'I'm here to rest,' he said. 'No water. How are you, daughter?' 'I'm just fine,' I said. 'From now on things will go very well with you,' he said, lifting a palm in blessing. 'I'll be back again later.'"

Ba's hand remained frozen in blessing. She looked at us sternly. "And then he dissolved," she said. "There was no one there."

I loved imagining Ba as a girl out in the jungle by herself. "How old were you?" I asked.

"I was eleven years old," Ba stated.

I was still taking in the idea of Ba having once been just a little older than me when Deven asked, "Ba, do you know who he was?"

"He was Dattatreya, guru of the gods," Ba said. "He did appear to me again, just recently. Taking Mani Driver, I had gone on pilgrimage to Pandharpur and then Gangapur, a place where Dattatreya is worshipped. We visited Akkalkot Swami, who is a very perfected being. Some other women cooked, and he fed us. Then we went on to Poona in the car. We stayed for the night with the great singer Hirabai Barodrekar. We were sitting down to eat when a *sadhu* arrived.

"'One Kamla-bai of Nasik who came to Gangapur. Where is she?' he asked. 'She's eating,' people said. Then they told me, 'Some man is here for you. Come out and meet him.' I went out, and there was the same old man from the jungle. He was carrying a shoulder bag. He was really ancient. I bowed. 'Take twenty rupees from me,' I said. 'From my bag I will give you hundreds of thousands of rupees,' he told me. "*Khush raho,* stay happy. I came for you all the way from Gangapur.' And then he vanished. Even Mani Driver said so: one moment you could see him, and then he had disappeared."

"Yes, I have lots of blessings from the gods," Ba affirmed, resuming the stirring of the sweet, which was supposed to make us all strong through the winter. She motioned toward the room where once again Paw had remained home, drinking and reading, rather than going to the office. Her voice lowered conspiratorially. "If there's no work, no business, in this house, how come we're still eating? This is the blessing of the saints."

:::

I was disoriented by my mother's absence and began to spend more hours each day writing my way into the life of Princess Snow Rose. Snow Rose had first joined me when I was about six, and her family was as familiar as my own. She too had older siblings, but unlike me, she also had several younger brothers and sisters to boss around. Her mother, Queen Snow, had died giving birth to twins, but her father, King Augustine, adored her and often showed his appreciation with fabulous new gowns. Joined by her orphaned cousin, Rosemary, and aided by her Fairy Godmother, Snow Rose embarked on all kinds of adventures: she crept down secret passages, spied on the Enemy King, and even lived among witches, learning powerful spells that allowed her to escape and rescue others too.

As Christmas neared, Rahoul set up our usual decorations: two coconut fronds bound together along their stems and trimmed into an elongated triangle, making a four-sided tree the shape of a fir. We balanced this tree in a big brass water pot filled with sand, then hung the flat fronds with shining red globes left by Nani and gold origami birds that we folded and threaded ourselves. We also cut big symmetrical gold stars that we taped along the vertical slatted windows separating the living room from the porch.

Ba's birthday was on Christmas Day, so she had always felt a special sympathy for this "Kar-ees-chan" holiday. Rahoul reminded Ba that it was our custom to give and receive presents; however, he had little money to spare from running the household. On December 24, while Paw was at the office with his car and Chanda-phui was at the dentist's, Ba gathered up her khaki tote bag and announced that she and Rahoul were going shopping. She sent out a servant to fetch a taxi from a nearby tourist hotel.

"Are you coming, Baby?" Rahoul asked me.

"Okay," I said, shutting my notebook.

Ba, Rahoul, and I drove across town to the suburb of Matunga and entered a ready-made clothing store. "Bring clothes their size!" Ba ordered, waving a tattooed forearm at a sales attendant. "Choose something!" Ba instructed us.

Ready-made clothes were an embarrassing luxury. Even my panties were sewn by Maw's tailor, Zareena, down the beach. How could I choose anything with price tags attached? Then too, how could I choose anything that was synthetic, with machine-stitched embroidery? When I was small, my favorite piece of clothing was a frilly pink party dress Nani had bought me at Bambino's downtown. But since Maw took charge, when I wasn't in school uniform I mostly wore block-printed, vegetable-dyed, Maw-designed handloom dresses.

The sales attendant scurried about, bringing piles of possibilities. Rahoul located a few cotton shirts for himself, Deven, and Tashi, but the girls' selections were a jumble of pastel synthetics. The shopkeeper flung more and more clothes in my size over the counter as I looked away and shook my head.

"Are you worried about the money, Baby?" Rahoul asked me in an undertone.

I couldn't bring myself to answer. I stared at the blue bands of the rubber *chappals* emerging from between my big toes and second toes.

"Ba can afford it," he murmured. "You know, she has her own money, separate from Paw's. You'll make her happy if you choose something."

He picked up a pale green *kurta-churidar* set, with a black inset with chain-stitched embroidery at the chest. *"Kitna accha hai!"* Rahoul said enthusiastically for Ba to follow. "It's so nice!"

I knew, just knew, that Maw would find the green insipid and the machine-made embroidery crass. With us children, Maw never hid her opinion that Paw and his family had bad taste. Maw had already warned me about developing Chanda-phui's voice; I hated to imagine her thinking I'd caught bad taste.

"Accepting a present is a kind of present to the person who's giving it," Rahoul whispered in my ear in English. In Hindi, he continued. "Isn't this pretty? Kirin likes it!"

I hung my head, still staring at my *chappals*. I could not bear to look up and see Ba extract hundred-rupee notes from her roll.

"Put it on when we get home, okay?" Rahoul urged as we followed Ba out the door and he took my hand to cross the road. As though he was reading my mind, he said, "This is for Ba. Don't worry about what Maw thinks. It's not a big deal. Listen, like Swami Prakashananda says: In life it's good to make other people happy."

:::

Just as Davina and Georgina had moved on with their own lives, after a few weeks Ba and Chanda-phui left to return to other obligations. By this time, Paw was drinking heavily and making no attempt to hide it.

Paw usually arrived home late at night, having spent a few hours at the soirees of the writer Mulk Raj Anand in the company of his friend Dolly. We'd have bathed, eaten our dinner, and done homework under Rahoul's supervision when Mani Driver honked from the driveway and everyone rushed out to greet the car. Paw staggered in, stumbling through the living room to his own room and armchair. Once there, he fumbled open his briefcase and brought out the *Playboy* magazines that some hanger-on must have found for him at the black-market stalls near his office. (Paw never bought anything himself; he always sent someone else and never checked the change.) He left the magazines out in plain view for children, servants, or visitors to leaf through.

I occasionally took a *Playboy* to my favorite corner seat. I studied the

strange blonde women with pink udders, wondering about their lives. Seeing them made me uncomfortably aware that I was the only female in the
house; even Dobeyboy and our old cat Soda were male. I also scrutinized
the cartoons, with the same baffled confusion I brought to those in Maw's
favorite magazine, the New Yorker, which had arrived by sea, three months
late, ever since she moved to India. I couldn't understand what was funny
about naked people chasing each other. Obviously, the word "adultery," repeated in so many cartoons, had to do with being an adult. How did this
relate to the adults I knew best—Maw and Paw? I thought of asking Rahoul
but felt that I should be sophisticated enough to know. I didn't want to make
a fool of myself, as I had done by admitting I didn't know the meaning of
"streetwalker."

Foreign liquors in heavy bottles came home along with the magazines.
Like the magazines, these would have come from the black-market stalls. I
knew that anything foreign was expensive, and I tried not to think of how
Rahoul sat with notebooks, working out how to pay the bills. As the bottles
lost their labels, lining up to hold boiled water instead, Paw stopped going
to the office. He woke later and later each morning, irises stained red: somber, the antithesis of gods' eyes. He was usually reading in his armchair, radio playing beside him, when we returned from school. He seemed friendly
but sad, with little to say and no interest in going down to the beach to
watch the sunset. He was hardly eating anything, and his sweat had begun
to smell fermented.

Since Paw's psychiatrist didn't seem to be helping, Rahoul decided that
something drastic needed to be done. He had heard of places that helped
people give up drinking, so he telephoned family friends, doctors, and hos-
pitals. Juhu phone lines, strung between coconut trunks, required repeated
dialing, returned only busy tones for hours, often crossed into other people's
conversations, and sometimes went suddenly dead. Still, Rahoul persisted.

"I've taken Paw to the hospital," Rahoul announced one afternoon,
pouring out foaming glasses of banana milk when Deven and I came home
from school. "He's sick. Nobody wants to say it, but he's an alcoholic. It's a
sickness, and he needs medicine. He didn't want to go to the hospital, but he
was too drunk to resist. I had to take him in a taxi because Mani Driver said
he wouldn't drive without Paw's orders."

Deven and I were still staring.

"Look, don't worry about Paw," Rahoul said. "He has lots of pretty
nurses from Kerala looking after him. Everything's going to be okay. We'll
go see him this weekend."

The Holy Spirit Hospital was located far out in the suburbs beyond Andheri. When we visited that weekend, Paw seemed to have shrunk. He looked like he hadn't slept for days, and his hands shook. He seemed uncertain of what to do with his hands without a glass, his usual prop, and so he clung to his trembling pipe. He had renamed the place the "Wholly Spirits Hospital."

Rather than sit in his small room, he took us out to the garden, where marigolds and yellow asters were blooming. We trailed along, humoring and flattering him, enjoying the novelty of being on a walk with our father.

When visiting hours were over, we said good-bye to Paw, leaving him in his room. On the way out Rahoul suddenly said, "I want to show you something," and led us into the premature baby ward. This was a small, warm room, flooded with artificial light, with half a dozen cots under glass covers. Beneath the glass, skinny, hairy red babies were tied down with tubes. We peered at them, but they were too inwardly preoccupied to know we were there. I had no idea that anything human could be so hairy. There were no mothers in sight, but the room seemed so infinitely safe under the kind eyes of the nurses that I dragged my rubber *chappals,* not wanting to leave when Rahoul prodded us toward the door.

:::

When Paw came home, he started rereading a thick book from his college days called *Fear and Trembling.* I couldn't help wondering if his unsteady hands were behind this choice. Accountants from Sethji's nineteen apartment buildings sometimes arrived to have him sign stack upon stack of receipts for tenants. The milkman camped on the porch again, waiting to be paid. Eventually Paw set off for Nasik to sell more land.

Maw wrote regularly from America: letters cramped with excited handwriting that filled the page, then swirled around the margins with last-minute additions. She sent the happy news that Maya's operation had been successful. I had never figured out what exactly was wrong with Maya and almost superstitiously didn't want to ask, as though talking about it might make her condition worse. Anyway, the important thing was that she was getting better. Maw wrote that she planned to stay the full term of her four-month round-trip ticket. She was thrilled to be meeting old friends and was making new friends too. On her way back to Bombay, she intended to stop in Europe to visit various friends and museums.

Maw's long absence was starting to feel dangerously like a desertion, and

I couldn't help brooding about Nani's departure. Old fears I had once been able to keep underground tormented me. Then I began running a fever and had to stay home from school. I threw up repeatedly in the scratched enamel tub that Rahoul set on the floor beside one of the living room divans. Rahoul telephoned our family doctor, Tony De Souza, who arrived once his evening clinic was over.

Doctor De Souza stroked his goatee, then made me bend my neck forward. "Watch the fever," he told Rahoul. "If her neck gets stiff, it could be meningitis. Have you tried spoon-feeding Coca-Cola?"

The doctor snapped shut his black leather briefcase and departed. Meningitis? I remembered that Ved Mehta, the New York–based writer who wrote for the *New Yorker* and had once visited our house, had gone blind from childhood meningitis. But I lacked the energy to be scared.

Rahoul sent a servant out to fetch a bottle of Coca-Cola. He sat beside me holding a cool, wet washcloth to my head, soaking it in ice water, then twisting it out. Instead of Bob Dylan, he put on a recording of Wanda Landowska playing Bach on a harpsichord. The order and precision of the notes quelled the nausea briefly, but then the urge to throw up drowned out the music and I was retching once again, and again Rahoul was holding my head over the enamel tub. I wanted to sleep, but my belly heaved from deeper and sourer recesses.

"Just one spoonful of Coke," said Rahoul. I opened my mouth, a meek baby bird.

I rolled the dark sweet fizz around my mouth. Maw rarely allowed us soft drinks unless we were traveling and had run out of boiled water. Coca-Cola reminded me of Nani's ice cream. A few times a year when she'd lived with us, Nani would bring out her eggbeater to whip up deliriously delicious vanilla-flavored ice cream, which she floated for us in bowls of Coca-Cola, the way children did "back in the States."

"Open wide," Rahoul coaxed. "One more."

I tasted a safer, sweeter time in my life. The few spoonfuls stayed down and I was able to sleep. The next day, Rahoul tried mashed bananas. "No," I said. But the day after, he insisted. "Just one bite," he said, holding a spoon by my mouth.

"You have to eat, Baby," said Rahoul, nudging with the spoon.

The thought of anything solid made me queasy. "No."

"You have to listen to me."

"No." An empty stomach promised peace.

"Look, I'm so much older than you that I changed your diapers. I taught you how to walk. Now you have to listen to me, okay? Just one bite."

I took a reluctant mouthful. To our relief, we didn't need to pull out the basin afterward.

I lay in the living room, day turning to night, night turning to day. Sometimes I stood up shakily and, holding on to the wall, shuffled toward a bathroom. I could have retreated into a bedroom, but it seemed safer to be at the center of household activity, near the record player. Visitors coming by spoke in hushed tones and moved to the porch instead. I had been ill for long stretches in the past, but this time around my spirit was cracking.

"I want Maw," I eventually wept, not caring that I was too old to cry.

"After America, she's going to Europe," said Rahoul. "I'll have to figure out where to find her."

"Tell her to come home," I sobbed.

More days passed. I identified new shapes in the blotchy monsoon stains on the rippled asbestos ceiling. Sitting made me dizzy. Anything but a few spoonfuls of mashed bananas turned my stomach. Doctor De Souza came by and rubbed his goatee, then tested my neck again to be sure it really wasn't meningitis. I drifted back into the shadowy space of dreams.

I woke from a long sleep, not knowing whether it was day or night, smelling potatoes. Rahoul sat on the edge of the divan, a plate of french fries still glistening with oil balanced on his knees.

"One bite, sweetheart," said Rahoul. He put a fry into his mouth and chewed, rolling his eyes. "Ummmm! Delicious. Just try one. Look, here's ketchup."

"No."

"You need to eat, Baby," said Rahoul, looking me straight in the eyes.

Through the lens of fever, his deep-set brown eyes seemed big, scared, and kind.

"You have to get strong," Rahoul said. "You're going to have to start eating. Do you remember how, when you were little, Maya and I used to grab you by each arm and run down the beach with you between us so you could fly?"

"I remember." I remembered the soaring giddy rush against the wind, the sense of being cherished and indulged, the crash of the waves, my big brother and sister laughing as they ran.

"We never let you go, right?"

"Never."

"So you have to trust me," Rahoul said.

Rahoul's six-year advantage on life had elevated him beyond any sibling rivalry, criticism, or blame. He had always seemed more like a benevolent grown-up: a powerful, almost godlike protector. I looked at his anxious face with its halo of messy curls and, as though from a great, calm distance, I understood that he wasn't godlike after all: he was a scared, uncertain, sixteen-year-old boy trying to do his best.

He pulled me up by the shoulders and readjusted the pillows so I was almost sitting up. Then he angled a french fry bright with ketchup into my mouth. "Just one," he said. "For me."

The calm, distant part of me understood that even if I had come to fear food, I should try this to make my brother glad. "In life it's good to make other people happy," Rahoul had said, echoing old Swami Prakashananda.

I accepted the french fry from Rahoul, feeling its strange solidity. Crisp saltiness turned to moist substance as I chewed.

"One more," said Rahoul, reaching his hand to my mouth.

I chewed that too.

"I sent Maw a telegram to come home," he said.

"Really?"

"Really." He was smiling full-on, not with his sideways hint of teasing.

I sat up against the pillows and allowed Rahoul to feed me the whole plate of fries. He disappeared into the kitchen again and brought out another warm yellow gold pile with rich red on the side. This time I fed myself, and Rahoul ate some too.

: : :

A few days before Maw returned, I left the living room sickbed, energized by relief and excitement. Maw returned to find me well, though my ribs showed and my backbone protruded; for lack of any other explanation my illness was labeled as severe amoebic dysentery. Paw was home from Nasik and, for the moment, dry. The house was clean and ordered. Things were basically under control, and it was hard for Maw to understand why we had summoned her back.

"I don't know why you are all 'Hey Maw'-ing me when you managed by yourselves so well," Maw said. "This was my one chance in twenty years. You don't know how important this time was to me."

Maw's words seemed embarrassing, unseemly, deeply wrong: how could our mother possibly separate her own desires from our welfare? I hovered nearby as she unpacked, enjoying her mother-warmth and feeling confused. Was it appropriate for her to look radiant after she'd been away from us? She described how, after all these years, she had worn her thick brown hair curling around her shoulders rather than tying it up tightly like a good Indian wife. She talked excitedly about starting a business with a woman in New York exporting clothes in handloom fabrics, and her dream of finally being able to earn on the scale of the West. I listened, remembering how, in my hearing, Nani had disapproved of Maw's enthusiasm for travel and sociability. Observing my mother behave with what seemed like girlish exuberance, clearly absurd for a forty-year-old, made me feel as though somehow we had switched roles.

Maw had brought home a new shade of lipstick, Chanel No. 5 perfume, and special gifts for each of us. Among my presents was a troll with amber eyes, stubby brown arms spread out in greeting, and white hair standing on end. A real, imported troll was even more of a prize than the tiptoeing Barbies that occasionally found their way into our classroom. I immediately began taking my troll to school, where she could confer with other trolls from the apartment buildings on Malabar Hill. I lovingly drew portraits of her perfectly round beads of eyes, snub nose, beatific smile, and short arms. Soon I was drawing trolls in saris, in ball gowns, and in long princess trains. Every school recess, I drew more happy trolls for my classmates.

At home, Maw rearranged her *puja,* searched for misplaced clothes, rattled through cupboards trying to locate her saffron and ajinomoto. She became increasingly hot and bothered.

"Just a few more days and I could have seen some major museums," she lamented, sweat glistening on her forehead. "This was my only chance to see art I've only known through reproductions."

"Yes, Martyrji," said Rahoul sarcastically.

I looked at him closely: after that distant, dispassionate part of me had glimpsed that he was not all-knowing, I saw his strain and confusion. I had been waiting for him to teasingly tell me things like "I taught you how to eat!" and "I taught you how to stay alive," but he seemed tense and serious.

Obviously, it wasn't very nice to call Maw "Martyrji"—adapting Mataji, an address for a holy mother. Still, once Rahoul had coined the name, none of us, including Paw, could resist using it. And as soon as he could, Rahoul once again left home.

Fused Doubles

When Babaji first visited the West in 1970, his trip set in motion a kind of swami musical chairs. Old Swami Prakashananda moved from the Saptashring Gadh mountaintop ashram to the rice fields of Ganeshpuri to help manage Babaji's ashram. In turn, he asked a younger *sadhu*, Swami Pranavananda, to leave a goddess temple in the Khandesh region of Maharashtra to look after his own ashram and the resident children. Swami Pranavananda was twenty-seven and Rahoul nearly seventeen; they became good friends. To keep these swamis straight when we didn't want to say their full names, we started referring to grandmotherly Swami Prakashananda as "Old Swamiji" and to Rahoul's new friend as "Young Swamiji."

Babaji returned from what was now called his First World Tour, bringing along a jumbo jet full of foreigners, and the shuffle was repeated in reverse. Old Swamiji returned to Saptashring Gadh, and Young Swamiji went back to his Goddess temple in the jungle. Rahoul followed his friend.

"The temple's in this really remote valley," Rahoul reported during one of his trips home. His body was growing to match the size of his head, and his face was filling out around the nose; he looked more like a grown-up. He sat at the dining table, hand over the steel *thali* filled with food. "A valley filled with trees and with cliffs all around. The Goddess there is called Patane Devi; she's a form of Durga riding a tiger and holding all these weapons. During the day, the *pujari* comes to chant to the Devi and some villagers come for *darshan* too. At night, it's totally deserted. Lots of stars and silence."

"It sounds like a classic forest retreat," Maw approved. "I know that Babaji lived there briefly, years ago, when he was a wandering *sadhu* doing his *sadhana*. But where do you stay in a temple?"

"There's this tiny room. We don't have electricity, but we have a kerosene lamp and a kerosene stove. The problem is that the rats in the jungle all seem to depend on the offerings to the Devi that villagers bring during the day—you know, coconuts, sweets, whatever they set out. So all night long, the rats have these festivals. You have to pull the covers over your head so they don't jump on your face."

"Don't!" I protested, appalled. It struck me that this could be one of Rahoul's tall tales. "Really?"

"Please be careful that you don't get bitten," said Maw.

Rahoul nodded abstractedly, as though he hadn't heard, and wrapped an edge of hot *chappati* around another bite of vegetables.

Later, I went to find Rahoul where he was writing at his desk. "Are there really that many rats?" I asked.

"Look, it's a jungle," Rahoul said, closing his notebook. "Sure there are rats. And then snakes come out looking for rats to eat. There are tigers in that jungle too. If you go out to pee at night, shadows can make you paranoid."

"Don't!" I objected.

"One night when I wasn't there, a roaming gang of dacoits came to investigate why there was a light in the temple. But Young Swamiji wasn't scared. He talked to them, and they ended up sitting in a circle around the kerosene lamp, telling him their troubles."

"No!" Was Rahoul teasing me again? How could Maw and Paw possibly allow him to live in such a place? "What if the robbers come back and take his things?"

"That's just it, Baby," said Rahoul, smiling to himself. "Young Swamiji doesn't have to worry because he doesn't *have* things. That's sort of the point of becoming a *sadhu*. Anyway, Young Swamiji can look after himself. He's gonna be okay."

: : :

I had thought that holy people related mostly to Ba, Maw, and Rahoul, but meeting Young Swamiji, I was enchanted. I understood why Rahoul couldn't help smiling whenever he spoke of his friend.

Deven and I were playing *dabba-I-spies* near the Nasik cowshed with our cousins when Rahoul and Young Swamiji arrived. A servant came to find us, and we trooped into Paw's downstairs suite.

"Devendra and Kirin! I have heard so much about you two!" Young Swamiji called out as we entered. He spoke English in a high-pitched yet resonant voice. He sat on a divan, bald and beaming in his saffron robes. He looked simultaneously like a man and a woman; like a self-possessed adult, eager teenager, mischievous child, and gurgling infant. I stared, sorting out this startling impression.

Young Swamiji was small: about our size, I figured, taller than me but shorter than fifteen-year-old Deven. From the slight afternoon shadow darkening his upper lip and cheeks, I could tell he was a man, but his enormous brown eyes and bow-shaped brows were those of a stunning woman. With his big shaved head and plump torso he had the proportions of an adorable baby. As Maw would later say, "If you were to slice through any part of his body you'd always get a perfect circle."

Young Swamiji wore a pale saffron cloth tied round his neck in what looked like a halter-neck dress, falling to just below his knees. Looping down toward his chest, a brown *mala* of enormous fused double-*rudraksha* beads accented the beaming brown of his eyes. His skin was like polished sandalwood in gods' images that Ba brought from Mysore. A sun-at-sunset round circle of goddess *kumkum* glowed from the center of his forehead, and dimples marked both round cheeks.

"Come sit," Swamiji beckoned, patting the divan on either side of him. We sat and he thumped at our shoulders. "Tell me, what game have you been playing? Ah, *dabba I-spies*—how are the rules different from ordinary *I-spies*? What class are you in? When are your exams?"

Young Swamiji was comfortable in English, though with an unfamiliar Bengali accent that sometimes turned a *s* into a *sh*. His high-pitched voice was almost like a teenage boy's, filled with a warbling excitement.

"So what other games do you all play? *Kabaddi*? Cricket? Cards? Tell me, what are you favorite card games?"

He seemed genuinely interested in our answers, trilling, "It's goo-oo-ood," with his head thrown back, dimples deepening, and little white teeth showing in a perfect row.

Rahoul was continuing to Saptashring Gadh by bus. He asked us if we could give Young Swamiji a ride to Bombay and look after him for a few days, and Maw said that would be just great.

Young Swamiji sat beside Mani Driver in the front of the Ambassador, while Maw, Deven, and I sat in the back. As we descended past forests that seemed thinner every year, Maw and Young Swamiji chatted, and I listened in.

Young Swamiji told Maw that he had first become interested in "these spiritual things" when he was a boy in Bengal. His mother had died when he was three, and he had decided the goddess Kali was his mother. He was the only child in a big extended family of married and unmarried brothers. As a boy he performed long death ceremonies for a childless aunt, and then for an uncle, making him question life's meaning. After finishing school, he trained as a civil engineer. During a class outing to Rishikesh in the Himalayas he had met a *sadhu* who impressed him and made him eager to know more *sadhus*. He found a job with a British firm that had continued to operate in Calcutta after Independence and made a pact with the Goddess that if he were promoted to head of this firm, he would leave it all. "You see Maw, I was always testing Her, seeing if I could devote my life to Her." As a junior member of the firm, such a promotion seemed unlikely, but when he was twenty-six, it came to pass that the existing head resigned, and in the ensuing chaos he was temporarily offered the post.

So the young engineer left home to look for a guru. He wandered through India visiting many ashrams before meeting Babaji and taking *sannyas* at Ganeshpuri during the same sixtieth-birthday celebration that had drawn Rahoul and Maw. Soon after, he decided to leave the big institutional structure to pursue his spiritual practices by himself. Babaji had described a goddess temple in the jungle where he had lived briefly during his years of wandering, and because of Swamiji's closeness to the Goddess from childhood, that was where he headed. Babaji had been displeased, and Old Swamiji had tried to serve as intermediary to bring Young Swamiji back to Ganeshpuri. But the younger man wouldn't waiver.

"I've put myself in Her hands, Maw," said Young Swamiji, "What else can She do but look after me?"

I thrilled to how effortlessly he had said "Maw," as though he were already a member of the family.

"Rahoul is sometimes with me," Young Swamiji continued, "but otherwise when anybody says they worry about my living in the jungle alone, I say, 'Baba, who says I am alone? I live with my Mother!'"

Young Swamiji's voice swooped higher, almost squeaking, as he quoted himself, then burst into laughter, causing us all to join in.

"So Kirin Devi," Young Swamiji addressed me after a while. "What are your plans? What profession are you aiming for? Doctor or lawyer?"

"I want to be a writer," I mumbled, still so used to being an onlooker at the margins of family interactions with holy people that I was unsure what tone to adopt.

"A writer!" Young Swamiji trilled. *"Baap re!* I am very happy when I learn of a girl's ambition."

I flushed, haltingly confessing that I had written a novel about the adventures of Princess Snow Rose and her family. At 135 longhand pages, with Snow Rose having freed a pretty older relative from witches and installed her as a stepmother, I had declared the novel finished. But then, missing the space to which I had often retreated, I immediately started on a sequel involving the rescue of a kidnapped brother.

"It's goo-oo-ood!" laughed Young Swamiji. "One novel by age eleven! I am sure you will be writing many other books. Let me tell you, books can be on serious topics also, not only on love, stars, and all that."

Why did Young Swamiji think that my novel had to be about love, stars, and romance? Snow Rose regularly took on all kinds of adventures; she was brave, ingenious, and romantic only insofar as wanting to match up others. Would Swamiji be interested to learn about Snow Rose's powerful Fairy Godmother? But I was too tongue-tied to elaborate. I bowed my head and wriggled my shoulders forward, hands together, grinning, as Young Swamiji turned the sunny spotlight of his attention on Deven.

: : :

When we arrived in Bombay, Maw went off to instruct the servants on dinner and greet the latest arrivals from the ashram. Young Swamiji settled down with Deven and me around the big yellow square of the carom board balanced on a stool in the boys' room.

"See, carom is very good for learning concentration and control," Young Swamiji assured us, angling his middle finger against his thumb to flick the round shooter, sending chips careening toward the corner nets. By the time Maw called us out to eat, he had shared choice tips on how to powder the board and the best angles to shoot from. "We can play cards after dinner," he promised.

As we emerged to wash our hands at the sink, I overheard Maw explaining to the guests why our robed visitor was devoting himself to our company rather than theirs. "As Old Swamiji from up on the mountain says, 'If you want to change the world, start with children. With adults it's too late.' Great beings have a talent for meeting people on their own level, you know, and so when they're with children they act childlike. Have you ever noticed that whenever His Holiness the Dalai Lama is posing in pictures with Tibetan children, he squats down to be at their height?"

I personally thought that Young Swamiji was playing games with us because he enjoyed it and we presented an excuse. He seemed wary around the young Western devotees from Ganeshpuri, and I remembered that Babaji had not wanted him to leave the ashram. He observed without comment as Maw started in on a moment of silent prayer that she had instituted before meals. All the urugs shut their eyes too, while Swamiji, Deven, and I exchanged knowing looks.

Young Swamiji was still locked in Rahoul's room when we had to leave for school next morning. I assumed he was communing with his Mother. On the bus, I told Fatty Rasha about our unusual visitor.

"A swami who plays carom?" Fatty Rasha's eyes curled into new moons that matched the shape of her eyebrows as she laughed. "No!"

"Really!" I assured her, starting to giggle too.

Deven and I set down our school satchels in the late afternoon to find Maw already cooking up the special treat of a Western meal: steamed cauliflower, cheese sauce, fresh rolls, and baked potatoes. Young Swamiji again joined us at the dining table. As Maw started in on the moment of silence, Deven and I watched Young Swamiji reach over and transfer butter from the edge of Maw's plate onto his own. Maw picked up her fork to discover that she had no butter to melt over her potatoes.

Young Swamiji's dimples appeared. "This was the danger of looking inside when others are alert, Maw," he said.

"Oh!" Maw was taken aback, but then smiled as though she'd like to pinch his chubby cheeks. "So you're a butter thief just like baby Krishna."

Young Swamiji returned Maw's butter to her plate. "You must have heard about the snake who met a guru," he said.

"And stopped hissing?" asked Maw. "I think it's in *The Gospel of Sri Ramakrishna.*"

"That one," Young Swamiji nodded. He looked around at the rest of us. "See, the snake used to bite and everyone was scared of him. Then he met a guru and he began to meditate; he became nonviolent. The village children noticed this change. After a time they began poking him with sticks. Then they pounded him with rocks. No matter how much they troubled him, the snake didn't strike them. When the guru returned to the area, he found the snake hungry and bleeding. 'What happened?' the guru asked. 'You told me to control my senses and turn inside,' said the snake. 'You told me to practice nonviolence.' 'But did I ever tell you not to hiss?' asked the guru. See Maw, if you live in the world, it is good to be aware of the habits of the world. If you want your butter, you will have to guard your plate."

After that night, Maw no longer legislated moments of silence before meals. In the ongoing tug-of-war over how openly spiritual our house should be, Young Swamiji had surprisingly taken our—the children's—side.

The even bigger surprise was that when Paw returned, Young Swamiji chatted with him about civil engineering projects as a fellow professional. He laughed at Paw's jokes. I noticed that he addressed Paw as "Narayan-bhai" as though intuiting that Paw might not take the same pleasure Maw did in being an honorary parent.

"So those are Gauri-Shankar *rudraksha* you're wearing," Paw said, raising his chin to the series of fused *rudraksha* seeds, each almost the size of an eyeball, hanging around Young Swamiji's neck. These rare *rudraksha* had been a gift from Babaji at the time of Young Swamiji's *sannyas,* and he always wore them. "My God, I have never seen such a lineup. My mother Ba, you know, loves anything spiritual and rare, and *rudraksha* with unusual numbers of sides are a special fascination for her. She's acquired a single-faced one, an eleven-faced one, and so on, but she still hasn't found a double Gauri-Shankar. Those two fused sides are Ardhanarishwara."

I immediately recalled images of Ardhanarishwara, "Half-Woman-Lord": male Shiva on the right side, his beautiful wife Shakti on the left. Even if the combination of male and female wasn't so neatly split between Swamiji's two sides, I could see how it seemed to swirl through his every feature.

"Well, isn't that the best of both worlds, Narayan-bhai?" Young Swamiji joked.

Young Swamiji told Paw about meeting a disapproving old gentleman on a train. "Young man, putting on these saffron robes and living on donations, what are you doing for society?" the man had inquired. "How are you helping the future of our nation?"

Young Swamiji repeated his simple, dimpling reply: *"Family planning!"*

"Family planning," Paw echoed, laughing.

After Young Swamiji left, whenever he was mentioned, Paw started to smile and his voice rose into a falsetto: *"It's goo-oo-ood!"*

: : :

The two *rudraksha* joined neatly down the middle reminded me also of our own caste goddess, who took the form of twin women joined at the shoulder. I thought particularly of the printed posters that Ba hoarded in her treasury of spiritual paraphernalia, showing Vishwakarma's daughter Randhal Ma from the torso up: two beautiful, identical women with dark hair, gold-bordered red saris partly covering their heads and offsetting their embroidered, forest green blouses. They glittered with dangling gold earrings and many gem-encrusted necklaces, and gold rays rose from their heads.

Paw said that the story explaining why we worshipped Randhal Ma in a doubled form existed in Hindu mythology as far back as the *Rig Veda,* which would make it almost thirty-five hundred years old. The story, as I gleaned it from various adults retellings, went something like this:

Vishwakarma Bapa had four sons. He also had a daughter, Randhal. (We call her Randhal Ma because she's a goddess.) She has two names: Samjna (symbol/name) and Chhaya (shadow).

Daughters, you know, must be married off. Vishwakarma Bapa had constructed the Sun's chariot for riding through the heavens, and he thought that the Sun would make a good groom. So Vishwakarma Bapa arranged his daughter's marriage to the Sun.

Randhal Ma lived with the Sun and bore him children, but this life was difficult for her. The Sun was hot and bright. So Randhal Ma placed Chhaya, her own shadow, in charge of everything in the house. Then she herself went off to the jungle to meditate. She turned herself into a mare because she didn't want anyone to disturb her.

At first, the Sun didn't notice that his wife was gone because her shadow was identical. Even the children didn't see any difference in their mother. But then, while she was serving food, one of the children, who was making trouble, kicked her. She got so angry that she cursed his leg. When do mothers curse sons? He suspected that she was not really his mother and alerted his father.

The Sun could not completely undo Chhaya's curse. But he questioned her, and she confessed who she was. Then the Sun went to Vishwakarma Bapa to ask where Randhal Ma had gone.

Vishwakarma Bapa told the Sun, "How is she to live with you when you are so hot and bright?"

"What am I to do? This is my nature," the Sun said.

So Vishwakarma Bapa offered a solution: "You can shave off some of your brightness."

The Sun agreed, and his father-in-law put him on a lathe and shaved away some of that light. From those fragments of sun, all the shining weapons of the various gods were forged: Vishnu's discus, Shiva's trident, and all the other weapons later used in the great battles against demons.

Then the Sun went to find Randhal Ma in the jungle. She was praying peacefully in her mare form. He became a stallion. They had more children, including the horse-faced twin gods who heal people—the Ashwins.

Because she existed in her own form and in the form of her shadow, we worship Randhal Ma with two faces. For special pujas we bring at least two coconuts and balance them in pots. We give them clay faces with cowries for their eyes and mouths, and we dress them in red saris. Then we say Randhal Ma has come to visit.

I once asked Chanda-phui, "So if we're all from the sons of Vishwakarma, doesn't this make Randhal Ma a kind of *phui,* a father's sister? Does her being our goddess mean that for us there's something special for us about a father's sister?"

Chanda-phui replied, "The love between a brother and a sister is very strong. So of course a sister loves her brother's children. That's why Randhal Ma helps us."

In wearing the doubled *rudraksha* beads, Swamiji carried the familiar benevolence of this twin image.

: : :

Back with his Mother, Young Swamiji began sending us plain yellow postcards stamped with three-headed lions, the cheapest communication from the Indian Postal Service. He wrote to each member of the family individually, using a blue fountain pen, in neat, matter-of-fact round handwriting. He usually ended his notes with *"Rest is Okay. Jai Jagadamba! Yours, Swami Pranavananda." "Rest is okay"* meant that things around him were okay, not that it was okay for any of us to rest: Young Swamiji, it turned out, was big on hard work, duty, and grades. He checked dates on letters against postmarks and chided us when we'd taken a couple of days to mail something.

"He is so damn bourgeois," Rahoul shook his head, smiling, on a return visit. "Now he's insisting that I have to go to college. He says that if I'm going to be his disciple I've got to listen to him."

"I bet there are lots of colleges in America that would be fascinated by your background," Maw urged.

"I guess," Rahoul shrugged.

Rahoul had left his sculptures and drawings behind, becoming interested in photography. Maw loaned him her camera, and Stella emerged from her darkroom to give him professional tips. He filled rolls of black-and-white film, bringing home photographs of Young Swamiji, the temple in the jungle, and the village nearby.

Some of Rahoul's pictures of Young Swamiji were informal, catching him in interaction with villagers. Other pictures were posed. Rahoul showed us *Swamiji as the Adi Shankaracharya,* referring to the great eighth-century saint, poet, and scholar who had helped revitalize Hinduism. Shankaracharya was familiar to us all as a shaven-headed, bare-chested *sadhu* with a covered head, a book in one hand, the other palm raised in blessing; in the same posture, Swamiji really did look just like him. In another, even more playful photograph, *Swamiji as Sharmila Tagore,* he smiled with a covered head, glamorously beautiful and dimpled as the female Bengali movie star. Rahoul's masterpiece, though, was *Swamiji as Buddha,* a color picture that adorned many disciples' *pujas* for years to come: Young Swamiji stripped down to just a loincloth and his loop of double *rudraksha.* Sitting cross-legged in a perfect lotus pose, hands resting in his lap, lashes spiking downward, he radiated a calm inwardness.

"God, you have such talent," Maw said to Rahoul as she looked over these prints.

"I had a good subject," Rahoul said. "With him, it's kind of hard not to get a good shot."

: : :

We always celebrated Divali in Nasik, the extended family gathering to honor Lakshmi, goddess of abundance. Her footprints were drawn beside doorways to direct her into the many wings of the house. Upstairs, the men and boys of the family sat cross-legged in a long line with Paw at the head, following ritual instructions from our family *pandit,* whom Paw had long ago unkindly nicknamed Haddiram Totaram (roughly translated, "Skinny-bones, Parrot-face"). They all faced a low table piled with account books for the coming year, open to the first page, inscribed in red with greetings to Lakshmi. Milk sweets, dried fruit, and crunchy white sugar *patasa* mixed with puffed rice were offered in silver *thalis* around the books. We, the women and girls, sat facing their ritual action as onlookers. For my cousin Yeshu and me, this Divali *puja* always presented a special challenge not to giggle. The more we knew we shouldn't, the more the rhythm of the chants and the poses of the boys would cause laughter to bubble up uncontrollably.

The next day was the Gujarati New Year, and Maw decided to visit Young Swamiji. As Ba said approvingly, this was a perfect day to visit a saintly person and collect blessings for the year ahead. She was tempted to come with us, but she had to stay home to receive the relatives and neighbors who would inevitably come by with boxes of sweets. Paw said we should deliver his *pranams* to Young Swamiji but that he would also stay home. Our cousins stayed back too.

Mani Driver bore Maw, Rahoul, Deven, Tashi, and me along the highway for several hours, through big towns and dusty villages. In Chalisgaon, the nearest town to Young Swamiji's village, bright saris were spread out to dry in long rows on the ground by the river. We turned onto a narrower road, proceeding through low peanut fields and scrub, then toward a mountain range.

Near the village of Patane, Banjara tribal women with full skirts, silver spikes pinned to the top of their heads, and ivory bangles all the way up their arms were washing dishes by the village well. They turned to stare. A crowd of barefoot children ran after the car in the dust; a few dogs lazing along the roadside chased us too, then fell away as we left the village behind. Rahoul directed us onward, through more fields, toward a small square cement building. Villagers who worried about Young Swamiji's welfare had finally convinced him to move closer to their settlement and had built him a one-room *kutir* in the peanut fields.

Young Swamiji came clattering out in his wooden sandals. "Welcome!" he called, his voice seeming higher, his dimples deeper, than ever. He greeted us all by name as we unfolded ourselves from the car. "Come sit, and the Boys will make tea!"

The Boys were a group of teenage village lads scurrying about a makeshift kitchen inside. To my surprise, the group included a thin woman with a haughty, weather-beaten face, wearing the short full skirt of a teenage girl but with a man's white shirt. I recognized her from Rahoul's stories as Raju, who had been a Maharashtra state long jump champion and who, after her father's death, took to farming and assumed a male role, marrying off her five sisters. She must have been older than most of the boys, maybe almost thirty, and the age difference seemed to win her respect and acceptance. She squatted by the kerosene stove, skirt trailing behind her, then stood up very erect to join the rest of the Boys in handing out tea and sweets and snacks.

As we sipped what Rahoul called our "hard-boiled" sweet tea, Raju stood in the background, arms crossed. She watched us interact with Young Swamiji as though she were his bodyguard. I saw myself through Raju's alert gaze as easily dismissed: too meek, too young, an uninteresting, un-exciting girly girl. Young Swamiji had recently instructed Maw to buy me silver anklets with little bells so that hearing their rhythm would help me gain grace. When I wasn't wearing my school uniform— black shoes, white socks, and a knee-length, blue green plaid dress (that had recently replaced yellow checks) —I usually slipped on the anklets with an ankle-length skirt, a modest blouse with sleeves, glass bangles from the Nasik bazaar, and a little red, painted-on *bindi* on my forehead. Under Raju's eyes, I saw my "traditional" getup as ridiculous.

"Kirin Devi, how is school?" Young Swamiji asked.

I flushed with pleasure to be addressed as a goddess. I reported that I had written a social studies essay on Rumi, a Sufi saint, using books recommended by an Indian-African-Canadian ashram visitor with a Harvard Ph.D.

"Baba, a school report on a saint?" Young Swamiji laughed. "It's good to write about saints! You can show me next time."

I couldn't bring myself to tell Young Swamiji that my essay, which received an A+, had vanished after Paw loaned it to the headmaster of his old Nasik school. I was torn between regret at having lost my prized document and pride that Paw might possibly be bragging about me to his friends. He so rarely noticed or admired anything I did; although he hadn't said anything about the report directly, the fact that he passed it on seemed a sign that he had approved.

Young Swamiji chatted with Deven about what he was reading, asked Maw about goings-on at the ashram, and interrogated Rahoul about whether he had decided which colleges to apply to.

"I've told Rahoul that it's time for him to rejoin the world," Young Swamiji said, patting his friend's bony shoulder. "He's had enough of us swami types, babas, gurus, and all. See, Rahoul, you can't give up the world if you don't know what the world is. Seventeen is too young to leave the world behind! You must complete your education and know how to earn, and then, if you still want to come live with us in the jungle, I will be the first to welcome you."

"But can't I earn by being a guru?" Rahoul teased. "I hear it's a very lucrative career."

Young Swamiji giggled, even white teeth lined up like jasmine buds tied together in the *veni* that women wore in their hair for special occasions.

::::

After tea, Young Swamiji announced that he would take us to meet his Mother. The road into the forest was too rough for a car, he said, so Raju had brought her bullock cart.

Raju sat in her *bel gadi,* presiding over two white bullocks with horns painted red, brass bells clanging around their necks. We climbed into the wooden cart and lurched into motion along the narrow dirt road, sending up a cloud of dust. Raju commanded her bullocks through clucks formed against her palate, clicks against her cheeks, and occasional stern shouts. We clattered and creaked, jolted and rolled, further and further into the pale green jungle rimmed with mountains on all sides. I remembered how whenever Paw was "on the wagon" he seemed so restlessly keen to jump off.

Finally we pulled up at the far end of a valley surrounded by tall cliffs, trees illumined along its high rims. Across a dry riverbed, the gray stone temple rose like a citadel with two stone towers flanking broad stone stairs. Swamiji explained that the towers were designed to hold oil beacons at their crowns on special occasions. The right-hand tower had partially tumbled.

Young Swamiji slipped out of his wooden sandals at the base of the temple's stone staircase. He scampered upward, and we tagged behind. Entering a roofed stone area, we sniffed bats.

"That's where I first stayed, Maw!" Young Swamiji paused in the doorway of a small room. "And Rahoul stayed here with me."

We peered over his shoulder. The room held a raised stone plank and a latticed stone window. Time seemed to be holding its breath.

"The rats probably miss us," Rahoul said.

Young Swamiji turned, strutting further into the shadowy temple, toward an alcove where a stone statue receded into the shadows. I assumed this must be Young Swamiji's Mother, Patane Devi, but he just bobbed his head in greeting, then continued to the left. We passed between carved pillars. Suddenly, he whirled right, reached overhead to clang a brass bell, and joined his palms just above where his belly curved out from under his halter-neck robes. He bowed his head, thick-lashed eyelids almost seeming to swoon. Then he fell outstretched to the floor, palms joined over his head. We crowded in, standing behind his prone body, facing the image illumined from above by a skylight and from below by an earthenware lamp.

Patane Devi was another staring, coral-colored goddess, her face filled with bright eagerness, her lips slightly parted. Her front two arms brandished a silver trident; her other sixteen arms, spread around her, wielded sharp weapons, balanced a pot of flames, grabbed a cobra's neck, gripped a demon's severed head, and so on. Several layers of cotton saris—red, green, green and red—had been draped and folded around her torso. She rode a fierce striped tiger whose yawning jaws bit into the head of a gray blue demon with bulging eyes and the lower body of a buffalo. Victorious, aloft, she radiated strength and fearlessness.

The air in this womb-space was close, filled with the familiar temple aroma of burning oil, charred wicks, rancid coconut flesh, and sweet incense. A soundless hum reverberated in my ears. I realized that this must be the sound of silence that pulled you inside yourself to meditate.

Young Swamiji stepped across a low wooden bar to touch the Devi's feet: first her right foot, then her left foot. Next he reached up, took a pinch of red *kumkum* from her forehead and pressed this onto his own. Behind him, we each went through the motions of salutation. Patane Devi's huge eyes gleamed in the dancing flicker of the lamp.

"So how do you like my Mother?" he asked as we started out into the sunshine to make a clockwise circuit around the temple.

"She's a marvelous example of folk art," said Maw with the eye of a self-trained art historian. "The temple seems to me to be about twelfth century, but the image must be a later addition. It's a classic Durga Mahishasura-mardini image, of course, and such interesting simultaneity—the demon is emerging from his buffalo form under the lion, while on her left, she's already holding his severed head."

"Baba, she's eternal and she's formless," said Young Swamiji, dimpling. "All this form and all, it's just for fun." He pressed his head against the wall directly behind the Goddess, at a spot where the rock was indented. How many centuries of devotees' foreheads, I wondered, had it taken to wear away the wall?

We completed our circumambulation, returning to the Goddess. Young Swamiji led us out onto a platform where an iron trident held stacks of green bangles on its tines. Raju took charge of the coconut we had brought as an offering, smacking the brown shell against a rock at the trident's base. Then she drained out the water, forcefully split apart the coconut with her hands, and scraped at it with a sharp stone. She set a few wedges of white coconut flesh before the Goddess, then distributed pieces to us. She also moved between us, applying spots of deep red *kumkum* to our foreheads with her finger, ensuring that we were all blessed. I admired her self-contained ease, wondering if I would ever carry myself with such confidence.

"The *pujari* only comes here in the morning to bathe our Devi and chant," said Young Swamiji, as though to explain why Raju had taken over the ritual action. "Except on full moon nights and holidays, when more visitors come. You know, this is a small place in the jungle, not like Saptashring Gadh, where thousands upon thousands come for big festivals."

"Yes, but just wait until you get more disciples," Maw teased. "I bet that buses will be chartered to come out into the jungle."

Young Swamiji laughed. "We enjoy the simple life," he said, exchanging a look with his Mother, whose parted lips seemed to be smiling directly at him.

::::

Back in his cottage after lunch, as our boys mingled outside with his Boys, Young Swamiji presented me with a small black-and-white photograph of Patane Devi. "Kirin Devi should have a Devi in her *puja*," he said.

I was too awed and shy to tell him that I didn't have a *puja* of my own. Maw looked on as Young Swamiji brought out a book in Devanagari script.

"You can read Sanskrit, no?"

"I can read Hindi," I said.

"Good, same alphabet. Come sit, it's Divali day, I'll teach you a chant for the New Year."

He held up the goddess epic, the *Durga Saptashati* ("Seven Hundred Verses to Durga").

"You see, she is formless, but from time to time she takes on a form to protect us," Young Swamiji explained as I settled beside him. I noticed that his hand-dyed saffron robes held an aroma of sandalwood, greenery, and wet earth.

"See, sometimes bullies take over the universe," Young Swamiji said. "One time, two very arrogant demon brothers, Shumbha and Nishumbha, drove out the gods from the three worlds. The gods remembered how Devi had saved them when that bullying buffalo fellow Mahishasura had thrown them out before, so again they requested Her help. They gathered together near the Himalaya Mountains and they sang Her praises."

Young Swamiji opened the book somewhere in the middle and began to chant in a melody similar to what I'd heard in the ashram. Maw closed her eyes to better focus on the sounds, but I was trying to keep up with the shapes of the Sanskrit words before us. Young Swamiji's sandalwood-colored index finger moved under the letters, guiding me.

Devā Uchuhu
Namo devyai mahādevyai shivāyai satatam namah . . .

The gods said:
We bend our heads with joined palms to you, the Goddess, the Great
    Goddess
We always salute you who brings good
to Nature, to our Protector
We bow before you with attention.

You are fierce and eternal,
You are luminous, you support us.
You are moonlight, you are the moon's form,
You are happiness: we constantly bend our heads before you.

The hymn went on to salute the Devi who exists in all beings. She lives in everyone as consciousness, as intelligence, sleep, hunger, radiance, power, and many other things, including error. Sung in Young Swamiji's emotion-filled voice, the rhythmic, repetitive verses built up an electric atmosphere. I felt as though my eyes were starting to water, a tension tightening my throat.

Then Young Swamiji turned to the end of the book and showed me how to chant for forgiveness in case I mispronounced anything. "Maw has this book at home," he said, "You can recite everyday. It's good for a girl to know some songs!"

"Okay," I agreed, overwhelmed. I thought that he might have also taught Rahoul and Deven these chants when they had stayed with him, but I wasn't sure.

Rahoul remained with Young Swamiji, but the rest of us drove back toward Nasik under the expanse of bright stars and the coming and going of truck headlights. Bumping along in the back seat, I clutched my photograph closer. The echoes of Young Swamiji's voice showed me how chanted images could pull me inward to glimpse goddess eyes within myself too.

6

Doorways

During the monsoon of 1970, after almost twenty-five years of marriage, Chanda-phui's stomach began pushing out under the front tucked V-end of her sari.

Ba claimed responsibility. "I asked the right *sadhus* to bless her!" Ba said. "I took her to the right temples!"

This was the first miracle I could remember witnessing. I listened, agog, when Ba visited Juhu with Chanda-phui and Sukhlal-phua. As we enjoyed the crunchy snacks that Chanda-phui set out on plates, Ba filled us in on how her own divine connections had set the stage for this astonishing turn of events.

"When Didi was in America and we were here in Juhu with the children, a *sadhu* called from the gate," Ba told us, presiding cross-legged from Paw's bed. "I went out and saw that he had a face of light. I understood that he was a god taking the form of a *sadhu*. I sent Chanda to give him an offering. I told him: 'Maharaj, bless my daughter.' 'She will have a son within one year,' he said."

Our uncle Sukhlal-phua listened, smiling, even though Ba granted him no role. His steel gray hair was receding further, elongating the "M" of his widow's peak, but he seemed younger and lighter. Chanda-phui sat hunched forward, her sari end tucked loosely so the billow camouflaged the swell. With her gray hair and bifocals, she seemed as uncomfortable with anyone noticing her changing body as the few "developing" girls in my class. Other women who had been married at her age were already grandmothers.

Ba continued waving her double-jointed fingers. "Then, after the *sadhu* spoke, I took Chanda to Kutch on pilgrimage. I took her to our temple in Kutch. 'Oh Bapa, have compassion,' I prayed to Khimji Bhagat."

"That temple is called 'Khimji Duvaro,' the doors of Khimji," Paw explained to us kids in English. He waved his pipe. "It was built by Sethji and his brothers in 1899, and it has an image you won't find anywhere else in India. It's unique, this image, and when I tell art historians, they are dumbfounded. Usually you see Vishwakarma as an old man with a white beard, but Sethji commissioned a statue of him as a clean-shaven young man."

Ba was approvingly nodding her chin, as she often did when she could glimpse familiar words bobbing in a stream of English. "Gods don't usually show their true forms," she reminded us, returning to the Hindi-Gujarati mix she used in speaking to us grandchildren. "Sometimes, they come in a *sadhu*'s form like that Mahatma at the gate. It is definitely going to be a boy."

No one dared point out that Ba had for decades been requesting blessings for Chanda-phui from scores of holy people and temples all over India. I was beginning to understand that if a story didn't draw attention to Ba's privileged relationship with unseen powers, she didn't consider it worth telling.

Later, I asked my brothers, "Did you see that special *sadhu*? Did you?"

None of them remembered this holy man with the bright face of a god.

"I guess we were all busy doing something else," I said, disappointed.

Had I been lost in reading? Or writing about Snow Rose? How could I have missed out on a god's visit to our own home?

: : :

Daughters usually joined their mothers for their first delivery, and so Chanda-phui had left her home in Ahmedabad to be with Ba. Since medical care wasn't as good in Nasik as in Bombay, they moved together into the family apartment in Byculla. Sethji had lived there before marrying Ba or moving to Nasik, and for years it had served as the family's Bombay base.

Ba knew all the right herbs and foods for an easy delivery and recovery. She had delivered all her own children at home and then watched over the births of Rahoul, Deven, and our Nasik cousins. She especially liked to recall how, when Paw was born, she had felt the pains coming and stood up to call for help. But the baby popped right out in the doorway. "I knew then that he had a special destiny," Ba said.

As we knew from other family stories, Paw's old father had been so over-joyed that he weighed the newborn in gold and then in sugar too, distribut-ing both in charity. He placed the infant in the arms of his own guru, Yogi Bapa, asking for a name.

Maw sometimes said that Paw's being born in a doorway was "very sym-bolic" because of all the thresholds he had since crossed: first person in the caste to go abroad, first to marry a non-Indian, first to receive a foreign de-gree. "But it makes him ambivalent too," Maw said. "He's never completely sure what he wants."

Whenever we visited Nasik and I played at the threshold of Ba's rooms with my girl cousins, we looked outside to the sunny courtyard of packed earth, the chattering neighbors lined up before the well, the rich green of the jackfruit tree where the buffalo Manik-bai relaxed, keeping an eye out for Ba. Turning suddenly to the interior, my eyes didn't immediately adjust: shapes flickered, colors disappeared. I thought of how Paw too could swing between bright, outward-facing laughter and jokes, and melancholy inner shadows. Like everyone else who loved Paw, I constantly wondered what it would take to pull him out into the sun, and whether I could do it.

Searching through our tall bookshelves for something new to read, I dis-covered a small cloth-bound copy of *Pride and Prejudice* inscribed with Paw's name. He must have acquired this book before he went to America, for he still spelled his name "Narain." The handwriting was precise and upright, in contrast to the scribbled signature he had developed over years of signing stacks of receipts for tenants in his father's apartment buildings.

Jane Austen: there was no doubt that the author was a woman. Usually, if Maw was reading something by a woman author—Virginia Woolf, Colette, Nancy Mitford, Isak Dinesen—Paw mocked, "Oh, a lady novelist." With a weary shrug, he informed whoever else was listening, "I've never liked lady novelists." Each time Paw used those words, a shadow passed over my heart. I wanted to write, but I didn't want to be a lady novelist forever stand-ing outside the door of the palace that Paw considered real literature.

I examined the stained and faded green cover, the yellowed leaves, greedy to know how Jane Austen had escaped Paw's scorn. A paragraph in and I was off to England. The reality within the pages grew vivid, the concerns around the character I thought was me faded, then disappeared.

"*Khana taiyar hai!*" I heard distant calls. "Kirin, dinner!"

Food, what food? I staggered to the dinner table and ate without tasting. As soon as I could excuse myself, I rejoined the Bennett sisters.

The next morning I read before breakfast, then walked to the bus stop with the book open in my hands for an occasional glimpse of what happened next. At my wooden desk in class, I took notes from the blackboard, longing for recess so I could continue reading. Good books often possessed me this way, but this book had the added fascination of being Paw's.

"Is this *really* your book?" I asked Paw shyly, bringing *Pride and Prejudice* to his armchair.

He stared blankly at the stained cover, and I realized I had found him in the confused twilight after his afternoon nap, a time he would usually start another round of drinks. This was often when the deepest springs of his unhappiness bubbled through him, seeming to submerge his sense of connection to himself and everything around him.

"I can't recollect," Paw said.

I showed him his name.

Paw shrugged. He looked at his feet, the square toenails so like Rahoul's. He began speaking slowly, as though from a great distance.

"Once I discovered books I bought them whenever I could," he said. "You see, in the Nasik house, we didn't have any books except for some religious volumes in Gujarati or Sanskrit. My father had his cataract operation when I was still a little boy, and he made me read aloud epics and Puranas to him in Gujarati. What stories! Then, when I learned to read English, the old man asked me to read aloud his legal briefs from all the different property cases. I was hungry for books. I looked everywhere for books in English. Whenever I visited Bombay, I used whatever pocket money the old man gave me to pick up used books from the footpath. 'Can you eat these books?' he would ask. 'Will they teach you about God? Then why are you buying them?' When I got to America, I went wild. I bought every volume I could of the Modern Library series." Paw waved at the wall of mildewing, insect-nibbled books to his left.

Guilt rose in my chest over the contrast between Paw's book-starved childhood and the abundant reading matter I had always taken for granted. Even now, the favorite family destinations near Paw's downtown office were the Strand Bookstore and the Bombay Branch of the Royal Asiatic Society Library. I wanted to tell Paw that that there was nothing I aspired to more than writing books that whisked people clear out of their lives, then returned them refreshed to resume whatever it was they had to do.

But his eyes had grown faraway as he remembered. Melancholy was rising around his ears, his eyes, the top of his head: rising, spreading, splashing outward. I picked my way backward through the door to avoid being spun in the current. Even from that distance, I could feel the tug of his longing for a drink.

::::

Once or twice a year, the line of waves pulled far back, exposing low expanses of rocks with sandy pools, slowly creeping snails, and waving sea anemones. During these rare, unusually low tides we loved walking out toward the horizon, jumping from rock to rock with bent heads. I enjoyed a similar sense of discovering a hidden landscape when members of the family got together to reminisce about the past.

The Rakshabandhan "Ties of Protection" full moon, when sisters tied bracelets on their brothers' right wrists, fell in August. Paw's nieces, our "cousin sisters" Narmada-ben and Heera-ben, arrived from their suburb, Matunga, to join me in honoring my brothers with *rakhis*. Chanda-phui usually sent Paw the simplest red, pompomlike *rakhi* by mail, but this year she had a chance to perform the ritual in person. She traveled from Byculla, along with Ba. Maw was still off on one of her decorating jobs, and Paw wasn't home yet either. As we all sat around waiting for Paw to arrive so we could begin the *rakhi* rituals, Ba started up a game of solitaire on the divan spread, and Chanda-phui, Narmada-ben, and Heera-ben began exchanging their favorite stories about Paw.

Narmada-ben and Heera-ben were the daughters of Vasanji-bhai, Sethji's son from the second of the three wives who had died before Sethji married Ba. Narmada-ben was Chanda-phui's age, Heera-ben a few years younger. In the possibilities that had been open to them as daughters of the family, though, they were a generation apart. Unlike Chanda-phui, they had been allowed to finish school and to pursue careers; now they were teachers in English-language primary schools. They were both unmarried, and they lived in Matunga with their own parents and the widow of Paw's half-brother from Sethji's first marriage. They referred to Sethji as Dada, or grandfather, and in their company that was what Chanda-phui called him too.

Narmada-ben was a handsome woman with the forceful voice of a teacher accustomed to commanding her class. Heera-ben was small and skinny, a perpetually deferring younger sister with a big smile, big glasses, and one mysteriously swollen "elephant leg" hidden under her sari. "Heera" meant "diamond," and Narmada-ben loved remembering how, when Paw visited their home as a child, he had referred to their threesome as *"Hun tun ane rataniyo*—you, me, and the Gem." Paw's sayings and exploits, it seemed, often had a mythic ring.

"Your Paw, *so* naughty he was," Narmada-ben told us in English.

"He peed from the balcony!" added Chanda-phui in Hindi, nose crinkling as she laughed. "You know how there are openings in the balcony wall there in Nasik? He stood and waited until Dada's solicitor was coming one afternoon, and then he aimed. He hit the man right on the turban!"

I had heard this story so often that I felt as though I could see it myself. I pictured the portico balcony over the round driveway, the designs that Sethji had laid out in Italian ceramic mosaic to reflect moonlight from the balcony floor, the flattened burlap sacks and steel *thalis* that on a sunny day would be filled with airing grains, drying papads, and dehydrating mango slices. The low wall around this balcony was perforated with clover-shaped openings. I imagined the small boy with an overly large head and intense brown eyes leaning forward, the excited *khi-khi-khi* giggles from his sister and nieces, the turbaned solicitor mopping his forehead and looking up for rain.

The story always ended there: in merry delight, never a scolding.

"And he shaved off your Chanda-phui's hair on one side," said Heera-ben, high voice cascading with glittery streaks of laughter. "Baba, she would do anything he told her to."

We looked at Chanda-phui, who nodded her head, eyes bright and shining. "I had to cut all my hair off, like a boy, after that," she said, smiling. "I really cried."

"And what all other mischief your Paw did, don't *even ask!*" continued Narmada-ben. "He was our gang leader and we just followed. You know how he has always loved music. He would sit and play the harmonium, singing away, and making us sing. How we would bray! And you know he tried to do an operation to cut off my nose? See? You see the mark here? He took out a razor and just like that he started cutting."

"Why?" I asked, staring at the bridge of her nose. No matter how often I heard the story, I couldn't make sense of it. All I could think of was that Nasik was supposed to have been the place where Ram's brother Lakshman sliced off the nose of Ravana's sister Surpanakha. Had Paw in some way been inspired by the *Ramayana*? "But why?" I repeated.

"Where is the *why* in naughtiness? You all are children; can you tell *why* you are naughty?" demanded Narmada-ben. She was still fingering the bridge of her nose. "Luckily my Mummy came and stopped it."

Ba was fierce in demanding that her grandchildren behave—I would never forget the uproar in Nasik when a child-size turd appeared on the floor of her Pears soap–scented bathroom. All of us, the guilty suspects, were soundly berated. But when Paw, her prized eldest son, behaved inappropriately, had Ba just stood back, certain that even his mischief proved him remarkable? Was Sethji just too old to rein him in? And if I was partly Sethji, did this make me responsible?

"And then the time he made us put our hands in the bucket with the electric heater——" Heera-ben began in her small high voice.

"Do you know we could have owned all of Worli?" Chanda-phui cut in. Worli was an area by the sea between Juhu and downtown Bombay. "Worli! Imagine how much property! Dada took your Paw for a ride in a horse carriage when he was five years old. That whole seaside area was for sale. Dada asked Paw, 'Shall we buy this?' And you know what your Paw said? 'No, it smells!'"

Everybody laughed. Though now densely built up, Worli still smelled, a combination of pungent sea air and what might have been fumes from the sewage processing station that Sethji had long ago built for the city. I imagined the old man in his maroon turban and black waistcoat, heard the clip-clop of the horses' hoofs, saw the little boy wrinkling up his nose along roads.

Sitting on a divan nearby, Ba had been laying down cards for solitaire, faintly bored when she wasn't the center of attention. *"Pagalpan chhe,"* she said, throwing up a tattooed wrist. "It's all madness. Why listen to a five-year-old boy? All that property could have been ours."

An awkward silence followed. Family property was an explosive topic in most extended families, and especially in ours. Long ago, when Narmada-ben and Heera-ben were tiny children, their father and uncle had apparently fought a court case against Sethji. Sethji hired the famous lawyer, Bhulabhai Desai, after whom an auditorium downtown was now named; his elder sons hired M. A. Jinnah, a man so persuasive that he later argued his way into the founding of a whole new country—Pakistan. Sethji lost the case. The family was partitioned, as India would be.

"Then when he went to school, you know what?" Heera-ben broke the silence, silvery laughter spilling out around her words. "It was a Parsi school, and in those days everyone wore caps. Parsis wore Parsi caps, Hindus wore all kinds of Hindu caps, and you could tell so much about a person from the kind of cap he wore. Your Paw, he liked to wear a white Congress cap. He was showing he was with Gandhiji, and against the British."

"In those days, with the British still in charge, your Paw got hold of a recording of 'Vande Mataram,'" Narmada-ben continued. "The song was patriotic and all, and it was banned. Your Paw took the Victrola and blasted it from the balcony for everyone in Nasik to hear! Dada got so worried that the police would come! Dada had great respect for the British, you know; he had worked so closely with them. 'Shut it off,' he said. But your Paw, he said this was just music."

"*So* mischievous he was," said Heera-ben.

"*Cricket mein acchha tha.* He was good at cricket," said Chanda-phui wistfully.

Hearing stories like this, I was glad not to be a son, especially not an eldest son like Paw or Rahoul. Watching from the sidelines as a daughter seemed easier than being under the spotlight of expectant, adoring attention. I stole a glance at the front edge of Chanda-phui's sari, wondering if everyone would be disappointed if the person curled up in there turned out to be a girl.

:::

Any mention of Parsis made me think of Dolly, who was possibly the reason Paw wasn't yet home. I sometimes wondered: was it because Dolly was Parsi that she had such a hold on his imagination?

As far as I knew, Paw's fascination with Parsis had started when he was the only Hindu boy and the rare day scholar in the English-language Parsi boarding school. Until that time, Paw had been "Narayan Ramji," taking his father's first name as his last one, just as his father was Ramji Keshavji. But old Sethji was also known as Ramji Mistri (*mistri* meaning "carpenter") and was sometimes ceremoniously addressed as "Mr. Contractor" when he made municipal contracts with British bureaucrats. In the small Anglicized, Gujarati-speaking Parsi community, names were also often based on profession: Doctor, Engineer, Daruwala (liquor seller), Junglewala (teak merchant), and so on. As a boy Paw decided that he would be Narayan Ramji *Contractor.* Ever since then, in the great Indian guessing game of using names to identify caste, region, and religion, Paw, and all of us who shared his name, had often been mistaken for Parsis.

As N. R. Contractor, Paw was also regularly mistaken for the great cricketeer Nari Contractor, and fans excitedly telephoned the Juhu house whenever test matches were under way. Paw told us that he was probably the only non-Parsi ever invited to build a Parsi fire temple (as non-Parsis are not usually allowed inside fire temples). He could joke with Parsis as though an insider, and each morning he read the *Bombay Samachar,* a Parsi-owned Gujarati newspaper. He claimed to have founded the Parsi-Watching Society of Bombay, dedicated to documenting Parsi quirks. For Parsi holidays, he sent boxes of sweets to friends like Dolly.

Dolly was a few years younger than Maw. Oddly, though, she looked a little like Maw, with pinkish skin and an edge of plumpness, flesh straining over her elbows where the sari blouse ended, her dark hair worn in one braid that she pulled forward over her shoulder. But while Maw would roll her eyes at Paw's sillier puns, Dolly exploded into obliging gales of giggles as he played around with language, switching deftly between English, Hindi, and, with her, varieties of Gujarati.

Dolly worked as an assistant to Mulk Raj Anand, a famous writer about twenty-five years older than her. She also helped produce an art magazine— "a career girl," Paw said. She seemed to belong partly to Mulk's household and to be good friends with Mulk's dancer wife, Shirin. Mulk was a squat, balding Punjabi man who had lived in Britain years earlier, befriending writers in Bloomsbury. He seemed to know something about everything and shared his opinions in a sputtering yet incessant rush of lisped words. He often wore a khaki beret, khaki shorts, and khaki shirt and sometimes a jaunty red scarf, which made him look like an elderly boy scout. I believed this was some sort of leftist military uniform: perhaps the Soviet army, the Cuban army, or the anti-Franco brigades from the Spanish Civil War—at one time or another, I had heard Mulk mention all these groups.

From my early childhood, I had memories of Mulk, Shirin, and Dolly coming over on weekends to play Scrabble or go for walks on the beach with whoever else had assembled, Mulk holding forth all the while. At the time I was struck by how, when the day grew hot, Dolly calmly stripped off her sari and chatted unself-consciously in her front-buttoning *choli* and petticoat with the dangling drawstring. I had also noticed that Maw turned away sternly when Dolly laughed at Paw's jokes.

At some point, Mulk, Dolly, and Shirin had stopped visiting us in Juhu so frequently. Instead, Paw visited them at Mulk's home in downtown Cuffe Parade—not far from Paw's office—or at Mulk's weekend retreat in Khandala. Paw was perfectly open about where he was going, and I continually tried to figure out why he preferred to be with them than with us.

Was it the Cuffe Parade salon that most attracted Paw? Mulk was connected with writers, artists, art historians, dancers, filmmakers, and government officials across India, many of whom dropped in at his house. On the days that Paw went to his downtown office, he picked up Dolly at her office after work and together they went over to Mulk's for a few hours. By the time Paw had dropped her off at the apartment she shared with her parents, then driven across town to Juhu, it was often close to ten o'clock.

Or was Khandala the lure? I had memories of the enchanting green and misty hill station near Poona from a distant time when Paw had taken us all. I could see the appeal of leaving Bombay for cool air and wide green views over a ravine. I had been especially struck that there were no doors inside Mulk's two adjoining cottages, not even on the bathroom. (Maw's theory was that Mulk did not want doors separating him from an audience, no matter what else he was doing.)

I noticed that Paw bought Dolly Cadbury chocolate bars, which he never bought for me. He seemed boyishly energized in her presence. What did it mean when he said they were "good friends"? I watched, I wondered, and I could never find a complete answer for why Paw did not stay home and spend time with us, his children. As an eldest son whom no one had ever scolded, he seemed to hold the right to make his own rules.

∶∶∶

The doors of our house are open to everything, Rahoul wrote in his left-handed scrawl, then crossed it out. Young Swamiji had sent him home to work on college applications. He was applying to a few small, unconventional liberal arts colleges in the United States that might be willing to overlook his never having finished high school.

Rahoul sat on the porch facing the pipal tree, curly head bent over a red-bound, Divali-blessed account book that had never been used and eventually was passed along for other kinds of writing. Beyond him shades and textures of green melted together in the heat. This was a Maw-designed porch: less a space stretching into the garden than a room without a front wall that drew the green luxuriance inside.

Both occidental and oriental cultures are—— Rahoul started, then scribbled a line through that too. Then he wrote:

My home East and West. Books + people + ideas.

His brow furrowed, he was writing fast.

Career—film maker, painter, writer, photographer, mystic, or guru.

Under the heading "A Teacher," he started in on the first draft of a college application essay.

> What I have always been looking for is a teacher. First I felt that a teacher would have to be a living person, but the more I search [the more] "teacher"

means an abstract ideal—an image of perfection that need not have any form. A teacher is like a signboard or map which helps one cross the confusion of life. He only guides you—you have to do all the walking and toil. A true teacher is a catalyst to inner growth or evolution. He helps and awakens but never takes part directly. Writing about a teacher is the hardest thing for me to do in completing this form. It is like trying to paint a picture of shapeless sunlight.

Rahoul had a lot at stake in this application. As Maw often reminded us, college in America was our way out from all the uncertainty of depending on Paw. Once Maya had received a scholarship to St. John's College in New Mexico, the rest of us lived with the expectation that we would also someday attend American colleges on scholarships. The scholarships were key: even if Paw had found some way to get around the Reserve Bank of India's rules against rupees leaving the country, the cost of tuition in dollars was out of the question. Nani had invested money from the sale of her Taos home in a fund to grant each grandchild about a thousand dollars a year toward tuition: nowhere near enough to cover costs, but a token to be dangled before admissions officers.

Ironically, while college was supposed to rescue us from Paw, it was Paw who had been the family pioneer in leaving India for an American college. In 1946, Paw had filled out application forms for the air force and waved these at his father, threatening that unless he was allowed to attend college abroad, he would enlist. Sethji countered that he would send Paw abroad on the condition that, as a son of Vishwakarma, he trained in some aspect of building. Paw wasn't particularly interested in architecture or engineering, but he agreed. In the spirit of Indian independence, he chose America over England, arriving in 1947.

Amid the postwar push for education under the G.I. Bill, Paw had found the University of California at Berkeley too crowded (Maw hinted that he had a sort of nervous breakdown). After two years, he transferred to the University of Colorado at Boulder to study civil engineering. According to Maw—this was not a story that Paw told—when Paw applied to transfer to Boulder, he was found to *have the highest IQ ever recorded for a foreign student and the lowest aptitude for engineering ever recorded for any student.*

Paw's college pranks among the Americans made for stories that he told more readily, his cheeks rounded with amusement. I had heard these stories of my trickster-father so often that I could recite them too. For example:

Paw was greatly entertained by American men's custom of carrying snap-
shots of their girlfriends in their wallets, and then sitting on them! When
men gathered in bars near campus showing off pictures of their girlfriends, he played coy, bashfully reporting that his girlfriend was a beauty
queen, that she had long curling lashes, marvelous curves, and beautiful,
milky pink skin. Then he produced a snapshot of a prize pig, her snout in
close-up.

When Paw and Maw began seeing each other seriously, she took him to
meet the chairman of the art department at Boulder. The chairman's wife
was ordering her spring bulbs from a catalog. Not knowing what to say
to an Indian, she pointed at her catalog cover and asked, "Do *you* have *tu-
lips* in *India*?" Paw stretched his hands about a foot apart. "*Big!*" he said.
Maw squirmed, trying to coax him to show his brilliance, but the evening
proceeded with this sort of stilted exclamation. "Do *you* have *elephants* in
India?" "*Big!*" As Paw later said, "If someone wants to talk pidgin English
with me, I'm very happy to talk it back!"

This story was supplemented by another.

A few months later, Paw was lecturing on Hindu philosophy to a small
group. The same chairman and his wife arrived and stood just behind him
at the open door. Maw could see them but Paw couldn't. They looked, they
listened to him speak with ease and sophistication, and their jaws dropped.
Very slowly, they turned around and left. "Needless to say, this didn't ad-
vance my career," said Maw.

While Rahoul prepared packages to mail, I was already wondering what
acts my brother might put on for the Americans.
—Do *you* have *gurus* in *India*?
—Yes. Actually, I *am* one.

: : :

In January, Chanda-phui gave birth through caesarian section in a Bombay
hospital. The next day, Maw and Paw arrived outside our school in an un-
precedented joint appearance, just after the 3:30 bell had released Deven
and me for the afternoon. Rahoul was off with Young Swamiji so couldn't
join us.
   We found Chanda-phui in a private room with filtered winter sun drift-

ing in through one window. She sat at the edge of the hospital bed, looking radiant and shy—too shy to accept the role of patient and lie down. As soon as we appeared, she pulled out snack-filled plastic containers from under her bed, urging me and Deven to have some *nasta*.

Sukhlal-phua sat stunned in a chair, unable to stop smiling. Ba occupied another chair, khaki tote bag in her lap, basking in her accomplishment.

"Didn't I say it was a boy?" Ba demanded as the rest of us found seats.

The baby was sleeping. He was very fair, so milky white that even my Maw-lightened skin looked dark beside his. Black threads were tied around his wrists and black kohl was dotted on his face to divert the evil eye.

So far Paw had only been a *kaka,* or father's brother, though our Nasik cousins referred to him as "Didi Paw," which emphasized his connection to Maw. With the birth of Chanda-phui's son, Paw had an important new role as a *mama*—mother's brother to his sister's child. He brought out what appeared to be a bundle of cloth and waved it in the direction of the baby. "May he enjoy a life full of vices," he said ceremonially in Gujarati, handing the bundle to Chanda-phui.

Chanda-phui unrolled the gift, and we all saw that it was an embroidered bag for storing tobacco and betel nut. Even I understood that this was a bizarrely inappropriate gift for an infant. But Chanda-phui giggled from deep in her throat, beaming at her brother. Sukhlal-phua's smile didn't waiver either.

"Yes, a life full of vices, just like his *mama,*" Maw added, a little too aggressively in too-loud Hindi. Chanda-phui had always admired Paw with such unswerving loyalty that having a son like her brother might seem to her an admirable goal, but Maw's words sounded like an angry warning.

On the long drive back to Juhu, the streetlamps had come on, and roadside shops passed like color slides forwarded too fast. Somewhere near Shivaji Park, in a darker stretch of road with no shops, Maw tried to coax Paw into sharing memories stirred up by our visit.

"Remember, Narayan, when Rahoul was born?" she said wistfully from the back seat, where she sat with Deven and me.

Paw didn't turn his head. He looked out the windshield, mute beside the driver.

"Sethji couldn't believe it after that astrologer's prediction," Maw said. "Ba fed me almonds and cooked special dishes for strength. Remember?"

Paw still said nothing.

We all knew the story, but Paw had been present as a central character. Why did he resist remembering? I studied the back of Paw's neck, the outline of his right ear and glasses frame, feeling my way into his mind. He had once again slipped into the habit of an evening drink—so far, he seemed to be in control, but by this hour he would need it. Also, this rare return from town as a family meant that he had lost a chance to visit with Dolly. He was barely holding himself together, it seemed, and he needed to concentrate on oncoming headlights.

Maw reached forward, her married woman's gold bangles slipping and sliding. Her fingers rested on his white shirt. "They finally were willing to give me wedding jewelry," Maw said, but the bubbliness of her voice had gone flat. She pressed his shoulder. "Narayan, remember?"

Maw's words hung in the enclosed space. Paw didn't move. "I remember," he said finally, in a voice that stretched taut over whatever words and feelings he held back.

Maw pulled her hand close against her sari, as though nursing her elbow, and turned her head toward the window. Sitting beside her, my head level with her shoulder, I could feel the hurt of rebuff like a jab in the ribs. I didn't say anything, and Deven sat quietly too. What could an eleven-year-old or a fifteen-year-old say? But in remaining as still and silent as Paw, I plugged into the crackling current of annoyance under his skin. The Maw voice inside me pleaded: *Why does he turn away?* At the same time, the Paw voice demanded: *Why does she insist?*

Each parent's emotional force field repelled the other's with such vehemence that I could imagine the car splitting apart. I tensed my knee to press against Maw's and reached my palm toward the plastic back of Paw's seat. When would Rahoul come home to hold us together?

: : :

When Rahoul was in Bombay, he consulted with Paw's psychiatrist for lessons on how to act like a paranoid schizophrenic. "Look, I don't want to be drafted when I go to America," Rahoul explained speedily, looking over his shoulder after every second word. "I don't want college to be a stopover on the way to Vietnam."

Rahoul received high scores on his SAT exam. As we waited for news on his college applications, Stella took Rahoul on a trip to our ancestral region of Kutch. Stella claimed to have now "done India," and was moving to an apartment near Lincoln Center in New York. Since I had always stayed away from elegant, outspoken Stella—as instructed—I didn't yet know her well. Still, I couldn't help feeling that another piece of my world since childhood was coming undone. My own body was starting to change in small ways too, and all these transformations at the same time were like strong sea currents carrying me far from the familiar shore rimmed with coconut trees.

A thick envelope arrived from Reed College in Portland, Oregon. Rahoul had been admitted and granted limited financial support. To help pay for the first year, he would need a summer job to earn dollars.

Maya would have finished college by the summer. Through letters, Maw knew that Maya also wanted to save up some money before she returned to India after the monsoon. Maya and Rahoul made plans to share an apartment for the summer in New York.

"I'm gonna be wild when I get to New York," Rahoul happily predicted.

"It's a good place to be wild in," said Maw.

"See, Young Swamiji and I have this special deal to pool our karma," Rahoul continued with one of the joyous, mischievous smiles that left me uncertain about whether he was making up what he said. "I've told Young Swamiji that I'm going to be totally crazy and burn off all his worldly karma in America, while he stays here in the jungle and stores up all this spiritual merit for me. He's the one who insisted I do this college thing, and I've told him that if I'm going, that's the deal."

"Really?" I asked, wide-eyed. "You can share karma?"

"What do you suppose we're all doing together in a family, Baby?" Rahoul countered. "Why do you think we were born connected to each other?"

"You'll have a great time," Maw affirmed. "You know, when I was seventeen, I went to New York with my friend Franny. Our Greyhound bus fare was paid by this man in Taos who wanted us to stop in every city on the way to sell his recordings of American Indian dances. It was so incredible to be in New York, and see all those museums and cultural events."

Maw began paging through her address book to locate everyone she had ever met from New York, and I studied her *New Yorker* magazines, which were still arriving three months late. I stared at advertisements for perfume, fur coats, and Caribbean cruises, wondering: Just how could you share karma across parallel realities?

Festive, excited, and all dressed up, we accompanied Rahoul to the Bombay airport on a humid night in April 1971. Like most flights abroad, his was scheduled to depart in the early hours of the morning. Ba, Chanda-phui and her baby boy, the baby's ayah, and also the Mehtaji accountant from Byculla joined us in the send-off party. Paw's drinking was making him distant-eyed and elusive again, but he managed to put in a brief appearance before taking off with the driver.

The airport lobby smelled of sweat and flowers, and hummed with con-

versation, excitement, and staticky announcements over the loudspeaker.
Fans beat at the heat. Flashbulbs flared like lightning from all corners of the
lobby, as families lined up for the professional photographers who milled
through the crowds. Many of the men going abroad were marked like victorious heroes or bridegrooms—streaks of red *kumkum* on their foreheads,
garlands around their necks. Ba called over one of the photographers sweating in a jacket with a camera around his neck, and we posed for our departure photographs.

Rahoul stood at the center of our group wearing a high-collared black
jacket with black slacks and gleaming black Bata shoes. His hair was styl-
ishly cut in a compromise between the wild curls and short-cropped *sannyasi* look he had been alternating these last few years. His cheeks were
shaved, and curved with a happy smile. He shone like a prince ready to
conquer the world.

Lacking the gowns, trains, and tiaras I considered suitable for the sister of a prince, I stood at his side wearing the best available token of roy-
alty: a hand-me-down gray checked dress that had once been Maya's. This
dress had arrived from America before my birth, in one of Nani's seventeen
steamer trunks; Maya had worn it when I was a baby, and it had then returned to one of the trunks for a decade, waiting for me to grow. It was still
too big, but I loved anything that belonged to my barely remembered sister.
So what if this was a relic of the 1950s—its white bib trimmed with fake
black buttons, its puffed sleeves, the full skirt with a tie at the back? So what
if its elephant-hide color did not reveal me as the cute Baby Elephant I had
once been but instead made my complexion appear sallow and accentuated
the dark watchful circles under my eyes? At my conquering big brother's
shoulder, I held my head high, basking in his glow.

Pulling back into the driveway late at night, the house seemed unfamiliar, shrouded in cricket call and the distant roar and tumble of the sea. Our
latest visitors were already stretched out asleep on the living room divans.
I began brushing my teeth. Reaching back toward my molars, I wandered
through the darkened living room to peer in at Paw's open door. The lights
were blazing, a cheerful BBC male voice was holding forth on the radio, and
Paw was slumped in his chair, mouth open.

Ever since Nani and Maya had left for America, Rahoul had stepped in
as an occasional spare parent. What would happen to us younger children
now that Rahoul had also been swallowed up by the dark stretches between
continents? Quickly, before fear coiled tight around me, pulling me into
inner spaces of foreboding, I rinsed out my mouth. Then I stood before

Maw's *puja* alcove in the dressing room, where she had allowed me to prop the picture Young Swamiji had given me of Patane Devi.

Patane Devi beamed bright assurance as I began chanting the goddess hymn that Young Swamiji had taught me. Rahoul might now be flying on the path of "worldly life," but we were only beginning to understand all the ways that his quest for a guru had transformed us. In the years that followed, even though Rahoul wasn't living in Juhu anymore, the adventures that he had set in motion continued to shape what happened in our home.

Gurus and Urugs

The Bombay International School occupied several floors of an old downtown apartment building across the street from the Babulnath temple and near the foot of swanky Malabar Hill. Most of our classmates lived downtown too, in the new sky-rises veering up beyond the noise and confusion of life closer to the ground. During recess, the girls discussed fashion shows at the Taj, swimming at Breach Candy, eating European pastries at Bombelli's, or going to the latest Hollywood movie at the Regal, Metro, or Sterling. Usually, my friend Fatty Rasha and I listened in from the margins. Juhu was too far away and our household budgets were too differently scaled for us to join our classmates for most of these after-school or weekend social events.

But when the girls in our class decided that we should perform a Hawaiian dance for our school assembly, no one had any doubt that the best place to learn how to dance like Hawaiians was under the coconut palms of Juhu Beach. We gathered around our wooden desks at recess to discuss a plan, and before I quite knew what had happened, the plan had roped me in. The downtown girls would travel to the Bombay suburbs on a Saturday, stop first at Fatty Rasha's apartment building facing the sea, then stroll along the sands to practice at my house. *My house!* In my eagerness to hide that I didn't want them to visit, how had I managed to back myself into an

« Maw and Swami Prakashananda (Old Swamiji) at Ganeshpuri, 1970s.
  Photographer unknown.   :: 123

invitation? Fatty Rasha in my house was one thing; all the girls from our class was another.

Fatty Rasha and I had been friends since she was five and I was six, roughly half our lives. She wasn't actually fat, just solid, with eyes that crinkled into sleepy new moons when she laughed. We lived a short walk down the beach from each other and first met because her older brother was about Deven's age and in the same school. She and I also took piano and band lessons from the same Parsi sisters in the Theosophical Colony. Even before we joined the same school, we had visited each other in the evenings and on weekends. For years, I had especially looked forward to Sundays at her home. I knew that her father would be lounging in shorts, her mother preparing *aloo parathas* crunchy with pomegranate seeds and dripping with homemade white butter, her grandmother spinning *khadi* or reading the *Ramayana,* her brother playing and replaying his favorite record. He had recently moved on from a long-running Harry Belafonte phase, and his latest pleasure was the new George Harrison single, "My Sweet Lord," a song we adored for its melody and the surprise inclusion of a Sanskrit chant. (Fatty Rasha's grandmother Mataji also greatly enjoyed the song, as devotional music. She asked for it as *"voh* Hare Krishna Hare Rama-wala *bhajan."*)

While I found Fatty Rasha's home delightful in its predictable rhythms, she looked forward to coming over to mine for the constant surprise. We often spied on the guests, or asked them trick questions and then rushed off, bent over, shaking helplessly with the giggles.

As our classmates discussed the details of our Hawaiian dancing plans, my mind raced from room to room, identifying possible dangers. Even with trusted Fatty Rasha, I made sure to deflect our play routes from situations that might reveal my parents' separate bedrooms, Paw's drinking, the perpetual worry over money. By carefully managing what parts of the house my classmates saw, I might possibly continue this cover-up.

But where, I worried, would I hide the urugs?

: : :

Returning from his 1970 World Tour, Babaji had brought along a planeload of young Western disciples. Many of them soon spilled over from the Ganeshpuri ashram and into our home, joining Western seekers from other ashrams and gurus. Once Paw had invented the word "urug" for these guests, he found himself using it often. *"The urugs are coming, ah-ha, ah-ha,"* Paw chanted under his breath as Maw greeted new arrivals. They came to stay especially when they needed to accomplish errands involving visas, tickets, international calls, or money in downtown Bombay; when they were recuperating from tropical diseases or nervous breakdowns; or when they were longing for familiar comforts like peanut butter, rock and roll, and old issues of the *New Yorker.*

Our home rapidly became a crossroads for urugs sorting out themselves and their routes. Most of our urugs were disciples of Babaji—Swami Muktananda. But urugs arriving from the north told stories about how big-bellied, blanket-wrapped Neem Karoli Baba read their minds, or how they had stopped in to meet Anandamayi Ma, whose dark hair and blissful smile had been described by Yogananda Paramhansa in *Autobiography of a Yogi.* Urugs en route from Igatpuri, near Nasik, described ten-day silent retreats with a businessman turned meditation teacher called Goenka. Others, descending from Bengal, spoke of the powerful presence of Ramakrishna Paramahansa that still lingered in Dakshineshwar. From the south, urugs brought tales of the ancient French Mother with her scarf-wrapped forehead, in Pondicherry; of fiery Swami Janananda, who lived in a complex of caves; of Satya Sai Baba, who pulled Rolex watches from his Afro and stone lingams from under his tongue. Those urugs who didn't come from the Ganeshpuri ashram were usually directed there by Maw for the next stop on their spiritual itinerary.

Once Paw had created the category, I could also see how urugs had been arriving all along, some in the guise of hippies—Rahoul's old friend Broderick, for example, who had talked about the Maharishi made famous by the Beatles. Even beatniks, Peace Corps volunteers, and students of Indian classical music who had visited had sometimes had uruglike qualities. It was only now that enough of a wave had formed that we could classify them.

I still remembered our Happening, the Indian concert in the garden in 1968, and how the hippies had swarmed in. I had stared, aghast, at the *cholis* and petticoats minus saris; embroidered vests minus shirts; macramé tops minus bras; sheer skirts minus slips; cotton pajama bottoms minus decent crotch-covering *kurtas,* drawstrings dangling obscenely outward. That had been just the start of the wild-haired, strangely clad parade of people who exchanged Maw's address, as she said, *"all along the hash trail."*

Urugs on the guru trail were generally better washed and more neatly dressed than the hippies who had preceded them; they tended to dismiss hippies as "being stuck at their lower *chakras,*" absorbed in sex and intoxication. Instead of tie-dye, striped satin, and heavy embroidery, urugs usually went for the simplicity of cotton in block colors. Men tended toward white, yellow, or orange T-shirts and *kurtas* with *lungis* folded up around their waists, leaving their calves exposed. Women usually draped themselves in long skirts or crumpled orange saris, ankles showing, hair pulled tightly back into braids. Men and women alike wore beaded wooden or crystal *malas*.

The line between hippies and urugs, I noticed, was actually quite porous. People who arrived at our house looking like hippies sometimes emerged in the robes of urugs, and the urugs could suddenly revert to tie-dyed T-shirts. In this migration between identities, our visitors shed clothes. Maw gathered the occasional ill-fitting orange sari blouse, yellow macrame bathing suit, or white-on-white embroidered Afghani top into the Visitors' Trunk, which sat atop the Costume Trunk in a corner of the boys' room. Then, when our next wave of guests tried to figure out who they wanted to be in India, she opened the trunk overflowing with possible identities. The trunk also contained "straight clothes" for the transition out of hippie and urug gear: miniskirts, lace-edged slips, ties, jackets, and Burberry raincoats appropriate for visiting consulates and visa offices, and even flying "home." Though the Visitor's Trunk was technically different from the Costume Trunk (filled with oddities like Nani's graduation robe, Beatle wigs, and a Kathiawari shepherd's tunic), when we kids needed costumes for Friday assembly performances at the Bombay International School, we freely rifled through both trunks.

In preparation for my debut as a Hawaiian dancer, I rummaged around in the Costume Trunk to find Nani's old grass skirt. She had picked this up in Hawaii in the 1920s, at the start of a journey that later landed her in Munich studying art, where she met Maw's father. The dry grass rustled, smelling comfortably of dark, hidden, slightly mildewed interiors.

::::

"When the girls from my class come you have to get rid of all the urugs!" I ordered Maw. I had found her alone on the back porch, where she was cradling her favorite coffee mug and staring out into the patterns of pipal leaves.

"Sweetie, why are you so worried?" Maw asked, looking over at me with her blue green eyes.

"I don't want anyone to think we're strange."

Maw shut her mouth tight. "Well, okay," she said after a moment. "But I think you're overreacting."

I hid, feeling guilty, wondering how Maw would disinvite our guests. "Kids, you know, are so bourgeois," I overheard her explain. "Her classmates are coming and she's a little uptight, she doesn't want this to seem like too much of a scene. So just for next Saturday it would be good to do a little sightseeing. There's this marvelous *sadhu* who's stood up day and night leaning into a swing for twelve years. You might want to visit him. If you go past the ancient Buddhist monastery at Kanheri caves and then turn right where there's a garden. . . ."

Urugs, I knew, made Maw happy. Some called her Didi, others adopted her as Maw, and yet others formally saluted her as Mataji (never "Martyrji"). Among urugs associated with the Ganeshpuri ashram, she shone with the aura of an old-timer who knew the ashram in the golden era before Babaji first went abroad. Maw offered the urugs quick lessons in Indian customs—*use your right hand for food, don't extend your feet toward people or gods, don't sunbathe in public.* She freely dispensed names of doctors, travel agents, bank managers, and potential hosts in other parts of India and abroad.

Maw bloomed amid the ever-changing assortment of people. She reveled in learning about their backgrounds, and in return told them about her own life: Her early memories of Munich. Her parents' bohemian friends, like Hans Hoffman and Emma Goldman. Her father's taking a job in what he thought was "the Wild West"; it turned out to be a Baptist university in Waco, Texas, where they had moved when she was six. Her teenage years among the eccentric artists of Taos. Her marrying across cultures, and long period of living with in-laws in Nasik before she and Paw were able to build their own home in Bombay. These days, when she told these familiar stories, they usually led to the happy ending of her finding a guru.

When Paw was home, if he was in a genial and expansive mood, he sometimes decided to play "Swami Paw." He wandered out from his room, inviting urugs to join him for a drink. As Swami Paw, he offered teachings on Indian history, philosophy, and religion in relation to his favorite Western authors: Joyce, Kafka, Calvino, or Borges. He relished playing the urbane, slightly mocking Hindu insider.

On Yogananda Paramahansa's *Autobiography of a Yogi,* a cult classic for most urugs, Paw's comment was always: *"How can a yogi have an 'auto' to biograph?"*

On chanting: *"Aum Sweet Aum."*

On the *Bhagavad Gita*: *"Bhagavad Gita, Dolce Vita."*

Swami Paw sparkled with an audience. But a few drinks later, he could become impatient with his new disciples. Lifting the edge of his *lungi* with one hand, he would shuffle off to find Maw. "Who are all these people?" he demanded, gesturing toward his room. "Get rid of them." Maw ushered the dazzled guests from Paw's room, and they rejoined the conversations unfolding in the living room, porch, or garden.

Our neighbor Stella had always repeated that she was *"absolutely not into gurus,"* but her house was not immune to occasional urugs. A tough older woman who had ridden motorcycles with the Hell's Angels and then wandered through the Himalayas with naked, chain-dragging Naga *sadhus* showed up at Stella's house with a fluffy, flat-nosed little dog. The dog was named Susu, which in Hindi baby talk meant "pee." It was funny enough to hear her standing in Stella's garden calling out what sounded like "Pee pee pee!" When we learned that the dog was a shih-tzu, Deven and I laughed even harder. We adopted the word as we heard it, "shitso," and applied it to anybody who behaved like a shitty so-and-so, including urugs.

We children liked many urugs. Some became beloved honorary family, and we looked forward to their visits; the treats, like honey or fruit, that they brought as house gifts; and also the knowledge they shared, whether how to crochet, strum guitar chords, or make ratatouille. Other urugs were comic curiosities; the New Yorker called Howie, for example, laid out his theory of interplanetary travel through "anal propulsion" (or excessive bean eating) as we kicked each other under the table, trying unsuccessfully to keep straight faces. Shitso urugs, though, might liberally slather expensive jam onto toast without noticing that there was none left for the children. A shitso invited other, unknown shitsos to crash at the pad too; they would arrive empty-handed just when dinner was about to be served, so water had to be added to the *dal* and more rice boiled fast. A shitso advised that lights shouldn't be turned on for homework because the room was already glowing with the inner light of consciousness.

As more urugs arrived at the ashram, names started to overlap and new ways had to be developed to sort them. So we shared meals with people such as Cowshed Alan and Garden Mark (both British), South African Chris and Australian Chris, Big Bruno (Italian) and Little Bruno (Italian American). No sooner were the foreign names getting sorted out than Babaji also began granting Hindu names to a few special disciples—flowery names of gods, mythological figures, and medieval saints. Some of these names, like Nala, Maitreyi, and Janabai, sounded so quaintly old-fashioned that when Fatty Rasha and I were introduced, we rushed off, hands over our mouths to hold back our laughter.

Maw loved to talk about how Babaji's energy-charged presence sparked such experiences as visions of lights, involuntary movements, and ecstatic calm. "He gives *shaktipat*," Maw instructed those who weren't yet in the know. "It's this energy transmission that awakens the *kundalini* energy lying coiled like a serpent at the base of the spine." Urugs who had received this *shaktipat,* I observed, could be especially dramatic. Settling into what started out as composed meditation, they soon began to rock their heads or whirl from the waist, throw up their hands in classical Indian dance poses, or let out fierce snorts. "Oh, this is nothing," Maw said. "You should see what goes on at the ashram when the *shakti* is really powerful." These apparently involuntary movements and sounds were called *kriyas,* and when I learned that an elderly American *sadhu* with long, stringy hair whom Maw had invited to dinner was called Kriyananda—"the joy of *kriyas*"—I thought I would choke on my own suppressed giggles.

Paw's relatives and hangers-on from his office made their way directly to his room with silent, sidelong glances at the urugs. But our downtown Bombay friends—the artists, scientists, writers, filmmakers, and politicians who had been visiting on weekends for years—attempted to make conversation. Somehow, these exchanges never worked. While our Bombay friends wanted to discuss population control, the tragedies of Vietnam, the writings of Günther Grass, or even what Americans might possibly find compelling about *Jonathan Livingston Seagull,* many urugs tried to guide the conversation back to timeless Indian spiritual truths.

With time, our cosmopolitan Bombay friends started keeping to themselves on urug-free porches, muttering about the "nut cases" overrunning our house. Urugs, on the other hand, could bemoan how "Westernization makes people lose their culture."

"I will be glad to discuss enlightenment when every village in India has electricity," said a middle-aged male editor, smiling with strained patience at a pretty female urug. He sat in a butterfly chair wearing a homespun *khadi* bush shirt, trousers, and leather sandals; she was perched in the grass, bare feet folded under her orange sari.

"And do you *really* think electric lights will make people happy?" the young woman inquired.

As I imagined my Westernized classmates encountering Indianized urugs, I wanted to stop up my ears to block out the giggled exclamations about the crazy foreigners who lived with Kirin.

: : :

I had always had an overactive imagination, and as I began to run through all the things that could go wrong, the return of Bhagavan Das loomed large. Maw had been so awed by this particular urug that I knew she would resist packing him off with the others to the Kanheri caves.

Bhagavan Das was an extremely tall Californian who had arrived at our house in the getup of a *sadhu*: matted blond locks twisted on top of his head, long ropes of *rudraksha* beads on his bare chest, and a saffron cloth wrapped around his waist. According to Maw, he had once been a surfer, had done a lot of drugs, and at some point had acquired James Joyce's bottle-cap glasses to understand what the world looked like from Joyce's perspective. He had found a guru in blanket-wrapped Neem Karoli Baba, then spent a few years wandering through the Himalayas as an unusually lanky, golden-haired *sadhu* whom villagers sometimes mistook as an apparition of Lord Shiva. His visa had long since expired when Indian government officials located him in a sensitive border area and suspected him of cold war spying. In the course of being deported, Bhagavan Das had ended up under house arrest in our home.

Bhagavan Das called Maw Mataji and told her she was an embodiment of the Divine Mother. He said he would like to wash her feet—a proposition to which Maw reacted with girlish shyness (it made me recall Ba's exchange with her *sadhu* friend Godhadiya Baba). Most urugs were offered mattresses in the living room or porch, but Maw honored Bhagavan Das with the use of Rahoul's empty room.

In the evenings, Bhagavan Das emerged for audience. He sat cross-legged out in the garden and plucked at a one-stringed *ektara,* loudly singing Hindu chants. Maw sat beside him, clinking small brass cymbals. Other urugs followed his lead and gathered to chant too, while neighbors peeped in through the hedge to see what the commotion was about. I frankly preferred the chanting of another Neem Karoli Baba devotee, handsome, easy-going Jeff, or Krishna Das, who had also come through our house singing praises to the Goddess.

"Why does he have to be the center of everything?" I grumbled about Bhagavan Das after Paw had returned briefly from one of his business trips, decided he wasn't interested in playing counterswami, and taken off for Nasik.

"He's famous!" Maw admonished. "You can read all about him."

She brought out *Be Here Now* by Baba Ram Dass, or Richard Alpert, Ph.D. This was a book that urugs had recently been leaving at our home, along with the usual staples: *The Autobiography of a Yogi, The Prophet, A Search in Secret India,* and *Seven Years in Tibet.* As far as I was concerned, *Be Here Now* was a hippie scrapbook that only deeply deluded grown-ups might mistake for literature. I had leafed through it on occasion, appalled by the multicolored print, text running at odd angles over the page, drawings of naked women, and blue- and brown-tinted photographs of lamas and gurus.

Maw pointed to a chapter titled "Bhagwan Dass," which featured a blue photograph that was clearly of our guest, his bearded chin lifted and hair hanging over his shoulders. "You can read for yourself that Ram Dass says that Bhagavan Das is the only enlightened Westerner he knows."

"You think I'm going to believe anything written in *that* book?" I scoffed.

Next, Bhagavan Das's *shakti,* or consort, had arrived: a gorgeous American girl with ivory skin and a sleek black cloak of hip-length hair. She went by the name Bhavani and dressed in a white sheet tied halter-style around her neck. This was a way in which some holy people wore their robes, but with her full breasts poking through, and her creamy shoulders and shapely calves exposed, her outfit looked anything but swamilike. As Bhagavan Das sang, Bhavani sat at his feet, singing along, taking over the duty of playing the cymbals.

"He's a *sadhu* but not the celibate kind," Maw informed other awe-struck urugs. "They have tantric sex."

For a festive Christmas Eve dinner, Bhagavan Das had mysteriously decided to eat from a pale, curved dish, holding it in his lap rather than placing it on the table. Maw wondered if it might be the top of a skull: "Some *sadhus* carry them around, you know, as a reflection on impermanence."

Deven and I caught each other's eye. I guessed that, like me, he was thinking that we hardly needed to dramatize impermanence at our everchanging dinner table.

::::

At the Bombay International School, foreign mothers were common enough, and some consulate children had foreign fathers as well. Maw had helped found the school and liked to say that many of the founding members were Western wives with Indian last names. In my class of about thirty students, I could count at least two others with American mothers, two with English mothers, and one with a Dutch mother.

Yet even among these foreign mothers, I realized, Maw stood out for her exuberant adoption of Indian outfits, customs, and now religion.

"When the girls are here, don't come out, and if you have to come out, don't say anything, okay?" I sharply ordered the evening before my class-mates were due.

"Okay," Maw said, barely repressing a sigh. "I'll make a cake and disap-pear."

On Saturday morning, I inspected our neatly swept, swabbed, and urug-free living room, contrasting what I saw with my glimpses of classmates' homes. I was already aware that most of my classmates came from families with longer and deeper British associations; in my Indian family, education in English began with Paw, and his family wealth was recent. Between Paw's background and Maw's American bohemian values, we had never been re-spectably *pukka*. I understood that some of my other classmates might have the same insecurities, but all the same I worried: what would the group think when it was discovered that I lived without air conditioning, with-out servants in starched white uniforms, without giant horse paintings by the trendy Bombay painter M. F. Hussein? Would they find the divans with bolsters and handloom bedspreads charming, or would they consider us peasants who weren't sophisticated enough for formal, carved colonial fur-niture? Was it too late to take down the chain of goat-bladder attar bottles that Maw had hung by the porch door, empty but still exuding sweet fumes of vetiver and roses when one passed close? What about the pictures of Babaji, with his sunglasses and woolen cap, and his guru, Bhagavan Nity-ananda, wearing only a loincloth under his big bare belly—could I some-how pass them off as eccentric relatives?

I slunk miserably to the kitchen. "Maw, we have to do something about the living room."

"Sweetie, stop being so uptight, won't you?" Maw said, stirring at cinna-mon cake batter. "Just entertain them in the garden."

Midmorning, my classmates trailed in through the garden gate. Every-one seemed unfamiliar out of the school uniform. I couldn't help noticing that most of them wore pastel flowered patterns. As usual, I was dressed in one of Maw's A-line designs in a dark, block-printed, handloom fabric, an-chored at the front with a chain of silver Rajasthani buttons. Luckily Fatty Rasha provided earth-tone solidarity with her fine brown-checked cotton shift.

Servants carried square tables to the shady area near the bamboo grove, setting out cake along with pitchers of fresh, tangy *nimbu pani*. Fatty Rasha, always a fan of Maw's baking, led the class in declaring the cake "yum!" The group ate, admired the overgrown garden, and then turned to our current favorite preteen topic—the much anticipated monthly arrivals of "chums." Chums inevitably led us to another scandalous subject: "It." Someone quoted from a magazine claiming that all couples, including our parents, did It twice a week, a statistic I sincerely doubted. Someone else shared the latest "heights joke": "What's the height of patriotism? Gandhiji wearing a *khadi* Nirodh." *Khadi* was the homespun cotton that Gandhi had advocated for nationalistic self-reliance; Nirodh were much advertised, government-issued condoms. We put our hands over our mouths as we laughed. Oh, the shocking shamefulness of It!

Eventually we settled down to learning Hawaiian dance. Our teacher was Nandita's cousin Amita, half-American like several of us, but visiting from Honolulu with tanned legs and an American accent. Several other girls, including Fatty Rasha, produced grass skirts that relatives had brought home as exotic souvenirs from abroad. We tied the skirts over what we were already wearing, and Amita started teaching us the words to our song. Words mastered, she moved on to the steps.

"*Lovely hula hands,*" we sang, swaying in unison. The grass skirts sighed and rustled, whispering of faraway places. Sun drifted through bamboo leaves, speckling us with brightness and shadow. Our voices mingled, soft and high.

"*Graceful as the birds in motion.*" From the corner of my eye, I glimpsed maroon robes on the porch. My inner alarms began to clang. How had the banished urugs managed to return so fast? I glanced again, unable to recognize the Western couple in sacred getup who stared, disoriented, at our Hawaiian costumes.

"*Flying like the gulls over the ocean.*" I scanned the faces of the girls around me to see if anyone else had spied the visitors, but everyone was concentrating on keeping up with Amita.

"*Lovely hula hands.*" Maw appeared and whisked the robed strangers out of sight.

I continued waving my arms while monitoring the porch. Should I suggest that we move to the beach in order to have a view of the ocean? But there, we would draw the attention of gawkers who strolled the beach in hopes of sighting scantily clad tourists from the Sun 'n Sand Hotel. A group of young dancing girls would draw a whistling crowd. Worse yet, it might draw the solitary man who reached into his shorts to show us scary things we didn't want to see.

I felt no certainty that Maw was really standing guard against urugs.

: : :

My nerves were still thrumming high-tension wires when my classmates finally departed, chorusing jolly good-byes. Fatty Rasha went with them, promising to ring me up later.

I searched through the house, then made my way across the driveway. I peeked through the vines covering Nani's porch to find Maw in earnest conversation with the maroon-clad couple. I blazed with outrage over Maw's betrayal. The woman was crying. What could *she* have to cry about, I scoffed. She didn't have half her class judging her home!

I stomped off to find refuge in my current favorite book: *My Family and Other Animals* by Gerald Durrell, whom I knew as Gerry. Our Juhu shelves carried a few sophisticated-seeming books by Gerry's older brother, Lawrence Durrell, and reading another Durrell allowed me to affect the same literary airs I enjoyed when reading T. S. Eliot's poems about cats or Oscar Wilde's short fables. The book jacket described Gerry as having been born in India, like me, but *My Family and Other Animals* was set mostly on the island of Corfu, off the coast of Greece. In my imagination the glittering Ionian Sea soon approximated the Arabian Sea nudging the Bombay coast, the olive groves became fields of mango trees near Nasik, and the peasants took on Maharashtrian white caps or nine-yard saris.

I adored Gerry as a child of about my age, looking on as the enthusiasms of older siblings continually transformed his home, and as eccentric visitors passed through, trailing stories. In his account, an absent father, heavy drinking, intellectual discussions, and family chaos seemed entirely acceptable and often hilarious. I cherished the personalities and peculiarities of the pets Gerry described and loved his discoveries of teeming societies of creatures that remained mostly unnoticed by grown-ups; somehow, the spacious calm of this natural world echoed the mysteriousness of the inner, spiritual worlds that I sensed lay behind the dramas of gurus and urugs. (Maw, though, said that while *My Family and Other Animals* was "entirely charming" I shouldn't make too many analogies between the Durrells and us—mostly, I suspect, because she found Gerry's mother too vague. "Just wait till you read Salinger," Maw often said. "You'll see that we have *much* more in common with the Glass family.")

Later that afternoon, I emerged refreshed and soothed by a few chapters of *My Family and Other Animals,* all set to take on my mother. I watched from beside the Queen of the Night bush near our front entrance as the couple stood with Maw beside a taxi at the garden gate. The taxi driver and the servant who had fetched him both looked on curiously as the couple embraced Maw. Now that the woman had stopped weeping, I noticed that she was as pretty as a Hindi film star, her curly brown hair offset by maroon robes. But the ridiculousness of those robes, in full view of the neighbors, only rekindled my rage toward my mother.

The taxi rattled off along the unpaved neighborhood road, and Maw walked slowly back toward the house. I stepped out from behind the tall bush, poised to strike. "Couldn't you keep your urugs away just once?" I demanded. "Couldn't you *just for a few hours* pretend we are normal?"

"But sweetie, I didn't invite them."

"Then why didn't you just send them away? I *told* you not to have urugs."

"They came to me for advice. Their faith is shaken. It's terrible what they've been through!"

Maw came into the kitchen and heated up her filtered coffee mixed with buffalo milk. She explained that the young woman was pregnant after having had her *"chakras* inspected" once too often by Acharya Rajneesh, their suave, English-speaking professor guru. He had instructed the woman and her boyfriend to abstain from sex with each other since they became his disciples, but now he was denying responsibility.

"Poor kids," said Maw. "They need to sort themselves out. They need to figure out their relationship, their faith, their views on India, everything. Would you really want me to turn them away without at least listening to them and serving them food? Pumpkin, have a heart!"

My fury at not having control of the household's comings and goings was brought up short against my shock that a guru could do such things, and my horrified sympathy for this woman forced into doing It and now paying the consequences.

"But still!" I insisted, unwilling to concede. "But still. What if the girls from my class had seen them?"

"I wish you would stop caring so much about what your classmates think," Maw said, starting into the living room with her coffee while I trailed after. "It's a big energy drain to fret so much about other people's opinions. When you grow up, you're going to be very grateful to have had such an interesting childhood."

This was all very fine for Maw to say when my childhood stretched out with no clear horizon. I reached about for fresh ammunition. "When I grow up," I informed Maw, "I'm going to write a book called *My Family and Other Saints* and put you in it."

I even requisitioned an old notebook to get started. I planned to make entries on every urug and guru, with cross-references on who had sent whom and notes on every odd thing each urug did or said in my home. But giving words to the life around me turned out to be harder than I had imagined. Documenting the kaleidoscopic shifts in my family's interactions only underlined how little I could anticipate or control. I found it safer to embark instead on an uninspired story about princesses at Miss Pace's Boarding School for Young Ladies who formed a secret society to explore the network of passages under their castle.

8

Mrs. Contractor's
Eldest Unmarried Daughter

In the months before Maya returned after her four years of college, I often looked out across the silvery band of the Arabian Sea at sunset, watching closely for the flash of green a split second after the red orange sun disappeared. Like Nani, Maya, and even, for a while, Maw, Rahoul had been swallowed up by that western horizon. The flash of light seemed to hold the promise that people could return too.

My big sister Maya had been gone for more than a third of my life. I remembered her in fragments. I felt the reassuring grip of her hand under my arm as I flew along the beach between her and Rahoul. I remembered burying my face in her towel and inhaling the scent of the shell-shaped French soaps given to her by the glamorous new Yugoslavian wife of an old American mathematician friend. I heard her feet slapping the ground as she spun in circles under the direction of her *kathak* dance teacher.

"Maya is *such* a beauty," Maw would say in a hushed voice, handing around the occasional pictures she received from America.

"Didi, she resembles you!" her friends would reply. "She looks more and more like you each year."

"Oh, she gets it from her grandmothers," Maw would respond, clearly pleased. "On both sides, her grandmothers were great beauties."

Though resembling a stern grandfather hadn't qualified me as a beauty, I felt no rivalry with Maya. If Rahoul's six-year lead on life

« Mrs. Contractor's eldest unmarried daughter peeps from behind the bride and groom, 1972. Photographer unknown.   :: 139

had set him beyond judgment and reproach, then Maya's nine-year start had rendered her perfect. I looked out at the white fringe of waves sweeping over the sand, the benevolent evening sky, the dots of light from distant ships, wishing that time would speed up and bring her home.

: : :

To greet Maya when she stepped off the plane, I wore the same gray dress with a white bib in which I had seen Rahoul off, and this time it fit better. Maw, Deven, and I watched through glass as people emerged from immigration to collect their giant suitcases. When Maya appeared, she waved and smiled. I drank in her hazel eyes, striking dark eyebrows, and fabled chestnut brown hair swishing in a thick braid to her knees. She wore a navy blue scarf tied over her head, a white blouse, and a long dark skirt that buttoned down the front and was patterned with tiny sprigs of flowers.

"Kirin! You got so big!" Maya said when she appeared on our side of the glass and got around to hugging me.

Looking up at her, I was so awe-struck that words stuck in my throat.

Maya reclaimed her old room at Nani's house, which at different times had been occupied by Rahoul, Young Swamiji, renters, and even favored urugs like Bhagavan Das. As she unpacked, I hovered, enchanted by all that emerged from her suitcases and the neat, methodical way she set out her things. Maw sat on the edge of the bed, sipping coffee and eagerly catching up with the latest news about friends in New York and Santa Fe.

I listened in, mesmerized by the rhythms of Maya's words. She was an enchanting storyteller, with a keen ear for dialogue and funny details. I noticed how her years in America had changed some of her intonations: *dahncing,* for example, had become *daencing.* She especially brought news of Rahoul.

"He got a lot of mileage out of seeming sexually naïve," Maya reported to Maw. "You should have told him more."

"But he was living in ashrams," Maw said, trying to defend herself. "You know that's a celibate scene."

"Still," said Maya, "you could have told him something. Women were practically falling over each other to educate him."

Maw took this in, cradling her coffee mug. I watched how she seemed to be struggling for Maya's approval. Finally she said, "Well, don't you think that would be a father's job?"

As though seeing how easily this defense could be rejected, given Paw's general difficulties with parenthood, Maw tried another tack, "You *know* that Rahoul's always been a trickster. Don't you think this could have been an act he was putting on? For heaven's sakes, Maya, Rahoul's hardly lived a sheltered life! He was reading *Lady Chatterley's Lover* before he left, going on about how he would write a scandalous exposé about a Bengali Brahman's affair with a *mali* called *Lady Chatterji's Lover.*"

"Well, if it was an act, he was good at it," said Maya.

I listened, wishing I too was sophisticated enough to talk back to Maw with such authority.

Like all of us, Paw was delighted by Maya's return. I couldn't help hoping that my big sister—the very person who had first linked Maw and Paw as a family—might somehow glue them back together. But increasingly, even when Maw and Paw were in the same house, they stayed in different rooms, within different orbits.

Now that Maya was grown up, Maw was ready to abdicate her own claims to looking pretty and dressing up. She rifled through the Godrej steel cupboard, pulling silk saris off hangers. "This will look better on you," she said. Then she started sorting through Nani's steamer trunks to find her own clothes from the era in the 1950s when she wore dark lipstick and tight-fitting silk sari blouses stretching to the elbow.

One night, I was falling asleep under my mosquito net when Maw and Maya entered the dressing room and turned on the light. The curtain dividing the bedroom and dressing room wasn't fully closed, and from my bed I could watch them both twice over—mother and sister reflecting each other in coloring and voice, and the mirror reflecting them both back. I felt a pang remembering that I didn't really look like them.

"These are sari blouses I had made up when Rahoul was a baby," Maw said. "I was never so glossy and slim again. Before he was born I had a really limited wardrobe and was given few gifts, but after he was born I was lavished with silk. The silk is still perfect. Wow, that blouse could have been cut for you. You know, I just can't believe I was your age when I followed Narayan to India."

"You should have finished college," said Maya.

"Yes, sweetie, but you were in the picture."

I held my breath, wondering if Maw would explain the special arithmetic spanning the date of the wedding in late January and the date of Maya's birth in mid-September. But they moved on to discussing another blouse. I shut my eyes again, thinking through Maw's being married and a mother by the time she was Maya's age. Twenty-one seemed incredibly old to me as a twelve-year-old; I thought that by that age everyone should be settling into the grooves that would guide the rest of their life. I worried that in coming home to us my big sister's prospects were shrinking.

It gave me hope that Maya regularly received letters from a boyfriend. When the afternoon post arrived, she disappeared to read her letters alone, then reported back to us with a smile playing over her features. I learned that the boyfriend's name was Jonathan and that she had met him in Santa Fe, at St. John's College. I gathered that he wrote poetry, smoked a pipe, wore a leather jacket and little round glasses, and had a mane of blonde brown hair that could make him look like a lion.

"So why didn't Jonathan propose before Maya left America?" I stood near Maw as she kneaded bread dough near the kitchen window. "Don't they want to get married?"

She laughed. "Sweetie, it's 1971. People don't get married any more. Nowadays everyone lives together. It's a good thing, too. They get to try it out before they're trapped."

"That's not true," I said haughtily. "People do still get married. Even John Lennon and Yoko Ono got married."

"Anyway, stop worrying," Maw said. "She needs to figure out her own life, her own identity between India and America. I'm sure there'll be all kinds of candidates when she's ready."

Which candidates? I tried to think of men her age. Eligible distant relatives from the Gujar Sutar marriage circle? Scientists or advertising people from downtown Bombay? Not urugs!

"At least he's writing to her," I reported to Fatty Rasha on the school bus.

"It could be very romantic if they write to each other for a few years," said Fatty Rasha. She raised one eyebrow significantly—our new affectation, which we had practiced for many hours, using each other as mirrors.

I arched an eyebrow in return. "*Dahling,* he *even* writes poems! And you know what? He is a"—I rolled the words around my mouth for gravity—"a *con-scient-ious objector.*"

As Maya told the story, Jonathan had drawn a low number in the draft and at first had hoped to use his doctor father's connections to avoid Vietnam. But sitting among migrant Mexican farm workers on the bus from Pasadena to the draft board, he had decided that it wasn't fair to use his privilege. Jonathan had declared himself a conscientious objector and was looking for alternate service, hopefully in India.

War was now uncomfortably close to us in Bombay too. East Pakistan had rebelled against West Pakistan, and by December 1971 India had stepped in and we were pasting strips of black paper over our windows. Air raid sirens went off at night, and we ran along the narrow alley toward the beach, through the neighborhood gate, to sit in the sand and watch the curve of the silver waves in starlight. Our school bus sometimes got stuck in traffic beside trucks filled with soldiers in uniform who stared back curiously at the middle-class children staring at them. I had not yet fully understood that newspapers described actual human beings whose suffering was real. The war still seemed a story set in some other reality when India declared victory and the new country of Bangladesh was formed.

I had just turned twelve, and East Pakistan becoming Bangladesh seemed the most important historical event I had lived to tell about. As the youngest child, I had spent too much of my life trying to catch up on events I had missed by listening in on the relevant stories. I longed to witness turning points that could seed stories in our family history too. In the meantime, I began recording mundane goings and comings at Juhu in a magazine the size of a postage stamp called *The Family,* drawing on the style of a British society magazine left by an urug.

:::

Maw and Maya's conversations inevitably turned to the ashram, and I learned that Maya had already met Babaji during his trip to America. She went out to the ashram with Maw a few times. Then she started staying there for a few days at a stretch and wearing her sari with the *pulloo* demurely wrapped around her other shoulder. I loved the neat precision with which she tucked and folded her saris and wished I were old enough to wear saris too.

Babaji sometimes traveled to Bombay to meet with devotees. One afternoon, Maw and Maya picked up Deven and me after school, and we visited with downtown friends until it was time for *darshan.* We arrived after dark to find the rooftop terrace of an apartment building already crowded.

Some devotees said that Babaji had been a king in a previous life. He really did create a regal atmosphere around him. On this terrace, he presided from a thronelike sofa surrounded by silk, flowers, and a cluster of devotees playing musical instruments: a harmonium, a double-sided drum, a stringed *tambura,* cymbals. Well-dressed people in fine clothes were seated on large dhurries spread over the rough cement floor. A microphone near Babaji picked up his deep, textured chanting and his occasional exchanges with the people lined up to bow before him.

When we reached Babaji's throne, we laid down our offerings of fruit and stems of fragrant tuberoses, then touched our foreheads to the floor.

Babaji acknowledged Maw and greeted Maya. We were hustled forward by the male disciples directing the flow of people: Maw, Maya, and I to the women's side, Deven to the men's. We squeezed in on the dhurries, knees touching, in an area already crowded with Bombay society matrons and Western women in saris. Maya and Maw started chanting at once and I mouthed the words, looking around.

A core group of singers joined Babaji in the slow hypnotic chant, "O-o-o-o-om namah shivaa-aa-ya," and the larger group responded, repeating the same words. We continued to alternate, melody rising and falling with the stately rhythm of waves riding to the beach on a calm day. Around us, some people spun in deeper tides. Women with closed eyes swirled from the waist, waving their hands. Some snorted fiercely. Others shook their bodies like dogs drying off after a swim. These weren't just urugs but Indian women too. I looked over at the men's side to catch Deven's eye, but he was lost in the crowd. On his side too, heads were spinning and hands shooting into the night sky.

Since our visiting urugs sometimes burst into such movements, I wasn't too surprised. What astonished me was the sheer number of people making a spectacle of themselves, and how no one seemed to notice. The chanting continued, wave after wave of call and response.

I peered at Maw and Maya. They mouthed the chant's syllables, eyes closed. I shut my eyes, listening with my whole body. The music moved through me, regular waves gliding to the shore. *Om namah shivaya*. I relaxed, allowing my head to sway, feeling the well-being of being held by the ocean on a still, warm day. Since I liked to mimic Maya whenever possible, I decided I would try to meditate.

I pressed my gaze inward, hopeful, staring into the red warmth of my closed eyelids. My torso seemed to expand in the restful, spacious presence of my own attentiveness. I looked for a divine force inside me, as described in Babaji's teachings, and though I didn't sight the dazzle of a blue pearl, I found the red glow of an amused friendliness. I continued to sway to the chant.

"Kirin got *shaktipat!*" Maw announced to Maya during the long drive home, as we whipped through patches of shadow and light. "Did you see her sway? Just being in his presence did it. Children are sometimes so much more responsive than adults!"

Had I acted too openly uruglike? Stuck in the back seat between Maw and Maya, I anxiously turned my head to see Maya's reaction. Maya smiled faintly as she looked out the open window, sea breeze finally dissipating the day's heat. I tried to figure out if she thought I was funny or Maw was funny, or if she was just happy because she had been greeted by Babaji, whom she seemed to be adopting as her own guru.

I resolved that if I ever went chanting with my mother again, I would sit still as the cross-legged statue of Bhagavan Nityananda in the ashram temple.

:::

We clustered around the big table, steel *thalis* before us, hot puffed *chappatis* brought in periodically by servants. The front porch opened out into the darkness of the driveway. Mosquitoes and moths hummed around the overhead light; the occasional gray mouse, rat, or *chuchundri* went streaking along the edge of the walls. When the shape of a man loomed up from the dark driveway, I almost screamed. With a suitcase in each hand, he stepped up onto the raised stand at the porch's edge, where until recently a coconut tree had grown through the roof. If our porch had had a door, this would have been the threshold.

"Is this 13 Janki Kutir?" the man inquired as his round glasses caught the light. Wiry light brown hair parted on one side grew straight down toward his shoulders, and a shaggy beard covered his face.

Maya cried "Jonathan!" and leaped into his arms. He swung her around so her long braid flew out behind her. Maw stood up, exclaiming.

My spoon froze in midair. This skinny, long-haired, jean-wearing man did not quite match up with the heroes of my imagination—Mr. Darcy, Mr. Rochester, Professor Bhaer, Maxim-who'd-been-married-to Rebecca, Rhett Butler, and the others. But his lifting Maya right off the ground was the most romantic event I had ever witnessed outside a movie theater. I couldn't wait to tell Fatty Rasha.

Jonathan settled down at the dinner table and a fresh *thali* was set before him. He explained that as a conscientious objector, he'd been assigned to do alternative service teaching English at a missionary school in northern Thailand. He had decided to stop off and surprise us en route.

"Will you eat some more?" he asked, extending the dish he had just helped himself from toward Deven and me at the other side of the table.

"Oh no," I said with all the restrained delicacy I imagined that a little sister should display before an eligible gentleman. "I eat like a bird."

"Like a vulture," elaborated Deven, as he always did when I used that line. I kicked his shin under the table.

Jonathan laughed into his beard at our exchange. With that laugh and look of shy complicity, he won my devotion. Before we left the dinner table, I had already begun imagining the scene for the Proposal.

Maw assigned Jonathan a bed on the porch outside Maya's room in Nani's house. When Paw returned from Nasik, he said this was inappropriate.

"Are they going to get married or what?" Paw growled

"Kids of this generation don't do that anymore," said Maw.

Paw scowled, refilling his glass and grimacing after a sip.

Yet when Jonathan sat by his side sharing a tall bottle of Kingfisher beer, Paw was all charm and erudition. He began telling dramatic tales about his stint as a pilot in the British Royal Air Force, training to drop bombs on chosen targets. I listened in, not interrupting, trying to figure out whether Paw was honoring or mocking his potential son-in-law. Maw put in a brief appearance and glared.

"You know, he made all that up," said Maw later, out of Paw's earshot. "Narayan threatened to join the new Indian air force if his father didn't sponsor his studies in America, but he never actually signed up."

I held my breath: would Jonathan take offence? Instead he laughed. "You're kidding!"

"No really," Maya said. "He does that."

"He calls it his Walter Mitty syndrome," I explained apologetically.

Jonathan laughed harder. "Man!" he said. "Thurber, huh? Your Paw is a pretty convincing storyteller. He really should have been a writer."

I thought Jonathan's comment over. *Should have been a writer* . . . might Paw have been in competition with the lady novelists?

During the next influx of urug visitors, Jonathan had a chance to hear Paw chant, *"The urugs are coming, ah-ha, ah-ha."*

"I think it might be from 'The Campbells are coming, hurrah hurrah,'" Jonathan said. "It's a Scottish marching song. My father's mother was a Campbell, and he used to whistle that as he got dressed in the morning. When we visited the great pyramids in 1962, a Bedouin boy taking us on a tour sang it as 'The Camels Are Coming.'"

Smart, observant, sympathetic, well-traveled—I kept ticking off more reasons that Jonathan should become a family member.

: : :

My head spun with romance. I constantly imagined the Proposal, worried that Juhu didn't offer the right setting. No manor park, no sitting room with a cozy fire, no stately dances, no lookout point from which to admire European scenery. There was always the possibility of a big black umbrella like the one beneath which Jo and Professor Bhaer had jostled elbows, but the monsoon wouldn't arrive for months. The beach, I decided, was our best alternative. A sunset stroll by the waves would give Jonathan the privacy to tell Maya how ardently he admired her and to offer her his hand.

Whenever Maya and Jonathan set out for an evening walk, I held back. I knew that a little sister with big ears and a toothy grin would spoil the romantic moment. But as I looked down the sweep of sand after their retreating figures, I felt dismay. Schoolboys rushed around playing cricket or football, monkey trainers rattled drums over the heads of blinking langurs, horses with jingles and plumes left trails of droppings, and crowds of giggling young men enthusiastically pursued any foreign woman in a bikini who was misguided enough to step outside her hotel compound. How could you have the Proposal with all this going on?

We were running out of days before Jonathan was slated to join the missionaries in Thailand. Why didn't anyone intervene? I hoped that Paw might take Maya and Jonathan with him to Khandala, where an appropriately misty and deserted lookout over a ravine might inspire the Proposal. But then I realized that Mulk would probably never stop talking long enough for Jonathan to get a word in edgewise.

Instead they went off to the ashram. The ashram! I was beside myself: how could Maw allow it? How could chanting and eating and sleeping— that too, in separate men and women's sections—possibly lead up to the Proposal?

But when Deven and I came in from school on the day Maya and Jonathan returned, Maw was practically skipping with excitement.

"Maya and Jonathan are getting married!" she announced before we had even set down our satchels.

I drank my banana milk as Maya and Jonathan drifted in from another room and told their story. Apparently, when they had gone up to Babaji's seat in the Ganeshpuri courtyard to say good-bye, he had asked where they would be getting married: "Bombay, Nasik, or Ganeshpuri?"

Maya mumbled something, embarrassed. She did not translate the question to Jonathan, and they did not have a moment alone before meeting up with Maw's friend Mummy-la for a shared ride back to Bombay.

Mummy-la was a British woman who had become a Tibetan nun. "What was your Baba saying about gnostics?" she asked in her crisp British accent.

"Nasik," corrected Maya.

"He was comparing marriage to the spiritual life at Ganeshpuri, wasn't he now?" said Mummy-la, adjusting her maroon robes. "Yes dear, even if one has a worldly life, one is never too young to start on the spiritual life too."

Mummy-la went on about the virtues of a spiritual life while Maya and Jonathan meekly listened. Only when they were back at our house, sitting on the big bed in Paw's empty room, were they able to talk alone. Maya translated Babaji's question. "*Ganeshpuri, of course,*" was Jonathan's answer (endlessly quoted by Maw in years to come). "It's neutral territory."

Neutral for whom, I later wondered? But we threw ourselves into a whirlwind of preparation so they could be married in time for Maya to accompany Jonathan to Thailand. Despite Maw's assertion that no one got married anymore, the missionaries for whom Jonathan would be teaching English accepted only married couples. Ba had been married at around sixteen, and Maw at twenty; none of us questioned whether, at twenty-one, Maya might be very young.

:::

Paw took the news well. He assured his drinking buddies and hangers-on that Jonathan's father was a big doctor. We took Jonathan up to Nasik, where Ba also accepted the news with aplomb, saying, "In our family, it's become the *rivaj,* the custom, to marry Americans." She couldn't quite get her tongue around the *th* in Jonathan, so she called him "Jonaassen." (Young Swamiji would later Indianize the name completely, calling him "Janardan.")

"I'll be your chaperone, *dahlings,*" I offered, now that I no longer had to make myself scarce to encourage the Proposal. As Maya and Jonathan set out for a walk from the Nasik house down to the sacred Godavari River, I took Maya's hand and on the other side Jonathan's. The birds were falling quiet, bells clanged for evening worship, people turning on lights in their shops paused to salute the illumined bulbs.

"Just think, I'm going to be Mrs. Contractor's eldest unmarried daughter!" I announced, swinging at their hands, dizzy with excitement and self-importance. "No one else in my whole class has a brother-in-law!"

I was so radiantly happy that I didn't care about young men and small children who, seeing Jonathan's shaggy hair and beard, called out the latest greetings for hippies: "*Dam maro dam*" (an exhortation to inhale) or "*Hare Krishna!*" Thanks to *Hare Rama Hare Krishna,* a recent blockbuster film by Dev Anand that followed the adventures of the gorgeous new star Zeenat Aman among hippies in Nepal, any Westerner wearing Indian clothes was now presumed to be perpetually stoned and prone to dancing. If Ba had been with us, she would have shown these hecklers the edge of her palm, threatening to slap them. We just sailed on, ignoring their calls.

At the banks of the river, we bought leaf boats, each carrying a small clay oil lamp and some flowers. The river glistened, streaming silently in the darkness. We descended the steps at the ghat, shielding the flame as we struck matches to light the lamps. Then we each offered our lamps as offerings to the silver currents of the goddess Godavari, younger sister of the goddess Ganga. With the light, I sent a wish floating downstream—that this wedding would take place soon, before the strangeness of our family might scare Jonathan away.

Kaki, our aunt, did not seem pleased by this latest development. "How does it look for my children's marriages?" Kaki muttered through intermediaries. "Who ever heard of a marriage in an ashram? What about people from our caste? If the wedding is going to be in Bombay, why can't it take place in the caste hall?"

To reassure his sister-in-law, Paw had his hangers-on charter buses to bring members of the caste to the ashram for the ceremony. They also planned a celebratory feast at the caste hall in the Bombay suburb of Matunga. As we rushed to prepare for the wedding, Paw drank more and instructed the hangers-on to sell land and buildings to pay for the clothes, the jewelry, the feasts that a father of a bride should provide. We all understood that given the price of air tickets, Rahoul's attending was out of the question.

Back in Bombay, our ruddy-faced Doodhwala Bhaiya appeared at midmorning a few days before the wedding. Usually he delivered milk at dawn, ladling out our share from giant aluminum cans strapped to the back of his bicycle. That he came a second time that day was odd enough; that two other men from the dairy were also steering their bicycles toward the kitchen porch, cans clinking, was even stranger.

"Here is the *doodh pak*," beamed Doodhwala Bhaiya. "Congratulations on your daughter's wedding."

"What *doodh pak*?" Maw demanded. *Doodh pak* was a sumptuous dessert: sweet thick milk flavored with almonds, pistachios, saffron, and cardamom.

"The twenty liters that Sahib ordered."

Paw was still asleep, so he couldn't be consulted. Maw cross-examined the servants, but they knew nothing about the order. Nonetheless, twenty liters of *doodh pak* had been delivered and couldn't be sent back. The servants brought out clean steel vessels. When these were filled, they set to scrubbing dirty ones. Soon the washed vessels were brimming too, and Maw directed the servants to scrub out and disinfect basins and buckets. She mounted a desperate search for plastic bags without holes and double-bagged even more *doodh pak,* with rubber bands holding the ends closed.

In the midst of the confusion, Paw's office peon, Ramchandra, arrived, sweaty after taking the train and bus from downtown. Ramchandra often showed up at the house on days that Paw didn't go to the office, just in case Paw had any whims or urgent business transactions. He usually hung around until evening, sharing tea and meals with the house servants. Keen to distinguish himself from house servants, Ramchandra dressed in Paw's cast-off clothes, especially long pants, which stood out among the usual servants' shorts. He also wore frames from Paw's old glasses, and on his bony wrist was Paw's old watch, which he looked at frequently through the badly fitted glasses.

"Of course I know all about the *doodh pak,*" Ramchandra informed Maw in his semiofficious way, adjusting the glasses toward his forehead.

Apparently, a few days earlier, when everyone else was at school or shopping, Paw had decided that *doodh pak* should be added to the festivities. Ramchandra dialed the Doodhwala Bhaiya's dairy, and Paw, who had a flair for dialects, spoke to the Bhaiya in Banarasi Hindi, taking on—with increasing enthusiasm—the role of a minor noble associated with the court of the raja of Banaras. By the time he got off the phone, he was feeding not just family but hosts of royal retainers.

"We can't take *doodh pak* to the ashram," Maw fumed, "It needs to be refrigerated. We can't take it to the caste hall either. Does Narayan even know how much milk is in *one* liter?"

For the next few days, and after the wedding too, we drank *doodh pak* so many times a day that the very word began to cause a queasy thickening in my throat; more than thirty-five years later, I never seek it out. Maw offered *doodh pak* to urugs and to downtown Bombay friends who dropped in to offer their congratulations; she sent tubs of it over to neighbors; she squeezed plastic bags of *doodh pak* into the freezer.

Jonathan laughed. Watching my family through his eyes, I saw us all turning into characters in a story. I started cutting blank pages to staple together for another miniature issue of *The Family.*

: : :

Jonathan's mother was recovering from surgery, but his father, Doctor Lyman August Brewer III, flew in from South Pasadena, California. Doctor

Brewer was a strikingly handsome man with strong jaws, thick white hair combed back from his forehead, and a white mustache. He wore a white suit, though the distinguished effect was slightly diminished by his having to leave his shoes at the ashram gate and pad around in socks.

Jonathan submitted with amusement to the getup of an Indian bridegroom. He was dressed in a long silk *kurta* and baggy white pajamas, with a shawl around his shoulders and a tinsel crown on his forehead. Still, he looked like himself with the wire-rimmed glasses, beard, and hair sticking out over his ears.

Draped in a red and green tie-dyed sari, jewels running down the center of her hair and looping on either side of her face, Maya was breathtakingly lovely: to me, at that age, all brides were enchanted beings, but my big sister especially so. Ivory and gold bracelets covered her arms, and her hands were traced with intricate patterns of henna. Babaji had ordered thick ropes of jasmine buds for her hair, and she moved in an intoxicating cloud of fragrance.

The ceremonies were held in the main hall of the ashram with the huge, dark cross-legged statue of Bhagavan Nityananda, Babaji's guru, looking on. The two families sat around a low fire altar constructed for the occasion. Happy ashramites, uncomfortable caste relatives, and baffled family friends (many of whom had never before set foot in an ashram) clustered around us. Chanting Brahmans issued directions for Paw and Maw to give Maya away to Jonathan's family.

I found it unnerving to see my parents as any sort of unit, much less a ritual one, sitting side by side, and in the ashram of all unlikely places. Maw wore a heavy navy brocade sari as soberly parental as Paw's dark suit. Wearing a pink half-sari over a long silk skirt printed with Mughal flowers, I pressed as close to Maya as I could, soaking in her glamour and the scent of jasmine. Brahmans rumbled on, and our celebrity neighbor Papaji (the film star Prithviraj Kapoor) boomed out risqué commentary, teasing Jonathan as he fumbled while fastening the gold and black beaded *mangal sutra* of a married woman around Maya's neck.

When the wedding was completed, Maya and Jonathan glided out into Babaji's courtyard, weighed down with heavy garlands of tuberoses, auspicious coconuts in their hands. Babaji sat on a raised marble platform that extended out from his apartment and placed his hands on their heads as they bowed before him. Viju the ashram elephant arrived from the upper garden, ears flapping, to add further auspiciousness of the occasion.

Doctor Brewer stood near the elephant and began reading a speech from a piece of paper. Babaji was not used to being upstaged, but he listened patiently. A few sentences into Doctor Brewer's address, confusion spread across the faces in the crowd.

"Lyman Augustus Brewer doesn't sound like a Jewish name," muttered a Jewish American devotee to Maw. "But that sounds likes Hebrew."

"I don't think so," Maw whispered back, equally confused.

"It's Latin," murmured a British woman standing near me. "Americans never could pronounce Latin."

A French disciple turned her head. "It is certainly not Latin," she asserted. "It is Pali."

"What would you know about Pali?" asked the British disciple, aggrieved.

"I have heard the monks in Ceylon."

Ba, long an expert at maintaining her dignity around unfamiliar languages, nodded her head, pressed her lips, and occasionally raised a finger as though agreeing with Doctor Brewer's point. Chanda-phui beamed her sweet, broad-faced smile. Most other relatives shrank into tight clusters, looking around with uneasy suspicion as though a joke were being played specifically on them.

When Doctor Brewer looked up from his text, his audience clapped, impressed but mystified, then swarmed toward the dining hall for the wedding feast. Jonathan walked along beside his father, then with a big smile reported back to us, his new relatives, that the address had been in Hindi, translated by a scholar at UCLA. Apparently the ashram elephant had understood, for as Doctor Brewer read a line about how the Brewer family had always respected the sanctity of all beings, the elephant had gently reached its trunk out to Doctor Brewer's shoulder.

The incomprehensible speech added to the Brewer mystique: "*Baman chhe,*" Ba boasted. "Maya's father-in-law is not only a big doctor, he is such a pure Brahman that he speaks Sanskrit."

: : :

In the presence of Swami Muktananda Paramahansa . . . began the wedding announcement sent out after the fact on a lightweight, airmail-appropriate hand-made paper card. What Jonathan's relatives and parents' friends made of this announcement I could not imagine. Some of Maw's friends were puzzled as well.

Though an ashram wedding in a guru's presence might have spiritual cachet, it turned out to have no legal status. Maya and Jonathan discovered that to prove they were married, they would have to travel to an office in the suburb of Thana (within which Ganeshpuri lay), taking along alleged witnesses (who actually had not attended the wedding). The clerk at the Thana court typed up a wedding certificate declaring Maya to be legally wed to "Sonathan Brewer" of "South Paradena, Caliporninia."

We found this hilarious, but the aide at the U.S. consulate was not amused. "Are you aware that this is a legal document of the United States of America?" he demanded. He was familiar enough with the vagaries of Indian court typists, though, that he agreed to change Maya's last name on her passport. As Jonathan's wife, she could now teach English with him at the missionary school in Thailand.

For years the composition of our family had been shifting through departures, arrivals, honorary family members, temporary family members. I approved of the way we had acquired Jonathan: formally and legally, to the accompaniment of rituals that brought good food, new clothes, and plenty of excitement. Jonathan's joining us seemed to give the family substance and color, and he hadn't even been put off by the ashram frame around family events.

"I'm going to be a writer," I told Jonathan, sure that as a poet himself, he would sympathize in a way that no one in my immediate family ever had.

"I'm sure you are," Jonathan laughed into his curly beard. "You certainly have enough material."

Conjunctions

"When His Holiness comes south," said Mummy-la, sipping tea in the living room during one of her trips to Juhu, "you'll finally have a chance to meet him. He's planning to be in the Bombay area for at least a week."

I listened in from the corner where I was experimenting with braiding five strands of embroidery thread to make *rakhis* for my brothers. Maw and her friend sat together on the divan, Maw in stay-at-home *lungi* and top, Mummy-la in maroon robes over a sleeveless yellow blouse. Mummy-la was a Tibetan nun, and her head was shaved, accentuating her large blue eyes and the rosy roundness of her cheeks. The only His Holiness I had heard about until Maw became friends with Mummy-la was the Fourteenth Dalai Lama. But when Mummy Bedi used the title, she was referring to her Tibetan teacher, the Sixteenth Gwalya Karmapa.

Mummy-la was, like Maw, the foreign wife of an Indian man and had lived in India for many years. She was about fifteen years older, though, and originally British; her husband had been Punjabi. As a married woman, her name was Frieda Bedi, and she was also called Mummy Bedi. In the early 1960s, when Tibetan refugees poured into India, she had set up a school that taught incarnate lamas English. She also became a disciple of the Sixteenth Gwalya Karmapa, who had reconstituted his Tibetan monastery in the mountain king-

« His Holiness the Sixteenth Gwalya Karmapa at our neighborhood gate, Juhu beach, 1973. The Karmapa is at top center, with sunglasses; Kirin and Maw are seated at right; Dobeyboy stands in front. Photograph by Prafull Dave.

dom of Sikkim, to the northeast of India. When her children had grown up and her husband set off for Italy to become "Baba Bedi," a guru in his own right, she had decided to become a Tibetan nun. The tradition of initiating high-ranking nuns had apparently died out in Tibet some centuries earlier, but the Karmapa had instructed her to resurrect the status of Gelong Ma. She traveled to Hong Kong and received her investiture through a Chinese lineage, becoming Sister Gelong Ma Karma Khechog Palmo. For Tibetans, adding "la" to a name was a form of respect, like "ji" for Indians. So she was also known as Mummy-la. I watched her with interest but also some wariness, hoping that Maw would not get any ideas about initiation, shaved heads, or robes.

Mummy-la traveled to Juhu each year because her son Kabir Bedi lived down the beach, in an apartment upstairs from Fatty Rasha. Kabir Bedi was a minor Bombay celebrity. Everyone agreed that he was a great advertisement for how well genes could mix across cultures with his dreamy hazel eyes, black brows, and fine physique. He wore shirts usually sexily unbuttoned to the waist, displaying a hairy chest. So far he was a model and had starred in a successful historical play. He was married to the even sexier, full-lipped Protima, who made headlines by bringing the phenomenon of "streaking" to Bombay with a bouncing nude run down the beach. (Fatty Rasha and I deeply regretted that we weren't out for a walk at that glorious moment; we would especially have liked to witness the response of the Hare Krishnas galloping through the sand to the thump of their drums.)

But when Mummy-la and Maw got together, they did not talk much about acting, streaking, or other activities involving their children. Nor did they say much about their experiences as foreign wives in India. What they really wanted to talk about were their gurus' powers and peculiarities. For every miraculous tale Maw told about Babaji transforming someone's life, Mummy-la would produce one about the Karmapa—drawn from across his sixteen lifetimes. Mummy-la also visited Ganeshpuri on occasion—for example, the time that Babaji had popped the question about Maya and Jonathan's marriage.

"Wouldn't it be a dream if we could introduce our gurus?" Maw said when she learned that the Karmapa was coming south. "We'd be bringing together Hindu and Buddhist branches of the Siddha tradition!"

"It would be a deeply significant event in the history of religions," said Mummy-la with grave British precision, setting her cup and saucer down on the table as she and Maw developed a plan.

: : :

Ever since Maya had made it appropriate for an eldest unmarried daughter to go to an ashram, I had accompanied Maw to Ganeshpuri on occasional weekends and even vacations without putting up much resistance. As a result, I had enough of a sense of ashram culture to see that Maw was treading a fine line with her plans to bring one guru into another guru's space and circle of disciples. In fact, the more I learned about ashram precepts and routines, the more I worried. I sensed that at heart my mother was a rebel, with a tendency to draw other dissidents into her orbit.

I stayed with Maw at the ashram for as long as a week at a time, and sometimes Deven briefly joined us. I learned the ashram's morning routines: rising sleepily in the dark to a clamor of banging drums and blowing conches; crouching to bathe amid the clang, splash, and steam of the women's communal bathroom with its open stalls; lining up in the dining hall to receive a steel glass full of hot tea; and then, with sleep still stinging my eyelids, settling down for an hour and a half of group chanting until the sun was up. The structure continued through the day, with designated times for eating, for work, for rest, and for more chanting. The last chant of the day, which usually inspired the most spectacular whirling and rocking from the *kriya*-prone, ended around 8:30. After that, we walked through the cool shadows of the garden to once again visit the bathhouse and brush our teeth.

With the influx of urugs, Sanskrit chanting books were now supplemented with English books that alternated transliterations with translations. Both sorts of book were stacked by the doors of the newly expanded hall, but Maw bought me my own copy of *Swadhyaya Sudha: The Nectar of Chanting*. I stood shyly in line for Babaji to inscribe the first page. "*Shree Gurudev,*" he wrote, saluting the divine guru in a rushed red script at the top of the page, then signed below "Swami Muktananda" and handed the book back to me without further comment. I was still not sure whether he knew who I was.

Young Swamiji had taught me to chant by myself, but in the ashram an entire hall full of people chanting opened out magnificent spaces, like a beach sunset tracing high clouds and pouring colored light over the coconut trees. With men on one side and women on the other, we either sat cross-legged, books held in our right hands, or we stood with joined palms facing the gleaming black statue of Bhagavan Nityananda. Dozens—sometimes hundreds—of voices merged and blended into something larger than us all, erasing the boundaries of self. I found that I loved chanting. I memorized words through their sung rhythms with a child's ease. Even now, driving to campus through Wisconsin snow, if I start up a chant it will unspool from my mouth as though of its own accord.

As the Sanskrit texts rushed rhythmically forward, I eagerly took in their English meanings too. Maw scoffed at the translations, which she felt were inadequately modern—"All that Thou and Thee and Thy," she said. But I was grateful that the Sanskrit opened out into images and stories. Thanks to the translations, I learned that the 181 verses of the *Guru Gita* that we chanted each morning represented a conversation between Shiva and his wife Parvati, with Shiva doing most of the talking. Shiva elaborated on the glory, importance, and divinity of a guru. He assured Parvati that the guru was really an imperishable force shining inside each person's heart, and that the guru was a form of himself, Shiva, while also a manifestation of Brahma the Creator and Vishnu the Preserver. (It seemed to knit together my worlds nicely when I recognized the verse *"Guru Brahma guru Vishnu"* as having featured in George Harrison's "My Sweet Lord," which I'd heard so often at Fatty Rasha's house.)

The *Guru Gita* also drilled in the importance of the guru as intermediary: the guru's form as the root of meditation, the guru's words as the source of mantra. Most people living in the ashram seemed to interpret this literally as a focus on Babaji with his orange knit caps, sunglasses, and vibrant presence. Maw too spoke of Babaji as "my Gurudev." But Maw was also interested in stories about all kinds of gurus. She filled our shelves with books about saints from numerous religious traditions and went to visit other gurus if the occasion allowed. When Anandamayi Ma had come through Bombay, for example, Maw said she'd like me to have *darshan* of a great woman saint of the twentieth century. She and I set off to nearby Vile Parle to join the crowd gathered around the small woman with a presence soft as rose petals, dark hair cascading around her shoulders.

The ashram chants roused my curiosity about mythology. We began some chants by saluting elephant-headed Ganesh, who enjoyed munching on wood apples and berries: why these fruits, I wondered. The evening *Shiva Mahimna Stotra* ("Hymn to the Glory of Shiva") praised Shiva, citing episodes I'd not previously heard of: just when, for example, had Shiva become a pillar of fire that neither Brahma nor Vishnu could measure? I usually napped in the afternoon but on rare occasions took part in the optional chant of the *Vishnu Sahasranama* ("The Thousand Names of Vishnu"). Here,

Vishnu rather than Shiva became central, with many intriguing names alluding to his attributes and mythology. A name like "the source of all effulgence" was enchanting and intelligible, but what, I wondered, were the stories that went with a title like "dweller in the cosmic egg"? Learning these chanted words before I fully knew the accompanying stories seeded a fascination with Hindu mythology that much later, in college and graduate school, I studied more formally.

But even as I participated in these daily chants, I continued with the goddess praises that Swamiji had taught me. Each day, I spent some time alone on my dormitory bed reciting sections of the goddess epic. I was discreet in my practice, for I wasn't sure how acceptable such worship was at the ashram, where the guru and Shiva were clearly the primary deities. In *The Nectar of Chanting,* only the *Annapurna Stotram* ("Hymn to the Goddess of Abundant Food") saluted the Goddess, but I had never heard this hymn sung. A tape of Babaji emotionally singing goddess praises from the *Durga Saptashati* was sometimes played over the ashram sound system, but no one else seemed to chant these. Following Young Swamiji's way of worship once again set me at a slight distance, a partial observer.

I felt most acutely anxious for my mother when I tagged along behind her to the tea shop that was just a stone's throw from the ashram gate. This tea shop resembled hundreds of other establishments run by south Indian migrants to Bombay: the kind of place that we ate at when we visited the Strand Bookstore downtown or stopped at Shahpur midway through the four-hour drive to Nasik. All these places blurred together: rickety tables over which boys flicked a stained cloth, scattering flies before bringing you glasses of unboiled water; the hiss of a Primus stove, the clamor of orders called out to cooks, the low rumble of conversation; a mouth-watering blend of smells as *dosas* sizzled crisp on hot griddles, *dals* and curry leaves browned in oil, and coffee dripped through filters. On the wall behind the cash register, a black-and-white photograph of big-bellied Bhagavan Nityananda usually looked on; in addition to being Babaji's guru, he seemed to be the patron saint of south Indian fast food.

Ashram meals were served at strictly specified hours, but the tea shop remained open much of the day, a magnet for those restless people who sought release from rules and routines: the smokers, the talkers, the couples separated by single-sex dormitories, the would-be couples who longed for a chance to talk face to face. Many mornings, as soon as the *Guru Gita* recitation ended, people rushed for the tea shop through the slanting light of the early morning sun. With its rupee prices, the tea shop seemed especially inexpensive to urugs who still had savings, and Westerners rather than Indians usually dominated the tables.

For Maw the tea shop was a luxury but one she greatly enjoyed. Sipping milky sweet coffee and sneaking a cigarette, Maw joined up with urugs to chew over questions that I sensed might not be acceptable within the ashram: Could you gain from multiple gurus? Did a guru act in shocking ways to challenge the egos of disciples? How exactly were the inner and the outer gurus related?

Astrology often figured in Maw's tea shop discussions. After two predictions issued by a Nasik astrologer in the mid-1960s turned out to be astonishingly precise, she had become curious about how astrology worked. Returning from her trip to America, she met a French diplomat's wife in Bombay: a small woman with a stylish hairdo, high heels, pantsuits, and a Ph.D. in astrology. Maw became a student of Western astrology and, in the last two years, had become fluent in the language of charts, houses, planets, and transits.

Maw's interest in divination was nothing new. She sometimes talked about how she had read people's palms in Taos until she foresaw a suicide and was spooked. During the era when hippies were more prevalent than urugs, Maw had laid out tarot cards on the coffee table, and for a while, a delegation of jet-set Parsis visited on weekends to learn about their futures. Then too, Stella had handed down two thick volumes of the *I Ching*, and Maw assembled a bundle of broom straws (*jhadu* sticks, instead of yarrow stalks) to meditatively divide and redivide as a means of consulting the oracle.

Maw's Western-style charts were different from the Hindu astrological charts that Ba had ordered drawn up when we were born. Those diagrams, rectangles divided into four diamonds and eight triangles, Ba kept locked up in her treasury for periodic consultations with an astrologer. Maw's horoscopes were circles divided into twelve pielike slices and included three more planets: Uranus, Neptune, and Pluto. Otherwise, as Maw often explained, the same theory held. At the moment of a person's birth, the position of the planets in relation to each other, to zodiac signs, and to particular celestial houses determined an imprint that shaped one's character and potentialities. As the planets continued to circle throughout a person's lifetime, the shifting patterns set the stage for particular events and insights.

Having learned this language of signs, planets, and houses, Maw chatted eagerly with urug astrologers. Just what were the differences in how spiritual growth played out through planetary transits in the eighth, ninth, and twelfth houses? Was it because of compatibility between charts that a disciple chose one guru over another? Could Babaji's astrological chart, so perfect for a guru, possibly be fabricated? I anxiously sensed that all these questions didn't really fit in with teachings on the guru's grace as guiding and shaping each disciple's life. But the tea shop conversations continued.

: : :

Maw looked through her ephemeris for the days that the Sixteenth Gwalya Karmapa would be in Bombay and consulted with our new household resident, Cupboard Swami.

"Practically everything will be in Sagittarius!" Maw said, "Neptune's been in Sagittarius for a while, but just then the Moon will be moving into conjunction with Mercury, Venus, and Neptune."

Cupboard Swami seemed to know just what she was talking about. "And Jupiter is coming into conjunction with the Sun in Capricorn," he said, hunching over the ephemeris too.

"Capricorn is of course associated with ambition, accomplishment, India, and the Goddess of the Ganges," said Maw.

"Of course," said Cupboard Swami.

Cupboard Swami was one of the many urugs who had had a falling out with ashram authorities, then showed up at our house where Maw offered refuge. He moved into what had once been the boys' room, which Maw had requisitioned as her *puja* room once Rahoul went abroad. Since our guest tucked himself away into the innermost recesses of that room and rarely emerged into daylight, Paw had nicknamed him "Cupboard Swami."

Cupboard Swami was in his mid-thirties—a little older, more judgmental, and more sarcastic than the average urug. He had a ginger stubble of beard, hair cropped short, a pronounced Adam's apple, and stained teeth. He wore a piece of white cloth tied around his waist and sometimes hitched up at the knees, and a white loincloth indicating his celibacy. (The loincloth I knew about because of the outline under the robes, as well as the general lack of privacy for laundry, which was always dried in direct view of the kitchen windows.) When it was chilly, or if an occasion demanded formality, he wrapped another length of cloth around his shoulders.

Cupboard Swami slept on the floor behind a screen in one corner of the *puja* room. Maw had decorated this room with a long low tables spread with brocade fabrics. On the central altar table, she propped up photo-

graphs of Babaji and his guru, Old Swamiji from the mountaintop, along
with Rahoul's photograph of Young Swamiji meditating. Between the photographs, she assembled objects like a calm Thai Buddha head that had belonged to her German father, sealed copper containers filled with Ganges
water, and curved soapstone boxes brimming with maroon goddess *kum
kum* powder from the Old and Young Swamijis. On the walls, she hung a
German wooden Christ that had also belonged to her father, prints of goddesses, and other assorted spiritual paraphernalia. The array was completed
by large tenth-century sculptures of the Sun God and of Vishnu that an
American art historian had asked her to house until he could obtain permits
to take them out of the country.

Cupboard Swami's routine was to sleep all day. He crept out in the late
afternoons or at night, sending kitchen cockroaches scuttling, to prepare
strong black coffee flavored with cardamom and to locate the leftovers set
aside for him under a steel *thali*. Then he returned to the cupboard to smoke
Dunhill cigarettes and drink more black coffee. At night, Cupboard Swami
banged out prose on one of Maw's typewriters—the Hermes—which was
propped on a small stool beside his mat in the corner. Waking to visit the
bathroom, I sometimes stopped by the closed door to listen to the clickety-
clack of the metal keys, the bell that rang as the carriage reached the end of
the line, the grating sound of its manual return.

Maw said that Cupboard Swami had talent. Maw had always appreciated
talent, and as far as I could tell, this was the main reason he was allowed to
stay in the room she had staked out as her own spiritual space. So far, Cupboard Swami had been tapping out literary retellings of Hindu parables: for
example, the story of a *sadhu* preoccupied with the sins of a neighboring
prostitute, who learned at his death that she had achieved salvation while
he had not, since in all her actions her mind had been fixed on God. Maw
read through Cupboard Swami's prose with rapt attentiveness. I sometimes
also read the manuscripts, which she left lying around, both disappointed
and relieved when worldly activities like the prostitute's work were not re-
created in much detail.

Cupboard Swami's other talent was cooking. He took over the kitchen
during hours when the servants weren't around, standing by the counter
to produce a mouth-watering variety of breads, muffins, biscuits, pies, and
cakes. I never ceased to be astonished by his odd, undulating posture at the
kitchen counter. His knees locked farther back than his hips or ankles. As
if to compensate, his hips were rotated forward, but his stomach curved
inward while his shoulders, Adam's apple, and head bent forward, intent.

While the ephemeris was out, Maw pulled Rahoul's chart from a folder. Rahoul had just written, telling her that his draft number was thirty-three—scarily low. Like Jonathan, he had "filed a claim for a C.O.," and while he waited, he was practicing the schizophrenic act that Paw's psychiatrist had taught him.

"With Saturn and Neptune conjunct in the eighth house and exactly on Saturn's Degree of Exaltation, I worry about Rahoul," Maw said, laying the chart before Cupboard Swami. "It's what draws him to new frontiers. It's exactly the conjunction under which Tenzing and Hillary finally made it up Everest."

Cupboard Swami studied the chart too and assured her that Rahoul would not go to Vietnam. Sure enough, a few weeks later, Rahoul wrote that he had been declared underweight and physically unfit to be drafted. By then, preparations for the Karmapa's visit were in full swing.

:::

Ever since her trip to America, Maw had been trying to set up an import-export business, hoping to gain more financial independence from Paw. She designed chic ethnic wear, like tie-dyed *kurta* tops with bell-sleeves and swirling, hand-printed skirts with the proportions of the panels based on the golden mean. After overseeing the tailoring in Bombay, Maw sent samples in expensive airmail packages to the woman who had agreed to serve as her business partner in New York. The woman reported back that Bloomingdale's was interested but said she would need more capital. Having already borrowed rupees for the venture, Maw now borrowed dollars from the college fund Nani had established for the grandchildren. At first, her partner wrote to explain various delays; after a while, though, Maw's letters received no response. Maw spent anguished hours consulting with Cupboard Swami about what action she could possibly take from this distance. Planning the Karmapa's visit seemed to cheer her up.

"The Karmapa will be here at the house for breakfast on New Year's Day," Maw announced to everyone who came through. "Then we'll take him out to the ashram to meet Babaji."

"But Maw, who exactly *is* the Karmapa?" I asked as she sat at the slatted dining table that urugs sometimes called "the picnic table." On the back of an invitation from an art gallery, she was writing a list of ingredients for dishes she planned to serve our illustrious guest.

"'Karmapa' is a title," Maw looked up to explain. "Like 'Dalai Lama' is a title. The bodies in which they're incarnated come and go. His Holiness the

Dalai Lama is the head of the Yellow Hat sect of Tibetan Buddhism. His Holiness the Karmapa is the head of the Red Hat sect. The Karmapa's lineage started the practice of consciously predicting their return after death, so he's already into his sixteenth lifetime of being reborn into that same role. For the Dalai Lama, it's the fourteenth time around."

We knew the Fourteenth Dalai Lama, who took a special interest in Tibetan orphans like Tashi who had been adopted by families in India and other countries. For years, whenever the Dalai Lama visited Bombay, he sent his secretary, Tenzing Geyche, to our house to check in on Tashi and his difficult adjustment. We also sometimes went to the Dalai Lama's public audiences downtown. I remembered his smile raising his high round cheekbones under rectangular black spectacles, his deep, kind voice like burnished wood, and I began looking forward to a visit from another Tibetan teacher.

:::

"Well, it's not every day that an enlightened incarnate being comes to breakfast," Maw said, hanging one string of festive marigolds and mango leaves over the folding doors to the garden porch and another by the door to the porch with the dining table. The living room was still decorated for Christmas: stars cut from gold paper were pasted on walls and lamps, and our coconut-frond Christmas tree rose from a brass water pot filled with beach sand. Mummy-la had told Maw that the Karmapa would have to be seated higher than everyone else, so Maw balanced two beds atop each other, piling on extra mattresses, before spreading out her best orange and pink embroidered *phulkari* bedspreads.

Competing bands had broadcast New Year's Eve dance music from nearby high-rise hotels until well after midnight. All the same, Maw and Cupboard Swami were up before dawn, bustling about the kitchen. Together, they baked trays of cheese and herb scones, cinnamon rolls, and honey-soaked, crisply layered baklava. The servants helped too, boiling up vats of spiced tea and coffee flavored with cardamom, the fragrance mingling with Mysore sandalwood incense as we waited for our honored guest to appear.

In the ongoing uncertainty as to which was the house's front door and which the back one, His Holiness the Sixteenth Gwalya Karmapa chose to enter through the door leading to the beach. He was a man of about Maw's age, with a shaved head, wearing deep maroon robes over one shoulder and a high-necked, long-sleeved yellow shirt. He ducked under the marigolds and mango leaves, all bending graciousness and smiles. A retinue of maroon-wearing lamas, Tibetan men in suits, and a few Tibetan women and children streamed in behind him. Maw had also invited friends from Delhi and Bombay, so the room was quite crowded. The Karmapa climbed easily onto his high seat and settled down, cross-legged. We all bent to greet him. Even noble Dobeyboy lowered his head and stretched out his paws as though prostrating.

I immediately observed that neither the Karmapa nor anyone in his group was wearing anything red on their heads. Wriggling into the kitchen, I cornered Maw as she prepared to bring out the food. "Where are the hats?" I whispered. "I thought you said they are the Red Hat sect."

"They don't wear red hats all the time," said Maw, gathering up plates and directing servants, "just when they're doing rituals."

"What about the Black Hat?" I started to ask, for I had heard that the Karmapa would do a Black Hat ceremony at Ganeshpuri. But Maw had returned to the living room, where our guests were settling down on mattresses and mats spread out across the floor.

Maw offered His Holiness a generously loaded plate, and he accepted it with both hands, bobbing thanks. Then he set the plate beside him, shut his eyes, and began to chant. The lamas joined him, filling our living room with what seemed to be the deepest possible registers available to male voices. Their mantras rode out in formation, sometimes with one voice beginning or straggling. The mantras surged through the open doors between rooms and gathered under the asbestos roof.

Ba always said that saints were like wish-fulfilling trees; sitting under their wide boughs, you received what you most needed. From these rumbling moments with the lamas poured a sense of life's deep sweetness, a rich, amber possibility. For me, their chants settled into the form of a wish: that peacefulness would permeate this house, soaking like the honey in baklava through the jagged layers of accumulated anxiety and unhappiness.

:::

Later that day we traveled in cars to the ashram, where the Karmapa and Babaji finally met. I wasn't there, but I heard that they embraced like old friends and chatted through interpreters about secret knowledge in their respective traditions, while Maw and Mummy-la purred in the background.

To show the Black Hat, the Karmapa took his place at one end of the ashram temple hall, facing the holy statue of Bhagavan Nityananda across an expanse of marble floor. Babaji watched through the windows from his courtyard perch—one way, I figured, for each guru to retain his own space and seat without upstaging the other. A large group of ashram dwellers gathered for the ceremony.

The Black Hat was like a crown, patterned with gold, with a giant ruby at the front. As Mummy-la had explained to Maw, many centuries ago, the emperor of China had received a vision of the Karmapa wearing such a hat woven from the hair of *dakinis,* or celestial women, and had commissioned its physical counterpart as an offering. Setting this hat on his head, the Karmapa was taking on the form of the Buddha of Compassion to spread blessings.

The Karmapa sat raised above everyone else, cross-legged on a high square brocade seat, looking straight ahead into some faraway inner space, his right hand raised to balance the hat, the left in his lap rolling a crystal rosary between his fingers. The lamas stood around him, their instruments raised. Horns rose, looped, sustained notes that carried us upward, then, just when we seemed to have reached a place of rest, took us higher still. The Karmapa remained fiercely indrawn, as though in a trance, holding the hat firm. He seemed both majestic and completely detached.

When the ceremony was over, His Holiness returned the hat to its box, then regained his smiling sociability. He bent forward, extending a red silk blessing thread to each person who filed before him, palms joined in greeting. When I received my thread, a Tibetan girl of about my age showed me how to tie it around my neck. She was the niece of a high-ranking incarnate lama from the Karmapa's Rumtek monastery in Sikkim, and since she was on winter holiday from her convent school, she was traveling with the group.

Talking to my new friend, I had the liberating sense of at last connecting with another child whose life was shaped by her family's spiritual pursuits. Over the next few days, as we tried to keep up with His Holiness's busy schedule in Bombay, I enjoyed my visits with her. Near the end of the stay, she ushered me aside to give me a keepsake: a beautiful, two-tone triangular chunk of turquoise that had been unearthed at the Rumtek monastery in the early 1960s, when foundations were being dug for extensions. I started wearing this turquoise on one of the many red blessing threads that I'd accumulated after numerous audiences with His Holiness.

At home, our coffee table was piled high with books on Tibetan Buddhism, pulled off shelves, borrowed from Mummy-la, bought at the Strand Bookstore, and checked out from the Bombay Branch of the Royal Asiatic

Society Library. But peering in through the doors without really entering, did we have any hope of understanding this other tradition with its bewilderingly complex array of gods, Buddhas, sects, reincarnations, rituals, and prayers? I couldn't help wondering: to members of the Karmapa's retinue, did we seem like well-meaning urugs swept up in a new enthusiasm? I also continued to worry about what Babaji and the other authorities of the Ganeshpuri ashram made of Maw's newfound interests.

We stayed at home one morning to catch up on various tasks. I sat down to complete an essay assignment before the school term began. With pen in hand and my new favorite reference book, *Roget's Thesaurus,* at my side, I began drafting "What I Did for My Winter Holidays."

During the winter holidays we visited Nasik . . . I began as usual, even if this year that was not where we had gone. I flipped around through the thesaurus in search of fancier words, decking out the essay like a Christmas tree with adjectives and adverbs. *During the truncated and chill days of winter, my family undertook an excursion to my grandmother's spacious abode in the ancient temple town of Nasik. . . .* I forged ahead with my fiction, reinventing my family as happy and normal, making absolutely no mention of our unusual guests. As always, I took great care to present Paw as though he were present at all times, and especially during vacations.

Midmorning, we heard a car roll into the driveway.

"Memsahib," called an excited servant, running into the house. *"Jaldi aao!"*

I followed Maw out to investigate and was stunned to see His Holiness climbing out of the car in his black lace-up shoes and maroon robes. He had come with only his driver and translator. Without his retinue, he seemed more like a regular person, a kind friend, as he offered Maw gifts: a white silk scarf, a long, intricately woven Bhutanese hanging, and a picture of himself. He also invited us to visit him in Sikkim. Why not this summer, when the lama dances were held?

Holding the gifts close, beaming with what seemed like every muscle of her face, Maw agreed immediately that we would come.

The Karmapa stayed for a few minutes, then departed in a sweep of maroon robes. Maw disappeared into her *puja* room for an excited discussion with Cupboard Swami about how such a trip could be accomplished. I drifted in, fingering the smooth turquoise around my neck. So far, all I knew about Sikkim was that an American woman called Hope Cook had married the king years ago, and Maw's friend Marilyn Silverstone had photographed the wedding. (In the spirit of Princess Snow Rose, I was more interested in the neighboring kingdom of Bhutan, where a teenage prince had recently become king.)

"Of course as a mountain kingdom squeezed between India and China, Sikkim is a politically sensitive zone," Maw said. "Non-Indians need special diplomatic permission to enter, so we'd all better start applying for permits."

"Well, a personal invitation from the Karmapa should make the process easier," Cupboard Swami assured her.

They took out the gray *Raphael's Ephemeris* for 1973 and assessed the positions of the stars in April and May, searching for auspicious conjunctions advantageous to our travel. I watched, knowing that even if Rahoul wasn't directly responsible, his prior adventures had set us up for this one.

The Moon Pearl

As we waited for travel permits for Sikkim, Maw wanted to visit Young Swamiji in the jungle. But with school in session, I refused to miss classes.

"Pumpkin, in the long run, you're *never* going to remember a few days at school," Maw said, arms dusty with flour. She was making bread all the time now. Working the dough, she said, was the best therapy for anger and frustration. "Going on a trip is the kind of thing that will stand out when you look back on your childhood."

"But what if I have a test?" I asked, heating myself milk at the stove beside her.

"Is there a test?"

"Not yet . . . but there *might* be. We'll cover things that will be on a test later."

"Okay, so then you catch up when you come back. You can ask Fatty Rasha what happened in class. And you know what? Even if you miss a test it's not the end of the world."

Milk sizzled at the edge of the pan, and outrage scalded my chest. How could a mother be so irresponsible? Other children's parents sent them to tutors after school so they would shine on tests; some mothers coached their children themselves, poring over homework assignments or inviting recitations of memorized lists and formulas.

"I'm not going," I said, grasping with a steel *khenchi* to lift the

« *"She is looking after me so nicely!"* Patane Devi, Swamiji's Mother Goddess. Photograph by Rahoul Contractor.

:: 171

handleless steel pot. I stirred my milk over a spoonful of the special Dutch cocoa that Maw had bought for my thirteenth birthday at the black-market stalls downtown. "You can go if you want."

Maw and Deven had visited Young Swamiji without me before, while I went to stay at Fatty Rasha's. Maw had also occasionally sent Deven to live with Young Swamiji for a week. They each brought home more stories about Young Swamiji and characters associated with him, sequels to Rahoul's tales. They told me about the mysterious Mr. Moose, who lived near the Chalisgaon train station, took artistic photographs of windup toys, and had not left his house for twenty years. They described Badrinath Kalantri, the white-bearded trader with a large family who sometimes hitched up his bullock cart to bring Young Swamiji's visitors out into the jungle. They praised the three-course British meals served up by Mahadevji Baba, an army cook turned wild *sadhu* who lived in a ruined Shiva temple at the other end of Swamiji's jungle.

One story especially caught my imagination:

> Maw, Deven, and Young Swamiji were returning one evening from a visit to Mahadevji Baba across the valley. They walked through the jungle along a dry riverbank. Suddenly Young Swamiji froze. "Stand back," he said, gesturing for them also to be still. A big black snake slithered over his foot, crossed the path, and disappeared into the bushes. "It's go-oo-od," Young Swamiji laughed, and they resumed moving toward the temple.

I was content to enjoy Young Swamiji's presence through such stories and his letters. I regularly sent him double postcards with neatly self-addressed, stamped sides for him to detach for his reply. He responded immediately and sometimes inquired after the exams that served as my personal signposts and hurdles amid the flux of urugs, Paw's coming and going, Maw's anxieties and enthusiasms. He remained my chief supporter for all this studying.

"You must get it from Nani," said Maw, shaking her head as I set an alarm clock to prepare for exams in the morning. "God knows I've never pushed school at my children."

I didn't tell Maw that I was finding ways to combine her goals with my own. Looking through the spiritual books she kept stashed in her *puja* room, I had found a short Sanskrit chant that I decided would help with my studies. Since this chant followed the *anustubh* meter of Young Swamiji's goddess praise, I could sing it too and soon memorized the verses. The chant honored Saraswati, goddess of learning, whose image I was familiar with from calendar prints of the sort that looked down from the walls of Ba's room with Christmas lights around their frames. Wearing a white sari, she sat on a white lotus blooming in a lake, playing her stringed *veena,* dark hair falling toward her waist.

After the alarm clock rang each morning, I remained in bed for a few more minutes. I imagined the fragrant petals of Saraswati's white lotus at my head and inwardly recited her praises.

> *Shvetapadmāsanā-devi-shveta-pushpopashobhitā . . .*

> You sit on a white lotus, wearing white flowers
> white clothes, white perfumes on your body
> You hold a white rosary.
> Your veena is white; you yourself are white,
> and all your ornaments are white.

> Siddhas and Gandharvas bow to you
> gods and antigods worship you
> sages pray to you
> seers sing your praises all the time.

> Eternal Goddess Saraswati who carries the earth
> whoever remembers you
> three times a day with this hymn;
> that person masters
> all skills in the world.

The word "white" had, for me, no association to Maw's or any other person's skin; if I needed to color in Princess Snow Rose's face, for example, I used a pink or tan crayon. To me the word "white" evoked jasmine flowers, thickened sweet milk, the sparkling curl of waves in the Arabian Sea, moonlight on an edge of cloud.

∷

For Maw to ask me to miss school was heresy; for Young Swamiji to invite me was fine. When Young Swamiji's next postcard suggested a visit for the coming full moon, I gave up on my affronted muttering about tests. Young Swamiji wrote separately to Maw too, asking for help in painting a large portrait of Patane Devi to be placed beside him in the outer room where he received visitors. Maw had already located a wooden board the size of a door for this project, and since this was for Young Swamiji, Paw granted us the car and driver.

We strapped the board to the roof of the Ambassador and loaded the car with gifts for Young Swamiji: a pressure cooker, steel utensils, and tins of powdered milk; stamped postcards and inland letter forms so he could write to friends and disciples within India; pale blue airmail letter forms so he could write to Rahoul too. We stopped overnight in Nasik, and Ba also sent gifts of sweets and pickles.

Since my last visit, the dirt road extending beyond Patane village had been smoothed, and it was now possible for us to drive slowly into the jungle. A local bus service had been established so that people from town could visit the Goddess and Swamiji too. Swamiji had moved from the peanut fields to a low, thatched cottage on a raised embankment facing the goddess temple. A fence of thorn bushes, tree saplings, and a few rows of planted flowers staked out the property from the surrounding jungle.

"It's goo-oo-ood," Young Swamiji reported, leading us inside. He had grown plumper since I had last seen him and resembled an adorable baby more than ever. He gestured toward the mud walls and woven bamboo mats, rolling his long-lashed eyes in the direction of the temple and then back to the calm space around him. "She is looking after me so nicely!"

"It's beautiful," said Maw, who always approved of buildings made from local materials.

"But Maw! I hope you will be comfortable. We don't have any marble floors." Young Swamiji dimpled at Maw. He was referring to the Ganesh-puri ashram, where he had once lived but which had now become a focal point for his teasing of Maw. "No silver money box with reflecting mirrors for donations. If we had such a box, Maw, we could roll out one rupee notes lengthwise so they looked like hundred-rupee notes when they were dropped in."

"Right," said Maw stiffly. "That's *just* what we need."

Young Swamiji's outer room was bare except for an altar, a low square mat for him, and a few striped cotton rugs. This was where he met with visitors during the day, and at night it became a dormitory for any guests who were staying over. Behind this room Young Swamiji showed us his own smaller room and a kitchen with a stove. The pots and pans were all arranged on the floor. Outside, near the back door, buckets of water, coconut husks, and piles of ash marked out the space for dishwashing. I observed that there was no running water or indoor toilet, already anxious about how I, a self-conscious teenager, would make it through the daily routine in a jungle.

Young Swamiji settled down in the corner, natural light drifting in through the low window to his right. Only one side of his face was illuminated, but both his big eyes shone. His sandalwood skin and ocher robes echoed the dusky brown of the wall. Maw, Deven, and I sat facing him on strips of burlap placed along the wall. The Boys set down full steel glasses before us, then rushed in and out with snacks, which they served on folded squares of newspaper.

"See, archeologically speaking, what's happening tomorrow is very exciting!" Young Swamiji leaned forward, grasping the rosy sole of his foot. "There is a local story that Bhaskaracharya lived in this valley. You know Bhaskaracharya, no? The great mathematician? He lived in the twelfth century and wrote five–six books. The most famous is called *Lilavati*."

Young Swamiji laughed as we took in the name. "Why *Lilavati*? You'll say this is the name of a girl, and you are right. Lilavati really was the name of his daughter. Kirin, you will especially enjoy this story. How is the tea? Too sweet? Good, I'm glad it's all right. I especially told the Boys you all are city people and will not tolerate their level of sugar."

Holding the steel glass by its rim, Young Swamiji paused to sip his tea. I was all ears, already identifying with the girl.

Bhaskaracharya was not only a mathematician, he was also an astrologer—like Maw. Naturally, as a father, he was concerned for the future of his daughter Lilavati. He cast her horoscope and found that she did not have a good horoscope for marriage. He felt so bad. He wanted Lilavati to have a happy married life. He kept looking through the horoscope and the almanacs, trying to find some remedy.

Finally he discovered that, yes, there was one chance for her marriage. Just one moment allowed by the stars. If she didn't get married on that certain date, at that certain hour, at that exact minute, then it could never happen. He was a father, no? Of course he wanted to try for her happiness. He located a groom.

In those days there were no exact clocks. So on the wedding day, he took a cup, made a small hole at the bottom, and filled it with water. He had calculated exactly how much water to use so that when the cup emptied, they would know the auspicious moment for the wedding had come. He didn't tell Lilavati what he was doing. How could he tell her? She was dressed for her wedding—silk, gems, and all. Why unnecessarily make her nervous? He put the cup aside in one room, and he must have closed the door.

But Lilavati was always interested in her father's work. She went into the room, saw the cup, and bent over it to see what it could be. She didn't plan to disturb anything; she was only curious. But when she bent over, the string of pearls around her neck broke and one of the pearls fell into the cup, blocking the opening. The water was no longer draining out. The moment for the marriage came and went, and the cup was still full.

Lilavati's one chance was gone. She never married. Instead, she stayed with her father, and she too became a great scholar. Bhaskaracharya wrote a book about all the things he taught her: about zero, geometry, and all that. The name of this book is *Lilavati*.

Becoming a great scholar, known for centuries to come, made up for not getting married, I thought. But her father's care caught like a jagged edge at my heart.

"What to do?" Young Swamiji concluded. "Fate is fate." He looked out the window to his right and switched into Marathi to ask the perpetually rushing Boys what they were doing now. Satisfied with their answer, he turned back to us, resuming English.

"Anyway, that is all many centuries back. Recently someone from the Archeological Survey of India came to look at the temple. The Survey has too many monuments to look after all over the country, so they were thinking of abandoning protection and repairs on this site. I talked with this gentleman, and I asked him whether he knew this local story about Bhaskaracharya. He went away, then came back and reported that most records indicate that Bhaskaracharya lived in Ujjain, which you know is quite distant. Maybe he lived here for a time, who knows? Still, I encouraged him to do some digging. I said: if Bhaskaracharya lived here, in this valley, would he not have chosen the spot facing the temple? Why is the earth here built up like a mound? They have agreed to do just a small dig, just to see if there is anything on this property. They will be coming tomorrow. See, Maw! I wanted you all to be here too so if they find something of importance, you will also see it."

: : :

We unrolled our sponge traveling mattresses over the packed-earth floor. I lay awake, aware of everyone else settling into sleep in the small hut. I could hear mice scuttling in the thatched roof. Moonlight drifted in through the netted windows, trees sighed, and an insect orchestra started to serenade the forest that stretched around us.

The next day's excavation made me think of Ba, who for years had schemed to dig for treasure in our fields. She sometimes told stories associated with this hidden treasure as self-contained incidents, and sometimes she unfolded them like the panels of a painted screen. Remembering the stories, I could hear Ba's emphatic nasal voice and see her energetic, double-jointed hands. Like Narmada-ben and Heera-ben, she always referred to Sethji as Dada, or grandfather, when speaking about him to us.

> When I married into this family, your grandfather had only the Byculla property. Then he fell ill. We came and lived in a dharamshala in Nasik. First, he bought land, all this land for only fifteen thousand rupees—we picked it up so cheap! Dada planted twelve mango trees, and we held a big feast for all our relatives and everyone in the town. Then Dada built a four-room shack, where we lived for two years—the shack near the cowshed. Dada was still building the other bungalows when his health grew worse. The doctor visited. "Just take this medicine," he said. "There's nothing to worry about."
>
> One night around eleven o'clock, a snake began to cry. He cried like a small child. I went out to look, and I saw that he was a white cobra. He had a red ruby on his forehead and a big white mustache.

Ba always demonstrated, drawing her thumbs outward over her lip to mime a handlebar that made me think of the portrait of Sethji soon after he married her. I imagined her as a willful, lonely teenager married to an ill old man. Paw and others had later seen the albino cobra in our fields, but Ba was the only one who had ever glimpsed its ruby and mustache.

> The cobra started coming to the door every night. The rest of the time, he slithered around in our fields. (Ba lowered her hand toward the floor, making a gliding motion.) When I went out to walk in our fields, the cobra sometimes came along beside me. Slowly, slowly, slowly. I wasn't afraid. He was at least a thousand years old. He didn't have much strength, he was so weak and old. I learned that he lived inside an old well. He's still there, swimming round and round in the water. If anyone ever tries to attack him, he makes himself invisible.

The reason for the cobra's presence was bound up with another story:

> All our land had long ago belonged to the Divan, the prime minister of
> the Peshwa king. The king had given the land to his Divan, a Brahman,
> as a reward for his good deeds. The Divan had one daughter who liked
> to go to war, all dressed up in armor and waving a sword. (Ba sat upright,
> brandishing imaginary weapons.) When that girl wasn't fighting, she hid
> in two rooms inside the well. She hid all the Divan's treasure nearby. All
> the gold, rubies, diamonds, emeralds from those times are lying there in
> our property, and they are guarded by the cobra. Armlets, necklaces, many
> gold coins. Lots and lots of gold coins.

All this set the stage for one of Ba's most memorable encounters with
a god:

> One full moon night after the cobra had visited, around 10:30, I heard
> something in the fields and went out to see. I saw a donkey grazing. "Hey
> you, sala!" I called. "Everyone's asleep and you've come to eat?" I went
> forward to hit the donkey, but it vanished and I saw it was a bull. I raised
> a stick to hit that bull—it was eating up our millet, our corn! Then I saw
> Shiva Bhagavan sitting on the bull. This was Shiva's bull, Nandi.
>
> Shiva Bhagavan held a trident in his hand. He had a big round belly. He
> was very bright and huge, while Nandi was small. Then Shiva Bhagavan
> began to walk toward me, his feet sinking deep into the ground. I went
> forward to bow. He raised his hand and blessed me. "As long as you live,
> you have nothing to fear," he said.
>
> Back at the house, I told people I had seen something. They asked,
> "Was that a *bhut* or a *bhagavan,* a ghost or a god?" They were alarmed.
> "Maybe it's a *brahm,* an illusion," they said. "Maybe it's a *bhavana,* some
> feeling inside you."
>
> "Absolutely not," I said. "That was Bhagavan."
>
> I told your grandfather, Sethji. "*Theek,*" he said. "Fine."

Ba usually ended any of these three interconnected tales by bringing the
story back to her ongoing quest for a *sadhu* who could help her take charge
of all that gold, all those gems:

> Even now, that cobra still lives in the well. Many times I've dreamed that a
> little girl comes with her hands stretched out, full of jewels, saying, "Take!

I'm here. Dig me out." Then the place where the treasure is buried appears before me. That little girl is the goddess Lakshmi. "I'm here!" she says. "Bring me out!"

No one listens to my dreams. Your grandfather was an argumentative man. And your father, he's useless, he just laughs. I know exactly where that treasure is, though. Now there's a government so we have to hide the treasure carefully or they'll confiscate it. I'm looking for a man who can dig it out. You need a *mahapurush,* a great being, to extract treasure. Otherwise it will all turn to ash.

: : :

Full moon days were auspicious, so workmen bearing shovels and spades weren't the only ones to arrive the next morning. A Public Works Department team brought a truck with a gigantic rig to drill a tube well; with Swamiji's growing local fame and more pilgrims visiting the valley, the lack of water had become an increasing problem. A group of Brahman *pujaris* arrived on foot, carrying satchels, to chant before the Devi in the temple. Villagers who had also walked started flowing up the stone steps of the temple. As the sun appeared over the mountain range, the first bus chugged in, roaring and reversing with black clouds of exhaust, disgorging people from nearby villages and towns.

The Boys carried over the huge wooden board we had brought from Bombay and propped it up on the open platform facing Patane Devi. Sari covering her head against the sun, Maw stood mixing acrylic paints and daubing them onto the board. Patane Devi looked out at us with her coral-bright exuberance, lips slightly parted, as Maw sketched out her eighteen arms with their weapons, and pointed out places that Deven and I could color in. From inside the shrine, assembled Brahmans chanted the epic of the Great Goddess at top speed and arriving pilgrims rang the overhead brass bells. Across the way, the drill vibrated and clattered.

Midmorning, lanky Raju marched up the temple steps wearing sunglasses, a tight shirt, and green bell-bottom pants. Amid all the women wearing five-yard saris or nine-yard saris, and the girls in long skirts, Raju cut a figure almost as astonishingly androgynous as Swamiji—all dignified angles to his plump circles. Raju greeted the Devi, greeted us, and briskly took charge of smashing the coconuts offered by the latest group of pilgrims.

"*Rahoul chi ai,*" she informed people coming by to gawk at us after they'd made their offerings and circumambulations. "This is Rahoul's mother.

"He was very bright and huge." Ba telling the story of meeting Shiva Bhagavan, 1985.
Photograph by Kirin Narayan.

She's an artist, and she's painting for Young Swamiji. Rahoul's brother, Rahoul's sister. Rahoul's father hasn't come, no. Rahoul? He is in America. How many days by bullock cart? People fly in the sky; they don't take a bullock cart to America."

Standing with her arms crossed behind Maw, Raju also pointed out details that might be added to the painting. When more people came by, she resumed her duties as self-appointed guide.

"Rahoul chi ai, Rahoul cha bhau, Rahoul chi bahin . . ."

Everyone nodded and greeted Rahoul's mother, brother, and sister. Having been one of Young Swamiji's first long-term visitors seemed to have made Rahoul a legendary figure. In Oregon it would be night. I wondered: how could Reed College possibly compete with the warm sociability of these crowds, the air humming with the possibility of miracles and blessings?

By late afternoon, the Brahmans departed, carrying away bundles of cloth, fruit, and sweets that had been offered during the day. Patane Devi's enormous eyes watched us paint. She was dressed in layers of starched, new red or green saris that people had brought her. The triangular skylight above her head let in softer light now, and a series of burning ghee lamps made the space around her seem rosy and abundant.

Maw had blocked out a first complete sketch of the portrait. As the paint dried, we walked back through the warm sand in the dry riverbed. Young Swamiji was still giving audience to visitors, and we drifted out to see what was happening at the archeological dig.

The workers had opened out a space a few feet wide and a few feet deep near Young Swamiji's door. A few potsherds, some coins, and a bit of sculpture had been discovered earlier in the afternoon, but the workers were still digging, hoping for more.

"The coins do appear to be twelfth century," the supervising archeologist told Maw. "That is the period of Bhaskaracharya."

As we stood watching, Maw asked the archeologist about Pittalkora, a much earlier Buddhist site higher in the surrounding rim of mountains. "I've come across it in my readings on art history," she said. From there, they moved on to how Buddhism had once flourished in this area, and how a great Buddhist university had once trained students where now there was jungle. "In excavations on the other side of the valley," he said, "we found a fossilized ostrich egg. It may have been an African curiosity displayed for the students."

I was watching the earth being sifted, wondering if the workers would find treasure, and if they did, whether Young Swamiji would have to be present to ensure that it didn't turn to ash? But the workers struck stone rather than coins. They switched from shovels to spades, then from spades to brushes, their actions slowing into gentleness. What they were uncovering took shape: the edge of a plinth, then the base of a carved stone doorway with holes drilled on either side to hold a wooden door. Steps led up to the door. A sunken square space for fire offerings emerged inside the room.

As the sunken room came into view, the drillers nearby let out a triumphant yell. Raju rushed over, arms in the air, head thrown back as she leaped, setting Boys jumping and hooting around her. "Water! Water!" she called. "They've hit water!"

Young Swamiji clattered out in his wooden clogs with the canvas straps. When he saw the ancient doorway, he laughed, mouth wide, dimples deep. It was a few feet out, directly in front of his cottage door, at the same angle and the same width.

"So Maw!" he trilled. "Eight centuries apart. Would you call this coincidence?"

I wouldn't admit this to Maw, but I was beginning to see how life outside school could be richly memorable.

: : :

Young Swamiji refused donations. *"Naka naka,"* he waved at peasants extracting coins from inner pockets or the recesses of faded sari blouses. The person attempting to make an offering usually stopped still, perplexed. Holy people were supported through the goodwill of laypeople, and even the poorest peasants wanted at least to make the gesture.

Barred from giving money, village people vied to bring Young Swamiji other things: peanuts and seasonal vegetables from their fields; milk from their cows and buffalos; steel containers of home-cooked food. People who lived in town arrived with canisters of oil, *dals,* sugar, tea, and other staples or big cardboard boxes of milk sweets. On a full moon day like this, the Boys constantly rushed between Young Swamiji's reception room and the kitchen trying to find more space for offerings.

When not stashing away food, the Boys had been squatting and stirring by the kerosene stove. As dusk fell, they laid out mats and served dinner for the twenty or so people who lingered in Young Swamiji's compound.

Maw looked skeptically at the spread: the *dal-bhatti* and *puran poli* soaked in ghee, *parathas* glistening in oil, vegetables in pools of red chili, and box upon box of rich milk sweets. "I know that food equals love, but the way Young Swamiji's going, he'll be lucky if he doesn't develop heart problems." Maw grumbled. "I wish *someone* would translate Adelle Davis into Marathi."

The moon peered over the left edge of the mountain as we faced the temple, then rose with a wide halo of light. Moonlight glistened on Young Swamiji's shaved skull, glittered in the eyes of the seated visitors, floated in our glasses of freshly piped tube-well water. We were drenched in soft light and blue shadows, enveloped by the sounds of crickets and wind, of people contentedly eating and joking. Young Swamiji's high-pitched voice maneuvered between languages—English, Hindi, Marathi—and bursts of laughter.

We could hear people singing in the temple. Raju, who had taken charge of us, the Rahoul contingent, explained in an undertone that on full moon nights, exorcists arrived to treat possessed villagers in front of the Devi. Listening closely when the singing stopped, we heard muffled sounds of an exorcist's questions borne on the wind: "Who are you? Why are you in this tree?"

The moon observed us with smiling interest. I'd seen a rabbit in the moon often, but this was the first time I'd sat long enough in the moon's company to discern a womanly face. I wondered if Lilavati, who once lived on this spot, saw the same features. Was she happy, being a daughter and scholar rather than disappearing into history as a wife? I imagined her with searching eyes, always wearing white saris, enjoying fragrant jasmines, and keeping a clean house with few possessions so her time could be devoted to the mysteries of integers and fractions.

Did the full moon, I wondered, ever remind her of the pearl that had fallen, locking her into the embrace of these mountains?

At the Border

"HOLINESS SAYS COME," Mummy-la instructed us by telegram from Sikkim. April heat had begun to roast Bombay, school had faded into the hot sleep of summer vacation, and we had still not received our travel permits. Newspapers reported mass demonstrations in Sikkim after a recent election, and the Indian army had intervened. At home money was especially tight. Paw, who had so often left the office in the hands of his business partner, was now taking this partner to court for embezzlement. Maw too was reeling with the realization that her New York export partnership had fallen through; she had lost years of labor, preliminary shipments of clothes, and a few thousand dollars in investment. Still, the summons from His Holiness seemed to raise us above bureaucracy, political upheaval, and financial worries. By the middle of April 1973, we started preparing to travel north.

Maw had already figured out that the best route into Sikkim was from Darjeeling, north of Calcutta. She remembered that a family friend based in Delhi owned a house on a defunct tea estate near Darjeeling and wrote asking if we might stay there as we waited for our travel permits. He wrote back granting us use of the house, but cautioned that he hadn't visited it for a few years, that he couldn't vouch for its condition, and that it was unfurnished. Paying for hotel rooms was out of the question, so despite these warnings, Maw accepted.

« His Holiness the Sixteenth Gwalya Karmapa at his Rumtek monastery, 1973. Photographer unknown.

But when Paw's office peon Ramchandra went to buy our train tickets, we learned that, what with summer vacation and wedding season, seats for the long journey between Bombay and Calcutta were solidly booked. Traveling in the padded seats, berths, and enclosed cabins of first class was beyond our budget anyway, and second class was also expensive. Finally, after much juggling of dates and connections, Ramchandra procured eight reserved seats in the no-frills third-class compartment (still a step above "un-reserved third"). But he was able to book only two narrow wooden upper sleeping berths.

"Do you really think that six of us can sit up for all of two days and two nights to Calcutta?" Maya asked Maw.

"Sweetie, it's the best I can do for now," Maw said. "We'll take mattresses to spread over the seats. The main thing is that we get on the train, and then we'll work out some way to be comfortable."

Waiting at the train station, our group was already collecting crowds of onlookers and annoying greetings of *"Hare Krishna!"* or *"Dam maro dam,"* We stood on the platform surrounded by mountains of luggage—trunks, suitcases, rolled-up sponge mattresses, bathroom bags, biscuit bags, fruit bags, meal bags, water bottles. Maw was at our helm, loudly directing coolies. She wore her hair in an unruly braid, a big smear of red *kumkum* on her forehead, a *mala* of *rudraksha* beads displaying her spiritual interests around her neck, and her maroon-edged, finely-checked brown Maharashtrian "travel sari," which showed neither dirt nor creases.

At her elbow, Cupboard Swami also displayed a big spot of red *kumkum* and a *mala,* His white robes arranged over one shoulder seemed to confuse onlookers about his possible country of origin. A few fellow male travelers ventured up to ask, "Where you are hailing from?" or "You are a native of which place only?"—but Cupboard Swami declined to respond.

Jonathan and Maya were with us too, back from Thailand after there turned out to be some legal glitch in Jonathan's having been assigned to the mission for alternative service. With his John Lennon glasses, shoulder-length curls, handloom *kurta,* and amused smile, Jonathan drew stares, which turned to wonderment when people then saw Maya, dressed as a traditional wife with her neatly draped and starched cotton sari, perfect round spot of *kumkum,* gold earrings and bangles, *mangal sutra,* and thick braid down to her knees—could she really be married to this seeming hippie?

The teenagers in our group attracted less attention, but we too seemed to demand a second look. Deven, tall and handsome with hazel eyes, had just finished school and grown his curly hair out into a Bob Dylan halo, which he often squashed under a black cowboy hat. Tashi had flunked out of school and also liked to wear a cowboy hat over his straight, shoulder-length hair. David, the eighteen-year-old son of an American professor friend, had been sent to Maw to gain a "summer of life experience" between high school and college. He was clean-cut with dark hair and dressed conventionally, in T-shirts and jeans, but still he was a spectacle in his sheer foreignness.

Finally, there was me, wearing one of my best outfits: a paneled ankle-length skirt in blue *kalamkari* fabric (a by-product of Maw's export attempts) and a ribbed navy blue T-shirt, with silver anklets and a tiny painted-on red bindi. I was trying to grow my hair into a long braid, to copy Maya in whatever small ways I could, but my teenage awkwardness only emphasized how she was the beauty and I was not. I watched our observers watch us, and I burned with embarrassment for us all.

When the train slid into the station, we scrambled on and staked our claims to the seats closest to a reserved berth. Maw immediately began urging the ticket collector, sweating in his black jacket, to supply us with more berths, and coaxing our fellow passengers to swap seats so the family could sit together. Her powers of persuasion fell short of gaining us more berths, but we did colonize two facing sets of lower seats. Maw directed as we filled the space between the seats with our trunks, suitcases, and other baggage; then we spread our sponge mattresses over the pile to make a giant bed. While Cupboard Swami and David got upper berths to themselves, the rest of us squeezed into the big family nest.

Two days and two nights later, coal dust lining our skin, subcontinental dust deep inside our navels, we arrived at Howrah station in Calcutta. I thought I was a city girl, but Calcutta revealed new dimensions to words like "crowd," "heat," and "traffic jam." We stayed at the Ramakrishna Mission Guesthouse, which was clean, affordable, and had the added benefit of seeming ashramlike. As we waited for onward train reservations into the mountains, we toured pilgrimage sites like the great Kali temples of Calcutta and Dakshineshwar, and the peaceful room where the nineteenth-century saint Ramakrishna had once given audience.

Before proceeding toward Darjeeling, we needed to gather supplies for the unfurnished house where we would stay; it made more sense to buy basics like buckets and utensils at city prices than at a more expensive hill station. On the advice of Margot, Maw's sari-wearing British editor friend, we set off for Calcutta's New Market.

Maw led us along hot, narrow walkways between shops selling fruit, books, clothes, kitchen utensils, cheese, silk, tourist curios, and much more. Everywhere touts called out for our attention.

"Madam Sadhu Maharaj!" shouted a skinny man sitting on a stool under hanging buckets, watering cans, and inflatable toys. He waved excitedly at Maw, gesturing for her to enter. "Madam Sadhu Maharaj!"

"What did he say?" we asked each other, already beginning to giggle. "Madam Sadhu Maharaj" was a hilariously incongruous title: "Madam" connoted respect for a woman, especially a Western woman, while "Sadhu Maharaj" extended kingly honor to a holy man. To call Maw "Madam Sadhu Maharaj" was to jumble together male and female, worldly and spiritual, and to simultaneously mock and salute her spiritual aspirations.

Maw ignored the man and sailed onward, scanning shop fronts for items on her list. As we caught up with her, helpless with laughter, she insisted that the shopkeeper had said "Madam" to her and "Sadhu Maharaj" to Cupboard Swami, who was at her heels. "There was definitely a pause between the words," Maw insisted.

All the same, from that moment onward, we were Madam Sadhu Maharaj and party.

: : :

A few days later, Madam Sadhu Maharaj and party emerged from taxis into the cool, pine-scented air of the village of Tung with what had become a Himalayan range of luggage. A few men sat out on benches in the sun, and stray dogs napped nearby. The boys went off to find the caretaker of the house while the rest of us waited with the luggage. After a while, they returned with an old man who seemed distinctly unhappy to see us. He had received our Delhi friend's instructions to let us stay, and he helped arrange for coolies to carry our things.

In the plains, coolies tended to carry heavy luggage atop their heads, using both arms to stabilize the load; in this hilly countryside, they instead loaded the trunks on their backs, anchored with straps that reached over their heads, leaving their hands free as they bent forward up inclines. We followed our luggage up narrow stone steps that wound toward a pine forest shrouded in mist.

As we turned up the last twist of the pathway, Anselganj loomed up from the hillside: a mansion with slanted roofs and many chimneys. To one side of the house a level, neatly tended lawn interspersed with clumps of blue hydrangeas stretched to the edge of the forest. Around this ordered flatness were terraced patches of gnarled, unkempt tea bushes. Stopping to catch our breath, we could hear the call of unfamiliar birds and the rush and splash of a stream.

"Wow!" said Maw with pleasure. As we drew closer and saw that panes were missing or hanging jaggedly in practically every window, she added, "Oh boy."

"*Bacche log,*" said the caretaker, following our eyes. "Children—when they have nothing to do, they like to throw stones. Who can stay here all the time watching?"

He opened the creaking door, and we followed him into the big, bare rooms, which still carried traces of the house's past grandeur: parquet floors, ornate fireplaces, a paned sunroom, and patterned wallpaper, now fading, peeling, and stained. I had never seen wallpaper before. I touched it, feeling as though I had entered a novel. I wandered from room to room, both astonished to find myself in a real British house of the sort I had visited so often in the pages of books, and dismayed by the realization that I couldn't enter a past time.

Upstairs too, the rooms were bare. Light switches were set into the walls, but the sockets in the ceilings had been ripped out, the wires left dangling. The bathrooms held large bathtubs, and even Western-style toilets, but had been stripped of pipes and taps. The caretaker pointed to the stream flowing nearby. He promised to arrange a daily delivery of milk, gave us the key, and then shuffled off, muttering. Maw began deciding who would camp out in which rooms, and we started to unpack.

"It'll just be for a few days," Maw assured us.

By the end of the first day, we had learned to fetch water from the icy stream, to squat at its edge to wash our clothes, and to scrub at dirty dishes with ash from the fireplace. We carried brass water pots as we searched for bushes to squat behind. For light, we lit smoky kerosene lanterns and burned candles.

As soon as we had found our bearings, we rode the toylike narrow-gauge train to "town"—the pretty hill station of Darjeeling, where flowers grew in bright abundance from tin-can pots. We turned our backs on expensive tourist temptations, trekking between the District Magistrate's Office and the Foreigner's Registration Office. Maw made inquiries, and we all stood around her, filling out applications for permits to enter Sikkim. Then we returned to our shell of a house to wait.

In Bombay, servants had taken care of our cooking, cleaning and washing; here we learned that these tasks could take hours. As misty days passed, turning into weeks, Maw and Maya masterminded most of the housekeeping details. Cupboard Swami helped out, especially with lunch. One afternoon he tried his hand at making rice pudding, and since we didn't have any rose water, he sprinkled in some rose attar we had picked up in Calcutta. Meant for skin, the attar was so overwhelming in food that none of us could eat the pudding. We sadly scraped out the treat into the heap of garbage behind the house. A cringing dog with elongated udders came up from the village and nosed through what we had discarded. She gobbled up the pudding, then scuttled around letting out volleys of rose-scented farts. After that, we knew her as Rosie.

In the quiet moments between chores, Maw worked on astrological charts, Maya read and sewed, Cupboard Swami continued writing fables, and Jonathan and Deven played chess or joked about the fine points of a Tibetan philosophical booklet that Jonathan had packed along, titled *The Treatise on Coming and Going,* Deven and Tashi played the guitar. David stood out on the lawn, tenaciously practicing his baseball maneuvers with a stick and stone.

I often sat cross-legged at a low desk we had made by propping a board across two trunks. Wind rattled at the broken panes, and mists wandered off the hillside and into the rooms. I looked out over the lawn with its hydrangea clumps, up toward the pine forest, and tried to find purpose as if I had homework. I read, drew, and composed further miniature issues of *The Family,* But also, I daydreamed about the dances, dinner parties, and marriage proposals that might have once taken place in these rooms. Who were these tea-garden owners, the Ansels? I knew that if I were a character in a book, I would find some way to reach them. But having patrolled the house in search of old shoeboxes that might contain pictures, or loose floorboards that might hide love letters, I had only my own imagination to consult.

People from the village below seemed to claim their own rights to the property. They stayed away from the house while we were there but continued to bring their cows and goats onto the lawn to graze, or stopped to pick tea from the gnarled bushes. David began to swap smoldering glances with a pretty young Tibetan woman who came by each day, sometimes leading a cow, sometimes just fiddling with the tea bushes. She sang to herself, looking sidelong at David, *"Ek pyar ka nagma hai,* this is the song of a love. . . ." For years after, whenever I heard that wistful song on the radio, I saw mists rolling in and once again felt suspended in waiting: waiting for permits, waiting for excitement, waiting to grow up.

: : :

A few weeks passed. Maw sent letters to everyone she knew in Delhi who might have direct or indirect government connections. She and Mummy-la continued a brisk exchange of letters. To help our cause, His Holiness the Karmapa sent a secretary across the mountain passes from Sikkim with precious blessing pills and an official invitation that carried a giant maroon wax stamp.

"We have a personal invitation from His Holiness the Karmapa," Maw said, brandishing this invitation at the District Magistrate's Office in Darjeeling, then at the Superintendent of Police's Office, then back again at the District Magistrate's Office.

"Madam, with the current unrest, foreigners are not permitted," said the office worker who found himself in the way of her will.

"Yes, but how many foreigners have invitations from His Holiness himself? We're here for peaceful, spiritual reasons."

"That may be, madam, but under the current circumstances we cannot issue you permits."

"How long will these circumstances continue?"

"That we cannot say, madam. You can try again next week."

"But we'll have to go back to Bombay soon!"

"Madam, there is nothing we can do. Foreigners are not permitted."

"I have lived in India for twenty-two years, and all my children are half-Indian. How can you exclude me as a foreigner?"

"Yes, madam, but these are not Indian citizenship papers you are showing me."

"Where is your superior?"

Maw tried every tack she could; she put on her haughty, explosive act—what she called "doing a Memsahib"—and she brought out her rarely used *mangal sutra,* "playing the Hindu wife." But every official she spoke to was unrelenting. Maw sent more letters to Delhi and cabled Paw to send more funds.

As we whiled away the days in mist and drizzle, Maw looked around for other Tibetan teachers with whom we might make good use of our time. We had heard that one of the Karmapa's teachers, an incarnate lama called Kalu Rinpoche, lived not far from Tung, and one drizzling afternoon, we set off in a procession of bobbing black umbrellas to meet him.

Kalu Rinpoche was an ancient, ethereally thin lama with high cheekbones and close-cropped gray hair. He sat cross-legged on an elevated seat, radiating ascetic dignity. Madam Sadhu Maharaj and party crowded into the back of a room already filled with Tibetans, as well as Westerners in Tibetan dress.

"They're probably all waiting to visit the Karmapa, too," Maw whispered, looking around to see if anyone appeared interesting enough to befriend. She had always prided herself on being able to identify Interesting People. I realized that, stuck for weeks in this backwater with the same, small group, she was probably missing the distractions and sociability of our Bombay home.

People filed slowly forward for the Rinpoche's blessings. We hadn't yet reached him when suddenly Maw dived into a bow. Bent and lurching, but moving very fast, she waddled from the room. We made quick salutes toward the Rinpoche, and then, like a trail of ducklings, following her. We found Maw in the courtyard by the brightly painted cylindrical prayer wheels. She moved as though her knees had become bound together under the sari.

"What happened?" we asked.

"My underwear!" Maw said, giggling. "It snapped!"

Cupboard Swami distanced himself from this profane situation, and David looked the other way, patiently enduring the latest antics of these weird friends of his parents. Members of the family gathered around her, all opening black umbrellas at knee level and trying not to laugh too hard as Maw discreetly stepped out of her underpants and slipped them into her cloth shoulder bag. We debated whether to go back to the audience hall and take more formal leave of the distinguished lama, but we doubted our ability to keep straight faces and show the appropriate respect.

"Maw, next time we visit an incarnate lama, check your elastic, will you?" Jonathan teased.

::::

The Sikkim permits still weren't in hand, and for me the school term would soon start. Maw continued visiting assorted officials. One official looking over our papers pointed out, though, that Deven and I didn't need permits. We might be minors listed on Maw's U.S. passport (as Maya and Rahoul had once been), but as the children of an Indian father, until we turned eighteen and decided on the nationality of our own passports we were also considered Indian. This meant that at least the two of us could legally enter Sikkim.

"You can't send two kids across an international border," Maya said, back at Anselganj, as we sat cross-legged on the parquet floor, eating supper by candlelight from enamel plates. "They're too young to go alone."

"Nothing will happen to them," Maw said. "It's actually less than a day's drive. Once they get to the monastery they'll be fabulously taken care of. Mummy-la will be there. And look, they really *are* Indian. It's not like they're breaking any laws."

"I'm just trying to say that they're too young to travel alone," insisted Maya.

"You were sixteen when you went to America," said Deven.

"Yes, but I was with Nani. And I didn't have a little girl in tow."

"I'm *not a little girl,*" I objected. "I'm an *eldest unmarried daughter,*"

"Okay, but that just adds to the worries about what could happen to you," Maya said.

There's nothing like opposition to harden teenagers in their resolve.

"I'm definitely going," said Deven.

"Me too. Definitely," I echoed, staring studiously away in case Deven issued one of his withering looks that signaled I was not to imitate him.

"Everything is going to be just fine," Maw insisted. "This is His Holiness's invitation after all. His blessings will protect them. At least *someone* in the family will have a chance to see the Rumtek monastery."

So in early June 1973, Deven and I started out toward Sikkim. He was seventeen, and I was thirteen. We carried no identification or permits beyond our apparent "Indianness." Deven was dressed as usual in jeans and a short-sleeved cotton shirt, covered today with a sweater. I had insisted on wearing a block-printed white and pink sari that belonged to Maya, and Maw's red Kashmiri shawl with tiny embroidered blue flowers. I knew that how old I appeared would not determine whether we safely crossed the border, but dressing like a self-possessed grown-up made me feel less vulnerable.

A few other people had paid for seats in the taxi too. I watched our fellow travelers anxiously to see if they were watching us. I kept worrying: When Maw had said good-bye to us in Darjeeling, standing beside the Jeep's windows with last-minute instructions, might her fair skin and accent have given away our part-Americanness? Did we look Indian enough to cross unquestioned? I had become so used to being stared at and speculated about that I couldn't quite trust that Deven and I would blend in.

As the Jeep zigzagged down the steep incline through the misty green landscape, I held tight to the triangular lump of turquoise that I had been wearing ever since the Karmapa's visit to Bombay. We moved downward, from pine to teak, ferns, and wildflowers. Maya's warnings were still ringing in my ears, and my imagination had no problem supplying further dire scenarios. I could be separated from Deven. Our money could be stolen. We could be detained by soldiers at the border. I didn't even want to think about trafficked teenage girls. I hoped that the blue and green patterned stone from Rumtek would lead us safely to the monastery.

At the border, I held my breath. Deven caught my eye, reassuring me with a small nod as men in uniform came toward the taxi. They asked a few questions, which he handled, and then we were waved through.

I had never left India before. I looked out the window, trying to decide if there was any difference in the landscape between countries; crossing this invisible line, how might I have become different? Soon after, I recorded my impressions in decorative longhand and the cadences of my beloved Victorian prose:

Sikkim is a beautiful country—lush undergrowth, creepers + large flowers studded the sides of the road. After a while rice paddies began to be a frequent sight, the fresh poignant green of the young shoots dazzling the eye. The road seemed to go on forever—past various bends—sometimes level with the gray rushing alive depths of the Teesta River, sometimes high in the mountains, with the Teesta below us. Sunlight streaked in—the weather was fine and a trifle warm, unlike the mist and rain of Darjeeling.

We arrived in Sikkim's capital, Gangtok, at dusk, too late to go on to the monastery. The taxi pulled up in a main bazaar, and we picked our way through mud, straw, horse droppings, and stray dogs, trying to decide on a hotel that wasn't too expensive. Traders sat on the sidewalks with their wares spread around them, but we looked away from things that would require money. Groups of monks in maroon robes and laced black shoes passed us and I scanned their faces, irrationally hoping to be greeted by one of the lamas who had visited us in Bombay.

We randomly picked one of the many cheap hotels in the bazaar and ate steaming bowls of noodles for dinner. *"The food was awful but the view of the mountains was breathtaking—snowcaps after snowcaps stretched away far to the NW,"* I wrote. Settling in for the night, we discovered that the door of our room didn't really lock. The flimsy aluminum latch had a screw missing and could easily be pushed open from outside.

Light streamed in through cracks in the door and plywood walls. Groups of drunken men talked and laughed and sang in an adjoining bar. I lay awake, holding tight to the purse that Maw had loaned me since I usually had no reason to carry money of my own.

When I heard Deven stir across the room, I spoke aloud my fear. "Do you think they might come in?"

"We can barricade the door," said Deven.

We switched on the dim light and moved a chair against the door. We piled on our bags for weight too, though neither bag was very heavy.

"Tomorrow night we'll be at the monastery," Deven assured me.

"Tomorrow," I agreed, wishing for the bright safety of daylight.

::::

The bazaar was just stirring when Deven and I went looking for another Jeep that would take us to the Rumtek monastery. We met up with a young Englishman who spoke the local languages and was able to haggle with the taxi drivers. We didn't ask when or how he had been issued a visa. I summed him up as *"young, rather handsome, and pompous—not a hippie but a 'mod' type with boots, bellbottoms but a short haircut,"* We again curved through the hilly landscape, this time driving southwest. The road was in poor condition, with great pits and ditches, and sometimes streams rushing over the uneven asphalt. At one point, we started up a hill that, from its base, seemed bare and brown. As we drove higher, the brown separated into bands, revealing the pattern of terraces filled with green shoots of young rice. Climbing higher still, we looked down on the terraces. What had seemed barren from below had miraculously transformed into a fertile expanse of rippling green light, faintly outlined in brown.

"That was like magic," I said, turning to Deven.

"I know," Deven said. He had seen the same thing.

At the monastery—*"maroon with intricate, ornate designs"*—we found one of the young English-speaking interpreters who had visited Bombay. He led us through the enormous gateway. The gateway was, I noted, *"perhaps 20 feet wide, as the lamas have rooms in the outer wall surrounding the courtyard,"* Inside the immense courtyard, I observed a large white tent, *"sagging, with rain continuously dribbling through,"* Beyond the tent, the central prayer hall resounded with *"chanting, low + monotonous, accentuated by sudden crescendos with drums and cymbals."*

We were taken upstairs to Mummy-la's room. Mummy-la was startled to see us, though clearly disappointed that Maw was not along. After tea, she and an old lama with a wrinkled face and a wisp of beard led us down into the main prayer hall for an audience with the Karmapa. Row upon row of lamas in maroon robes sat chanting, some on the ground, others on seats of various heights. Midmorning light drifted in through the open door, but otherwise the hall was lit with flickering oil lamps. The burning lamps and the smoky incense together produced a golden radiance, deepening the saturated colors of the hanging brocades and painted walls. The chanting hummed forward, now and then punctuated by a clamor of cymbals, drums, and rising horns. As I wrote soon after:

Perhaps it was the shock of suddenly being in an ancient Tibetan environment— perhaps it was the pure joy of being there at last, but the hall was like something heavenly—the air seemed misty and it was like entering another world. As we were led around to the right, I had the brief impression of many old lamas sitting in rows at different levels, some with instruments, muttering like a beehive. And then there was a group of small lamas, no older than nine or ten, talking and sleeping on their own benches behind the elder lamas, who regarded us without interest.

We stopped here and the old lama handed us two silk scarves to present H.H. Then we went on.

There was a sudden crescendo with cymbals and drums as we were led to H.H.'s high seat, where he was perched benignly with a kind yet very holy face. The row of steps leading to his seat was big enough for only one person, so Deven went first to present his scarf + the gifts, then I. His Holiness took the scarves and put them over our shoulders in the traditional Tibetan fashion. He smiled and inquired about something, which we could not hear above the deafening din. Mummy was telling him something.

Then the music subsided and there was a brief quiet broken only by the voices of the young lamas who were supposed to keep a certain mantra going nonstop day + night, and we were led away.

Mummy-la was about to go off on a short trip of her own. But His Holiness assigned us to the care of a young incarnate lama, Bardor Tulku, whom we had met in Bombay. All laughing jollity, Bardor Tulku led us to the area at the edge of the monastery complex where lay people were housed and arranged for us to have a room in a secretary's house. Washing the dust of the trip off my hands, I watched cold water spiral down a drain as though in a trance, wondering if special laws of physics applied in this magical space.

When the lama dances began two days later, Bardor Tulku purposefully led us through the crowd of onlookers to a good viewing place. The world I was struggling to make sense of had morphed again, as many monks had changed from their maroon robes to elaborate costumes. In one dance, a kind-faced masked man—perhaps a Buddha—moved with slow grace, languorously waving a fan. In another, a fluffy white snow lion flopped and pranced on two sets of lama legs, making the assembled crowds roar with delight. Then dancers in brocade gowns and broad-brimmed hats knotted under the chin came out to twirl, holding drums like tall lollipops in one hand and strikers shaped like question marks in the other. What was that?

What did it mean? My own questions drummed too as I tried to memorize the images and find words to take back to Maw.

As children, we were allowed into backstage spaces. One morning as groups of visitors flooded the monastery, Deven and I were parked to eat our breakfast in His Holiness's meditation room. One afternoon Bardor Tulku led us up the hill and into the house where His Holiness, who loved birds, had constructed an aviary. A large brown bird—not a parrot—piously croaked a mantra that apparently asked for the Karmapa's compassionate gaze, "Karmapa Cheno, Karmapa Cheno." Another evening, when the monastery doors were closed to outsiders while a special *puja* was performed, we stood by an open window looking in on lines of lamas holding oil lamps, their faces illumined from below in quivering light.

Many of the high-ranking incarnate lamas at Rumtek were not much older than us. I watched with tongue-tied pride as Deven effortlessly charmed and connected with these boys about his age and they practiced their English. Each of these high lamas had his own quarters with his own cook and attendants. With each visit we were fed, and some mornings we ate multiple fried-egg breakfasts. Situ Rinpoche and Shamar Rinpoche gave us small black-and-white photographs of themselves as keepsakes, and we exchanged addresses with the promise to become pen pals.

In the dreamlike space of those few days, I often thought of how the bare brown slopes we had seen on our drive had metamorphosed into an abundance of growing green rice. Transformations, I thought, could happen in the flick of an eye—it all seemed a matter of perspective. I fingered my turquoise again, wishing I knew the secret of keeping the green constant.

:::

On the morning of our departure, Bardor Tulku ushered us into His Holiness's inner quarters. His Holiness was cross-legged on a sofa, and Mummy-la, who had just returned, sat on the beautiful carpet at his feet. I remembered Maw telling us that His Holiness sat up, cross-legged, through the night, for conscious dreaming. I imagined the past and future filing by in this space, paying their respects to his tranquil observation.

Mummy-la translated as His Holiness asked after Maw. He presented us each with a yellow Bhutanese hanging, red blessing threads, and packets of black blessing pills that reminded me of the beady pupils in the tiniest of Rahoul's gods' eyes. He also sent blessing packages for each member of our party who had been left behind. I felt his warm hospitality, and also a slight detachment, as though he recognized that in this lifetime we were nodding acquaintances, not that important to each other. Maybe later I would better understand the blessings unfolding for me from this experience; for now, I felt that I was Maw's representative. Deven, though, felt a deep connection and afterward said that he wondered why we had left Rumtek at all.

As a special gift to Maw, His Holiness brought out a plum-colored silk brocade Tibetan woman's robe that he explained had once belonged to his mother. As we accepted this bundle, I guiltily sensed that I should have more respect for Maw's aspirations. If even the Karmapa honored her like this, was it right that we mocked her as Madam Sadhu Maharaj?

(In no way could I foresee the day in 2004 when Maw discovered that the blessing pills that the Sixteenth Karmapa had sent her through his emissary appeared to have multiplied in their little silver container over the intervening years. She was then identified by an interpreter of His Holiness the Seventeenth Karmapa as perhaps being in possession of a rare, self-multiplying "mother pill." "Only people of rare faith can cause these pills to reproduce," we were told. Maw replied with a bemused laugh, exclaiming to her incredulous visiting daughters, "Well! You see!" The Seventeenth Karmapa, who had been born in Tibet and recognized by the Dalai Lama, had fled across the mountains to India as a teenager, then moved into a monastery quite close to the house where Maw lives in the Himalayas. Maya and I went down the hill on Mission Pill Return, offering the collection of tiny black pills to the strapping young Seventeenth Karmapa, who smiled but did not comment. In turn, he sent Maw a set of individually wrapped enlightenment pills.)

Usually it was Maw who returned home from spiritual adventures, overflowing with stories; this time it would be Deven and me. When we had finally crossed the border and could relax in the Jeep back to Darjeeling, we chatted in a low undertone, smiling at each other as we practiced the retelling of our adventures.

Twin Goddess

Maw and I returned to Bombay by ourselves. Maya and Jonathan set off to travel through eastern India, Deven and Tashi were visiting Tibetan settlements to the northwest, David had returned to the United States to recuperate from his bizarre summer experience before starting college, and Cupboard Swami was taking a break from our cupboard to do a pilgrimage.

Rahoul had unexpectedly returned to India. With only limited financial aid at Reed College, he had been working a number of part-time jobs and falling sick often. He had applied to transfer to the San Francisco Art Institute so he could focus on photography and filmmaking, and was waiting to hear whether he had been admitted. In the meantime, Paw had paid for a round-trip ticket for him to come home and Rahoul had flown in while we were still up north. *"BOMBAY,"* he wrote, *"hot, everything rotting, the house worn out, ugly. Paw—thin as a stick . . . drunk . . . two days and off to PATANE."* Rahoul was still visiting Young Swamiji when we came home, and Paw was away in Nasik. This left Maw and me—and an assortment of urugs—with the run of the Juhu house.

While we were up north, the garden had not been watered. This neglect followed several years of not having been able to afford a regular *mali,* and now only the hardy trees—pipal, bamboo, betel nut, coconut palm—carried green bounty. The butterfly-filled garden of my childhood was now a distant memory, like a mirage. "It's

« *"His eyes. His ears. Exactly his chin."* Kirin with portrait of Ramji Keshavji, her grandfather Sethji, 1985. Photograph by Rashmi Sethi.

too bad about my garden," Maw said sadly, sitting out on a cane stool and sipping coffee from her smooth, handleless mug.

"*Our* garden," I corrected, looking up from the chemistry homework I'd brought onto the porch.

Municipal water only ran through the taps for a short time in the morning and the evening. We now lined up buckets to fill as the taps sputtered and gurgled to life. "My water tank has rusted out," Maw explained to new urugs as she showed them around.

"*Our* water tank," I said, standing at her elbow. How had we landed in this situation? Were Paw's and Maw's finances really so bad after their respective failed business partnerships that we couldn't afford to fix the tank?

"Ever since I rented my mother's house to an American filmmaker who was having an affair with a union activist, we've been hearing strange clicks on the line," Maw told a visiting journalist friend. "Of course you can use my phone, but you should know it's probably tapped."

"*Our* phone!" I hissed. "I can't stand the way you go on about *my* this and *my* that. This is *our* house. We live in it together. You are so egotistical."

Ego was of course what ashram teachings said you should move beyond. I saw the gray green of Maw's eyes go flat.

"Just stop it, sweetie," Maw said, drawing in a breath. "I didn't mean it wasn't yours too. I'm sorry if that's the way you hear it. It's just that I'm trying to think of myself as independent from Narayan."

"Call him Paw, will you?" I stormed, turning on my heels.

When Maw was anxious she had always spoken louder, faster, at a higher pitch. I would have preferred to turn a deaf ear to her upset, but I couldn't help overhearing her confide in friends in the living room, consult with Cupboard Swami when he returned, or shout over the static and crossed connections of monsoon-damaged phone lines to friends downtown.

—*I should have seen the signs years ago. When we lived in Nasik, I thought it was just weekend relaxation. He worked so hard in Bombay during the week that I thought he needed the drinks to relax. It wasn't until I moved to Bombay eight years later that I understood it had become an addiction.*

—*My mother always thought this marriage was a terrible idea and was really upset by Narayan's drinking. I had to make it work just to avoid proving her right. It wasn't until after she died and there was no one around to say, "I told you so!" that I began to think of actually leaving him.*

—*I was too scared to leave when the kids were little. He used to threaten that since I'm a foreign wife, he'd take the kids and have me kicked out of India. I couldn't risk that. I tried to leave once and took the children to Delhi, but he said he would give up drinking and we came back.*

—I thought that at least I owned my mother's house, but it turns out that he transferred the papers into his own name. The wife's property is the husband's property—you know the logic. So it's his property now, and I don't have any security of my own. When Deven goes to college, Kirin will be the only one left at home. At least if there's a legal separation he'll be forced to help out more with finances.

—Divorce is too difficult with the current laws. I'd have to prove adultery, and that's just too distasteful. With charges of mental cruelty, I can at least get a legal separation.

Old family friends and newer urug supporters soothed Maw, agreeing that it was impossible to be married to an alcoholic. Cupboard Swami reassured her that she was right. Even Babaji agreed that separation was a good idea, Maw said.

At first I heard all this and went about my schoolwork, as though ignoring Maw's words might prevent them from becoming my reality. In Bombay in the early 1970s, parents simply did not divorce, let alone legally separate. I could think of just one classmate (also half-American, like me) with divorced parents, but the fallout of that divorce had resulted in her being adopted by an adoring uncle and aunt. Certainly, parents might argue, or not speak to each other for years, or even live apart, but they didn't advertise their disagreements through battles in court!

One Sunday evening, Maw and I returned from a trip to the ashram, squashed inside a second-class women's train compartment. At Andheri station, as we tried to step off the train, a press of women was trying to climb in. Maw made it forward to the platform, but a wall of bodies slammed me back into the compartment. The train lurched into motion, but I was still inside. In a last heave of bodies I found myself propelled from behind and fell out among shouts and screams. In the moment before I located Maw, I felt sheer panic. Already we were being stripped of many of the buffers that had separated us from the financial realities of regular people; my heart pounded with the knowledge that I could easily have been swept away in that anonymous, sweaty crush toward an unknown, unprotected future.

We rode a taxi the last stretch home, driving past the new developments that had recently erased the open fields of Vile Parle. Still raw and bruised, we reached the driveway and saw Paw's Ambassador. He was back from Nasik. I went into his room to greet him and found that his eyes were red, his speech slurred. Dobeyboy's energetically wagging stub of a tail pro-

vided a warmer welcome. I ran my hand over the heavy black hair along
Dobeyboy's back, and he closed his eyes, raising his chin. Then, still shaky,
I went to the opposite end of the house to wash away the dust and panic
of our trip.

I did not hear what preliminary words were fired between my parents.
But then both their voices were raised, and Paw's bellowing was louder:
"Get out of my house. If you want to go, just get out."

I began to chant to drown out what I heard:

> *Om jai tvam devi chāmunḍe jaya bhūtartihārini* . . .

> Om, victory to you, Goddess Chamunda,
> be victorious, destroyer of demons
> Victory to you, Goddess who pervades everything,
> Salutations to you, Dark Night. . . .

These were the opening lines of the *Argalastotram*, or "Bolt Hymn," a new
goddess chant that Young Swamiji had taught me. I continued chanting as I
washed my face and combed out my heavy braids.

Teenage blemishes were exploding across the startled face I saw in the
mirror. Young Swamiji had offered me prescriptions—*besan* chickpea flour
paste to replace soap, cowry shells dissolved in lemon as a night mask—but
I seemed too thin-skinned for any of these remedies. What adult stranger
was starting to emerge from inside me? I had recently developed a cutting
sarcasm and couldn't stop myself from saying flippantly mean things. Was
I on the way to growing a Rahoul-nose and matted leg hair? Or a heavy
mustache like Sethji's? Would I ever become lovable?

I turned to the dressing room alcove *puja* that had become mine once
Maw's *puja* had graduated to occupy an entire room. I had filled this small,
head-high space with Young Swamiji's Mother Patane Devi, Rahoul's picture of Swamiji as meditating Buddha, and assorted pictures of the Karmapa and young incarnate lamas that we had brought back from Sikkim. I
lit a stick of incense, trying to soak in the courageous optimism of Patane
Devi's form: eyes huge, weapons aloft. I was now in the part of the hymn
with the almost hynotic refrain

> *Rūpam dehi jayam dehi yasho dehi dvisho jahi*
> Grant me your form, grant me victory, grant me fame, destroy my
>   enemies.

As Swamiji had explained, enemies did not come only from outside but were also in our habits of mind. As the hymn continued, Patane Devi looked back steadily. Later that night, as Maw sobbed in the dark in her nearby bed, I continued to chant in an endless loop inside my head, leading my mind back toward the sacred words whenever it was tempted to rush off wailing.

Paw left the next morning without saying where he was going. The house was again quiet. Fatty Rasha was waiting near the school bus stop, her eyes crinkling with laughter. Class periods unfolded in predictable succession. The boys made the usual mean jokes about teachers' pronunciations or the regional background of our classmates, and the girls gathered for more whispered consultations on "chums," which by now we were all experiencing monthly. Once again, school was my refuge, and yet, after our trip north, I seemed to be watching everyone through the wrong end of binoculars.

Within a few days I developed a high fever. My body itched as though I could no longer stand being inside this half-Indian–half-American skin; my eyes hurt so much I could not bear to look around me. Worms of worry burrowed through my stomach. I tried to discipline my mind with a chant, but it continued to slump into inertia. With the resignation that comes with the lack of energy, I realized that staying away from school would spare me the reminder of how different I had become from everyone else with their settled, secure families.

Doctor De Souza announced that I had the measles. "What, she never had measles before?" he asked, snapping his black bag shut. "She's thirteen? Unfortunately at this age, the effects are more serious. Yes, for the fever you can use cold compresses."

I couldn't remember what I had written about the situation at home to Young Swamiji, but as I lay in bed with the measles his reply arrived on the detachable, self-addressed side of the postcard. When Maw brought in the afternoon post, I squinted at his words in the darkened room.

Patane, July 12, 1973

Sister Kirin,

. . . Have faith on Her. Hope you are doing the recitation regularly. Whatever will happen will happen for the best. Do not get worried at all. Face everything in a smiling way. It is life. Take it as a fun.

When Rahoul was here, I wrote to Maw and Rahoul also put a separate letter for her. Hope this reached her.

Please ask Maw to write to me with all the details.

Are Deven & Tashi back?

With love and best wishes to you all. . . .

Love. Yours, Swami Pranavananda.

Gradually my fever came down, though every comb or brush that touched my hair swept off bushy handfuls. Over the last few years, as my classmates and I became increasingly conscious of our changing bodies, my hair had been one of my strong points—it was not the silky, thick Fab Hair of our most admired classmate, but it filled the circle made between thumb and forefinger and so earned some admiration. Now my two braids were reduced to one wispy ponytail, and once again my ribs showed.

Maw lavished me with attention, producing a steady supply of the only things I would eat—sweet gruel or cream of tomato soup with the skins strained out. She also fed me spoonfuls of *gulkhand,* a mix of rose petals and sugar that our neighbor Usha-ben had sent over to reduce the heat in my body and stop my hair from falling. To keep me in bed as I recuperated, Maw read aloud every book wc had by Mary Renault. Reading usually transported me somewhere else, but now even ancient Greece seemed like another mirage, too insubstantial to grant comfort.

Rahoul returned from Patane, painfully thin but with a luxuriant black mustache that Sethji would have admired. He seemed wound up, in perpetual nervous motion, walking round and round a room even when he was having a conversation.

"Look, the camera is an extension of state of mind," Rahoul said to Maw as I listened in through the open door. "Photography is both the moment itself and an attitude toward that moment. I want my photographs to capture that essence of being. I've got to get it together to make films too, but everyone who makes films has money and connections. I could work on connections here in Bombay, but the way Paw is going I don't see any hope for backing from him. I've got to figure out how I can raise capital. If I could export old Hindu mythological films to America, I bet they'd have a big audience. . . ."

It seemed to me that I had fallen out of Rahoul's vision, he was so overwhelmed by worries about who he was, what he would do next, and how he would find the funds to do it. I waited for him to come through the open door and remind me that he had taught me to walk, to fly, and to read in mirrors. I wondered if he might fry up some potatoes and bring them in with ketchup. But when he wandered in to say hello, his mind was still somewhere else.

Maya and Jonathan, and then Deven and Tashi, returned. Paw, too, came home from Nasik, where he had cut down the mango grove and sliced up the farm into plots for "development." He remained segregated, off in his own room, avoiding Maw as she avoided him. We might all have remained in separate rooms if our Parsi friend Flukey hadn't dropped in for a visit.

Flukey was the self-titled "Sickest Man in Asia"—making light of the mysterious numbness and blindness that would sometimes keep him in bed. He was a tall, lanky man with a striking resemblance to Peter Sellers, and he always wore the head-to-toe white attire of a cricket player. After graduating from a British boarding school, he had spent much of his inheritance flying to every one of Maria Callas's concerts. Luckily, there was enough money left over that he could still afford a jet-set life in Bombay. Now he was friends with Lata Mangeshkar, the singing voice of most heroines in films. I had heard that Lata called him each day with a song (and on days that she couldn't, her sister Asha Bhonsle filled in). As Flukey worked up an appreciation for Indian popular and classical music, he sent his butler and a driver for music lessons so they could play outside the bathroom door as he lay soaking in his custom-made oversize bathtub.

The presence of a whimsical outsider is the best possible tonic for any strained family, and soon after Flukey unfolded himself from his long white sports car, everyone was rushing about to prepare for a group photograph. Even I got shakily out of bed to join the action. The Costume Trunk was thrown open, releasing the smell of mothballs; linen cupboards were ransacked, displacing cockroaches; props were pulled off walls, disturbing spiders. Soon we assembled in the bare space that had once been a garden.

Flukey posed at the center in his elegant white slacks, polo shirt tight around his sunken chest. He wore dark glasses and clutched a carved walking stick. Jonathan had twisted an oversize turban around his head and was wearing Nani's black graduation robe from the University of Michigan. His arm curved around Maya in her Tibetan dress from the summer. Ever the devoted mimic of Maya, I too was wearing a Tibetan dress, scratchy in the Bombay heat, and I stood blinking in the unfamiliar brightness of sunshine. Rahoul had wrapped his lean frame in a white sheet around his neck in imitation of Young Swamiji's robes. Deven brought out a Hopi mask but ended up holding it beside him. Tashi tilted the brim of a black cowboy hat. Flukey had coaxed Paw from his armchair, but no one could think of a costume, so Paw stood bare-chested, wearing a crumpled *lungi* and smelling of beer. Maw pointedly positioned herself as far from Paw as possible, still wearing her flour-stained apron from kneading and pounding bread. Dobeyboy raised his aristocratic head. Cupboard Swami was not yet awake for the day and so remained in the cupboard.

We posed. We preened. But when the roll of film was developed, all the frames were blank. "You must have exposed the film to too much heat," the man at the developing studio accused. Even film, I thought, reacted against the unhappiness simmering in the house.

I was back in school and couldn't join the others to visit Young Swamiji for the Rakshabandhan full moon. Maw was longing to go, but she stayed back partly to be with me and partly because she had already missed so many days of work on my account. I had braided *rakhis* for all my brothers, including Young Swamiji, and sent them along for Maya to tie on my behalf. Soon Young Swamiji reported back:

                                                              August 15, 1973

Kirin Devi,
Thanks! For your *rakhi* and the letter. It was very good.

   Yes we had a good time here during the last Purnima. You were remembered by all of us. On behalf of you Maya tied all the *rakhis* . . .

   Here everything is ok. All green. Rivers dancing. New addition—3 tigers. It is a fun to hear them roaring.

   You will get all the news from your crazy brothers. So, what else to write?

   Please keep me informed about all that happens there. Hope you are doing your studies well. . . .

   With blessings and love.

   Jai Jagadamba. Yours, Swami Pranavananda

I read the postcard while still standing in my school uniform, smiling with pleasure. Just handling the card connected me to rivers and tigers and good wishes for my studies. I thought of Rehana Ma's psychic vision in Delhi a few years earlier. *"Another person in the group hasn't as yet joined. You will meet up later."* Could this new family member, born outside the family yet belonging to us, be Young Swamiji?

But to recall Rehana Ma was also to remember other words spoken in

"Yes we had a good time here during the last Purnima." From left: Deven, Rahoul,
Young Swamiji, Jonathan, and Maya, 1973. Photograph by Rahoul Contractor.

her frail voice. *"Just one or two lives ago, you were all together in a building when
it collapsed."* Here we were again, our home tumbling around us.

Rahoul left for San Francisco, then Maya and Jonathan went to Los An-
geles. Dobeyboy, alert barker of the night, was poisoned during an outbreak
of thefts in the neighborhood. I knew that soon Deven would be applying
to colleges in America. Tashi spoke of going to a Tibetan settlement in the
north to study Tibetan painting. Maw again talked about the possibility of
moving away from Bombay. I huddled close to my homework.

:::

All along the curve of Juhu Beach, cottages and coconut groves were coming down. Apartment buildings with stretches of balcony facing the sea
were rising higher than any of the trees they replaced. Hotels were booming, partly thanks to oil-rich Gulf Arabs. Many of these big hotels channeled
their sewage straight into the sea; Paw shrugged: "After all, it's the Turd
World—what can you expect?" Seashells were disappearing, and plastic
bags gathered like deflated jellyfish along the shore.

I hated the ever-present sounds of construction: the clink-clink-clink of
stones being broken into gravel, the crunch of gravel being shoveled, the

chop and crash of trees being felled, the vroom and beep-beep-beep of big reversing trucks, the bells marking the ends of work shifts, the whistles warning of imminent blasts. Most of the construction workers were refugees from distant, drought-stricken villages. I walked past construction sites unable to look too long at these men and women, displaced from their homes, living in makeshift shacks, thin limbs baked by heat. The men squatted on scaffolding, the women carried open basins of building materials on their heads, and malnourished, orange-haired children played in the heaps of sand.

Deven started studying each day from Rahoul's SAT book and began drafting essays for small liberal arts colleges. The SAT exam was to be given downtown, in a place hard to reach by public transport. Deven and I formed a delegation, taking several changes of bus to Byculla, to ask Paw if we could have the car on that day.

Byculla used to be a fashionable Victorian suburb with a zoo and botanical gardens, but by the 1970s it was run down, filled with cotton mills and big bristly sewer rats that trotted along the sidewalks even in broad daylight. The Byculla apartment occupied the upper floor of one of the many buildings Sethji had built in the early part of the century; downstairs was a school. The apartment was furnished with Japanese Victorian furniture that Sethji had bought wholesale at the docks, heavy carved pieces that made for a somber atmosphere. Sethji had tiled the floors in a black and white pattern that suggested boxes either endlessly stacked or endlessly descending with Escher-like energy. Some of Sethji's previous wives had lived in this apartment too, and one bed was said to be haunted, certain to toss you among the boxes if you made the mistake of sleeping there. (Ba indignantly discounted the rumor of previous wives' ghosts: "If there were ghosts in this apartment, do you think your grandfather would have been able to make the kind of money in Bombay that he did?" She did, however, blame the breakup of our 13 Janki Kutir household on an unidentified ghost who came with the property and lived in the pipal tree that faced the back porch.)

Paw sat in a shadowy upstairs room beneath a dangling light bulb and beside a tall bottle of beer. The sound of children chanting times tables drifted up from the school below, competing with the honking of traffic and cawing of crows. It was midday, but Paw was still unwashed, unshaven, in a grimy sleeveless undershirt and a *lungi* speckled with holes burned by his cigarette ash. Cockroaches occasionally emerged from edges of the room to scuttle across the floor.

The Byculla cook served us strong, overly sweet tea in little stained and chipped cups, and Paw retold his favorite joke, which Maw had never found funny: *"You look melancholy,"* one man said to another in a bar. *"So do you,"* the second man responded. *"Head like a melon, face like a collie."*

Then we asked for the car, and Paw's bloodshot eyes turned away.

"It's too much trouble for the driver," he said. "Too much driving."

Deven and I took turns explaining why having the car would make it easier to take the exam. Paw wouldn't budge. "The driver can't be expected to do this," he said. "Bombay has too much traffic. Byculla to Juhu to town is too much."

My tongue swung out of its scabbard. "What kind of father are you?" I demanded. "Do you care more about your driver than your children?"

Deven looked away forbearingly; I feared that once again, I had managed to embarrass him when all I was doing was trying to help. Paw stared out through the open doors and over the wrought-iron balcony. Anger was still shaking and roiling me, but I also wished I knew how to offer apologies: the soft words of a loving, lovable daughter. In our perpetual lurching between feast (recently sold property) and famine (money running out), was Paw too proud to tell us that he currently didn't have the money for petrol?

An insight hovered, indistinct, not yet accessible to words. I understood that to Paw, his children could seem like extensions of Maw. In the rift that had opened between them, we had ended up on her side. His anger toward her also singed his perceptions of us. We were loud, self-absorbed, demanding, unsympathetic toward his "health." We had callously turned our backs on him, and it was because of us that he sat here alone and abandoned as cockroaches scuttled.

In the dim mottled mirrors of this room of exile, I glimpsed Paw's helplessness, his desperate clinging to Mani Driver as his regular supplier of bottles. Paw needed his alcohol so badly that if we stood between him and his supply, he couldn't allow himself to need us.

Paw broke the long silence, barking for the Mehtaji accountant, a man with the sharp face of a bandicoot. Mehtaji unlocked a cupboard and produced a bundle of stapled notes that Paw extended toward us, notes fluttering in his unsteady grasp.

"Take a taxi," he said. He attempted to smile. "Take a taxi home too and buy something for yourselves if you like."

I hung my head, miserable with the reminder that children were a burden and an expense. Paw had not granted us the use of his car, but his attempt to make an effort played at my heart like the poignant asymmetries between the ascending and descending notes of his favorite raga, "Bhatiyar."

::::

For my December examinations, I set my alarm for five o'clock each morning, then bathed, chanted goddess hymns, and studied until it was time for breakfast and the 7:30 bus. Maw looked on, astonished as always that I was bent on such a bourgeois goal as good grades. I kept my focus on reporting those grades to Young Swamiji, whom I knew I could count on for applause.

During our winter visit to Nasik, Ba was startled afresh by how, having lost some baby fat, my face resembled Sethji's. *"His eyes,"* she repeated as if mesmerized. *"His ears. Exactly his chin."*

Seeing my thinned hair, Ba diagnosed *nazar,* the evil eye. Her buffalo Manik-bai looked on blandly as Ba directed me to stand in the sunny courtyard. She circled a lemon counterclockwise around my head, muttering incantations, then cut up the lemon to throw in different directions. Next she sat me down on the upstairs balcony and took on Chanda-phui's role, soaking my scalp with oil. "If you want your hair to grow back, you have to feed it good things," Ba clucked. "I don't know why girls these days think they can have nice hair if they don't feed it properly!"

I continued chanting my goddess hymns each morning, and in Nasik I settled on the low square mat before Ba's *puja* cupboard. The narrow shelves were lined with all her favorite gods, goddesses, and gurus. Since she did *puja* first thing in the morning, fragrant flowers that she had offered already mingled their scents with the smell of *agarbatti* sticks and the smoke of ghee lamps. The deities looked on.

Viewing these familiar images with fresh eyes, I noticed *"Jai Chamunda Ma"* written in Gujarati over a framed black-and-white photograph of twin goddesses, leaning together with long black hair, nose rings, and crowns. I also noticed a square, flat silver *yantra* inscribed with a six-pointed silver star in an eight-petaled lotus.

Chamunda was another name for Kali, and Kali was the goddess Young Swamiji had first connected to as a small, motherless child. I recalled the images of Kali we had joined our palms before in Calcutta: her dark skin, fierce eyes, and protruding tongue. Young Swamiji said that Kali was related to *kala,* or time; as the power of time, she undid things as they were, making new creations possible.

"Ba, why is Chamunda here double, like Randhal Ma?" I asked.

"Because that's how she is," Ba declared. "See, this is our *kuldevi,* our lineage goddess: Chamunda of Chotila. Her temple is on the Chotila hill near Ahmedabad. We can visit there sometime."

I was excited that sacred mythology from Paw's family and from our Goddess-worshipping Young Swamiji intersected in the figure of Chamunda. Back in Bombay, I tried to figure out the riddle of why she too was double by looking into Maw's English translation of the goddess epic *Durga Saptashati.* I found Chamunda in the third major demon-vanquishing episode.

Two arrogant demon brothers, Shumbha and Nishumbha, have taken over the universe. They have evicted the Gods from heaven and usurped their roles. The Gods gather to pray for help. They praise the Goddess, honoring her as existing within all beings, in many forms.

As the Gods offer up their chanted petition, Shiva's wife Parvati, daughter of the mountains, comes to bathe in the river Ganga. "Who is being praised?" she asks. Another lovely, shining goddess emerges from her body, saying, "Me!" Parvati turns dark, becoming Kalika, and withdraws into the mountains.

The goddess who leaps out from Parvati's body in response to the Gods' praise is called Ambika, Durga, or Chandika. Chanda and Munda, henchmen of the demon brothers, notice her stunning beauty. They suggest to Shumbha and Nishumbha that since the brothers now control everything fabulous and powerful in the universe, it is only appropriate they should acquire this gorgeous woman too.

So Shumbha sends Chanda and Munda with a marriage proposal: if not for himself, then for his brother.

The Goddess smiles and replies that unfortunately she's vowed to marry only someone who defeats her in battle. Chanda and Munda report back to Shumbha, and he is enraged. He sends his top general with sixty thousand soldiers and the command to drag her in by the hair. But when the general advances, the Goddess snorts contemptuously, reducing him to ashes, and the lion she is riding tramples, dismembers, and kills all the troops.

Shaking with rage, Shumbha dispatches Chanda and Munda with further battalions of demon soldiers and instructions to drag back this uppity woman. The demons swarm around the Goddess in a giant attack. The beautiful Goddess becomes angry. She scowls, and Kali bursts from her brow: an emaciated, sunken-eyed, terrifying goddess who roars with a wide-open mouth.

Kali sets upon the demon troops. She stuffs them into her mouth, crunches them between her teeth. Chanda and Munda also attack her with their arrows and discuses, but Kali just laughs and roars more, teeth glittering as she swallows the weapons they hurl. The goddess riding the lion, Chandika, rushes at the two demons and with her sword beheads them.

Kali lifts the heads of Chanda and of Munda, one in each hand. Roaring with laughter, she presents them to Chandika, saying, "Here are the heads of Chanda and Munda as animal offerings in this sacrifice of battle. You'll kill Shumbha and Nishumbha yourself."

Chandika playfully responds to Kali, "Since you've brought me both Chanda and Munda, from now on you'll be known as Chamunda."

The epic moved on to describe how the other demons were killed and order and calm restored. I thrilled to see these powerful female figures set the universe back into order. But I was also puzzled: which of the two goddesses really killed Chanda and Munda? If it was Chandika with her sword, then why did Kali make the offering? Was Chandika honoring Kali's crucial help in distracting the two demons? And hadn't Parvati earlier split into Chandika and a different form of Kali? What did the twin image really mean?

: : :

Maw's feminist lawyer was making progress in drafting a legal separation and financial settlement. "He doesn't have cash for a settlement, though," Maw said. "The only way to do it will be to sell the house. Then if you go to boarding school, I'll go to the ashram. You have just a few more years before you write the SATs yourself and go to college in America."

"If you wanted to dump me in a boarding school, why did you even have me in the first place?" I demanded. Then quickly, in case she responded that I hadn't been her idea at all, but the product of Sethji's and Nani's combined wishes, I pressed my attack. "I'm tired of your being this big Martyrji, this great Madam Sadhu Maharaj, when you're not even being a responsible mother! All you want to do is gallivant around trying to become a saint."

"Sweetie, figuring out what to do is hard for me too," said Maw.

"I am absolutely not going to be dumped in a boarding school," I stormed.

What was this nonsense that Rahoul had started? What made Maw think she could renounce the world just because he went off to an ashram? Maw often observed that it was normal to be furious at your mother at fourteen, which infuriated me further. If she was the person most immediately responsible for knocking down the walls that gave me shelter, I felt she deserved no sympathy.

Maw talked more to Cupboard Swami, other urugs, and assorted family friends while I glared from afar. She took out my chart.

"She has this difficult Moon-Saturn opposition to start with," Maw reported to Cupboard Swami. "And now Saturn is transiting the moon in her first house, opposing her natal Saturn. Her whole sense of personal self is being constricted and undone."

"Don't blame the stars," I exploded from the next room.

Maw decided to appeal to Babaji's authority. On a Sunday when she had managed to procure a ride to Ganeshpuri for us, she led me to Babaji's marble perch. As usual, smiling, moist-eyed devotees stood around him, drinking in his presence. The courtyard smelled of incense, marigolds, and tuberoses. The marble floor was cool beneath our feet.

Maw stepped up to tell Babaji that I was objecting to her joining the ashram. I stood mutinously behind her, acutely aware of my own angular unattractiveness in the midst of this regal spectacle. Pulling me up like this before Babaji was unfair. If I were to show any spiritual sensitivity, I would surely agree that my mother should devote the rest of her life to her guru and her pursuit of enlightenment. I reminded myself, though, that Young Swamiji had stood firm and not given in to the ashram scene.

Babaji's head turned in my direction as Maw spoke. He might have been examining me through his dark glasses, or he might have been looking over my head. His beard had developed more gray in the years that I had known him. "Why don't you let your mother come to the ashram?" he asked.

I wanted so much to say something about how it was a mother's duty to look after her children; to this day I am not sure if I actually muttered it aloud. More likely, I held my ground by just not answering, by reining in every impulse to be sweet and agreeable and to release my mother to become a saint if she chose.

Babaji remained turned in my direction. It was possibly the first time he had paid attention to me as me, not as Rahoul's sister, Maya's sister, or Didi's daughter. I held my back straight and tried not to drop my eyes from the dark reflecting surface of his glasses, but already I was breaking down, apologetically smiling.

"She said that if I want to send her to boarding school I should go along with her," Maw reported.

Babaji's mustache and beard parted to show perfectly white false teeth. Maybe the image of Maw's going back to school like an overgrown teenager had tickled his sense of humor. Then he waved a hand. It was time for us to move on so that others awaiting audience could step up. "You should go to 'boarding' too," he instructed Maw. "Then, when her schooling is finished, you can come to the ashram."

The guru had spoken. Our destiny seemed set.

::::

If we were going to find a new life at a boarding school, the first question was which one? After all the years during which my family dismissed my studying as "little Kirin doing her thing," Maw now brandished my good grades as trump cards that would allow me—and her—to get into the school of our choosing.

Deven received a scholarship to St. John's College in New Mexico, which Maya and Jonathan had attended before him. We saw him off in May, and then Maw and I began traipsing around southern India, trying to decide on an English-language boarding school we could afford and where she might possibly teach art. We traveled by train and overnight buses, staying with friends whenever we could.

After meeting school principals in the hill stations of Ootacamund and Kodaikanal, we visited Rishi Valley School, near Bangalore. Maybe because *rishi* meant "sage," and because the philosopher J. Krishnamurthi had founded the school, Cupboard Swami decided to join us.

"I can't show up with *an urug in robes*," I objected in a panic.

"He's only with us for part of the trip," Maw said defensively. "You know, you have to stop living by what other people think."

We arrived at Rishi Valley during summer vacation, so luckily no students were around to gape at our odd threesome. We stayed in the school's guest house. To reduce expenses, the three of us shared a room. Around us, the summer heat blazed so strong and dry that when we washed our clothes by hand under a cold tap each day, they were perfectly crisp and ready to be folded within ten minutes.

The principal offered Maw a job teaching art and the use of a tiny unfurnished cottage. "Can you see yourself here?" Maw asked me.

I liked the landscape, a range of low hills strewn with boulders, and the sense of a wide high sky. I already loved the several-hundred-year-old banyan tree so enormous that it framed an outdoor stage for student performances. I had worried about attending a convent school, being ignorant of Catholic hymns and rituals, but here at Rishi Valley, I could learn more Sanskrit chants and how to play the *veena* like the goddess Sarasvati.

All the same, I refused to give Maw the satisfaction of a positive vote. "I don't know," I said, looking out the window, past the drying clothes.

"That means yes?" asked Maw.

"*I don't know!*"

"Rishi Valley looks like the best solution," said Maw. She still seemed worried. She appealed to Cupboard Swami: "What do you think, is this a good place?"

"For a school, it's not bad," he replied.

"Sweetie, what do you think?" Maw appealed to me again.

"Do what you want."

"Rishi Valley?"

"I don't care."

"Okay, so we're moving to Rishi Valley," Maw concluded. We prepared to return to Bombay. Cupboard Swami traveled on to explore other temples and ashrams in the south. To my relief, he chose somewhere else to live.

On learning of our planned move, Young Swamiji also played on the meaning of *rishi*: "*I am sure when you come out from the Rishi Valley,*" he wrote, "*you will be like Gargi, Maitreyi, and other great Lady Saints who realized the TRUTH.*"

Becoming a great lady saint was not on my agenda; other family members could work on saintliness, thank you very much. But I remembered that Gargi and Maitreyi had been wise, confident women described in the *Brihadaranyaka Upanishad* that Rahoul had once left lying around in English translation. I didn't think that Young Swamiji really expected me to realize the TRUTH in full capitals, but his joking confidence seemed a good omen for the exams I was now focused on writing from Rishi Valley School.

: : :

Maw was permanently drenched in sweat as she packed up fourteen years of her life—and my entire lifetime—in the premonsoon heat of 1974. I couldn't bear to be near my mother. Her agitation filled the space around her like a toxin that crossed into my own veins. I refused to help pack. As she sorted through our things, I lost myself in Agatha Christie mysteries and Readers' Digest Condensed Books borrowed from neighbors. Maw distributed some objects, art, and furniture among friends and directed servants to move other things across the driveway to Nani's house, which Paw had claimed as his own. She filled and sealed boxes for a freight truck to take south, and I continued reading. Every morning I woke up hoping I had imagined all the changes.

I was terrified by this move. I didn't like myself anymore, and the discomfort of being in my own skin raged in an angry infection across my face. How could I be the new girl forced to explain myself, my sari-wearing American mother, the absence of a father, and possible visitations from urugs who found their way south? Why had I taken the cross-cultural mix among my Bombay classmates for granted? What were the chances of finding another group where my own half-ness didn't stand out? Where would I ever find another Fatty Rasha? I could no longer connect to Young Swamiji's chants; they seemed to belong in some other, more hopeful parallel universe from which I was now in exile.

All around me, storylines I'd hoped to record in *The Family* were foundering. Maya and Jonathan were not strolling through rose gardens on a country estate in the hazy glow of happy-ever-after, as I'd hoped, but were struggling to find the right professions on which to focus their abundant creativity and skills. In the meantime, they were moving into one of Babaji's American ashrams.

Rahoul had enrolled at the San Francisco Art Institute to study photography and film. He was working several jobs simultaneously and wrote fiercely to Paw that he wanted to be officially disinherited as the eldest son from any stake in the dwindling family property. To Maw, he wrote that he was coming out as gay, news that she accepted with aplomb. I took this in as yet another of the endless interesting surprises that Rahoul brought us.

Deven's absence was still so fresh that I felt it mostly as an emptiness when I wondered what to do next and realized I couldn't check to see what he was reading so that I could read it too. He had left behind a guitar, though (given to him by a South African urug who had ended up in a Canadian jail for importing sitar boxes lined with marijuana). I opened to the first lesson in *Teach Yourself Classical Guitar* and started working on developing calluses.

Tashi continued to be in limbo. He had abandoned his plan to study Tibetan art and was back in Bombay, smoking heavily and spending long hours with friends from the Juhu village. His latest thought was that he would move to Switzerland and join up with his siblings from his birth family, who now all lived there. In the meantime, he would stay on in Bombay with Paw.

Ba still hadn't located the right holy man to help excavate her treasure. Though our Nasik fields had grown rows of ugly apartment buildings, Ba insisted that the white serpent was still guarding the buried hoard. Yet Ba's supreme authority was slipping. Her Nasik grandsons had grown tall, shifting household power toward their mother. Manik-bai's milk had dried up and she had retired to the *panjrapoli,* an old-age home for cattle, so Ba no longer had a reason to croon toward the well. Now she was preparing to leave Nasik and move in to Nani's house to look after Paw.

Chanda-phui's miracle baby had turned into a willful toddler, and the main word in her vocabulary was now an elongated, threatening nasal *"Na-hiiin!"*—"No!" The afterglow of triumph I had imagined she would always carry had given way to dazed exhaustion. As she continued to grind at *supari,* her teeth were being further reduced to stubs.

Paw's hangers-on were handling the sale of the house, which surely meant that he was getting swindled. I tried to imagine what it would be like to continue living in Juhu with endless money shortages, the barren garden, the broken water tank, the apartment buildings towering above us. I thought I would prefer surviving among known difficulties to taking on the unknown, which to me seemed as rough and treacherous as the gray monsoon sea.

Paw arrived from Byculla one evening to meet up with the Gujarati family that was buying the house. The buyer pontificated on his intentions to add walls, grills, doors, and a high fence. In his plan, the deep porches opening out from the front and back of the house would become enclosed rooms.

"The architectural design will be completely spoiled," Maw said, almost in tears. Behind her words, I heard the complaint that her artistic vision had never been appreciated, and especially not by Paw. In forcing her to vacate the house, he was once again desecrating her creative spirit.

"Bombay has changed," the owner-to-be warned. "Nobody lives like this anymore, without proper doors. You must have many locks."

"They want the latest prison look," observed Paw after they left. "I suppose it will be an interesting experience to live beside a prison." Behind his words, I heard the self-pitying accusation that Maw's headstrong energy, her running off to an ashram and now leaving him, was forcing him to live in an ugly, constricted space not of his choosing.

On the train headed south, I refused to talk to Maw. I wanted to blame someone for dismantling life as I'd known it, and Maw was the closest target. As we pulled farther and farther from Bombay, I became more and more agitated, unable to focus on the passing scenery or the novels we had packed. Maw, though, had become very calm, enjoying the views of flooded rice fields through the window. When the cries of tea vendors—*chaiwala chai-e-ee*—turned into calls of *coffee-coffee-coffee,* we knew we had crossed into the complex of languages and regions that Bombay people usually lumped together as "the South."

We had to wait for a few hours at a small junction where our bogie would be attached to a connecting train. The platform outside was almost deserted, except for a family of curious, light tan lungur monkeys with wrinkled brows and blinking yellow eyes. The ground was still moist from a rain. Unwilling to chat with Maw, I started to sketch a monkey mother and the baby clinging to its neck.

"Things aren't going to be so bad, sweetie," said Maw, watching me. "Within a week you'll have new friends."

"I don't want to think about it," I growled through clenched teeth.

"At least allow yourself to imagine things that could make you happy," Maw said. "Even if they don't come to pass, you'll have had the pleasure of imagining them. You can at least hope for things, you know?"

"I don't want to imagine *anything*! Why hope for things you can't count on happening?" I was incensed that Maw could so happily rely on her imagination. Since when were children supposed to be the sturdy realists, bringing down parental castles in the air?

Maw tried again. "Okay, so let's not even think about the future. Right now is pretty good, isn't it? We're not in a big steamy city anymore. Here are the monkeys watching us, and it's just rained. Isn't wet earth a great smell?"

I breathed in the moist, dark, green-growing smell. I didn't say it, but if I focused right here on this little platform, with jade green weeds growing abundantly along the edge, I had to agree. The past and future fell away; this moment wasn't that bad. The monkeys watched, already expecting us to move onward. As Swamiiji said, *"It is life. Take it as a fun."*

Leaving my home was my first big lesson in letting go of the story and setting I thought appropriate to my life; I had yet to learn that a revised plot could also work out. In the bag at my side, I was carrying my picture of Young Swamiji's Mother sheltered between the pages of the goddess epic. I pressed the bag closer as though trying to absorb blessings. Inside my head I recited the last lines of the goddess hymn that Young Swamiji had taught me, slowing to a different tempo, his voice saturated with emotion.

Yāh sāmpratam chaudatadaitya tā pite . . .

Now, at this moment, tormented by demons
We worship you as the gods worshipped you

When we remember you, at that instant you destroy our calamities
With devotion, we bend our heads to you.

It was at this point, just as the hymn ended, that Parvati appeared to ask who was being praised, and a goddess appeared from her own body to answer.

: : :

If I could swoop in from the present, I would murmur in my own ear, cupping my hands among teenage Kirin's dark curls to assure her that the girls in her new class will arrive in a friendly delegation the first evening; that gregarious Maw will bond with many students, making friends on behalf of her awkward daughter; that one morning that girl in the long, paneled blue skirt will walk through winter sun beside the old and still handsome sage Krishnamurti, affectionately called Jiddu by Rishi Valley students, adding him to the possible saints she has known. I would tell Kirin that she will like Rishi Valley School and be grateful for the cultural knowledge and experience she would not have gained in Bombay. Above all, this school will be a doorway to college in America, the first step in the sequence of degrees that can make a skinny girl into a scholar with a professional excuse to enjoy the many shapes and colors of stories.

The Clasp

"The image of the 'gods' eyes' wrenches my heart," Maw wrote by e-mail from the Himalayan foothills, responding to the first chapter of this book. She was reminded, she said, of "the hard stare, as though already from the other side beyond the boundary of suffering, imposed as though pasted on the frail face."

She didn't have to name Rahoul. I could still picture his disoriented gaze as his strength and eyesight failed. He died from AIDS-related complications on the Sunday after Thanksgiving in 1985, just a few months after he turned thirty-two.

Throughout Rahoul's life, ways of seeing remained central to his creativity. "For me, the most important function of art is to evoke a contemplative state of both ecstasy and transcendence," Rahoul wrote in a 1984 graduate review statement for his M.F.A. in photography at the University of New Mexico. "Altered states entail altered perception of color visual coordination. I strive to imitate and emphasize the process of meditative visual reaction to the color of light."

After transferring to the San Francisco Art Institute in 1974, Rahoul dedicated himself to photography over other kinds of art. Today a few of Rahoul's striking photographs hang on the walls of his siblings' homes. A few are wrapped in plastic to protect against monsoons and insects in Nani's trunks, which Maw sorts through from time to time. Some are with his friends, and some are buried deep in

« *"Whatever happens, face it fearlessly."* Swamiji and Rahoul, early 1980s.
Photograph by Rahoul Contractor.

the climate-controlled archives of small museums, seen only by the occasional intern.

I have entered Rahoul's name in a Google search. Perhaps a gallery
where he had once showed his photographs would mention him in its records? Maybe a museum would note the acquisition of his work? Rahoul
Contractor. Rahoul Narayan Contractor. Rahoul N. Contractor. I tried these
combinations, as well as Rahoul Ramji, a professional name he briefly used,
bypassing Paw in favor of Sethji. So far, my brother seems to have left no
trace in the brave new cyberworld that he never knew.

I wrote my Indian Certificate of Secondary Education exams from Rishi
Valley School at sixteen, then followed the family tradition of studying for
the Scholastic Aptitude Test from Rahoul's now well-worn textbook. Rahoul wrote cautioning Maw that I was really too young to go abroad by myself. Maw considered the possibility of our proceeding together to a college
in India, but Paw was drinking heavily again and, with inflation, the financial settlement she had received was shrinking all the time. When I was
offered scholarships, I chose Sarah Lawrence College in Bronxville, New
York, and Maw moved to the Ganeshpuri ashram. I arrived in the United
States in June 1976 with the usual allowance for travelers from India at that
time—eight dollars. By the fall I was caught up in studying and work-study
jobs.

Maya and Jonathan drove me to college as my honorary parents. Later,
they lived in New York near Babaji's Manhattan ashram. During my junior
year, Rahoul moved from San Francisco to Manhattan with his boyfriend,
an African American ballet dancer. They broke up soon after the move; over
the next few years, Rahoul looked for connection in the bathhouses, piers,
and discos of the 1970s gay scene in New York. I continued keeping company with the rattling radiators in college dorm rooms, going to bed at ten
o'clock each night so I could be up before dawn to meditate and chip away
at my studies.

"You're still such a baby!" Rahoul said, seeing my life. "How'd you get
to be so square?" When I came into the city to meet him one weekend, he
poured a rush of sugar from a steel and glass container into his coffee, then
looked up to compare my circumscribed routines with those of efferves-
cently sociable Stella, fifty years my senior, whom he teased as his "good
God!-mother." "Even Stella has more fun!" Rahoul said. "You know, death
isn't as frightening as old age."

"Don't!" I responded.

I still wasn't sure when Rahoul was making things up to tease me. How much should I believe of his exuberant descriptions of popping "uppers" and "downers" to modulate his mood, or his mentions of other drugs? What should I make of his accounts of the theme parties and tableaux at his favorite club? How enthusiastic should I be about his ideas for films he hoped someday to gather the backing for: the Ramayana rock musical; the story of the mad woman who was recognized as the Mother of Creation; the confessions of an aged temple dancer?

Whenever gurus were mentioned, Rahoul said that if he'd gone into that business he'd be a millionaire by now. He stayed away from large ashrams but remained close to Swamiji, exchanging letters and visiting Patane now and then. During one of these visits, he and Swamiji posed together in yet another playful photograph, both wearing robes anchored around the neck, Swamiji's in ocher and Rahoul's in white. "Sure I meditate," Rahoul said to me once. "My whole life is a kind of meditation. I see the blue pearl all the time when I'm in the darkroom."

During the early 1980s, when I was absorbed by graduate school in anthropology at Berkeley, I knew Rahoul mostly by phone. His voice would burst over the line on occasional Sundays: "Hi darling, how're things going?" Hearing him rush from subject to subject, I often felt slow and unimaginative, still the staid younger sibling, her nose buried in homework. He too started graduate school, moving to New Mexico in 1982 to formally study photography. For a while we were not that close. After receiving his M.F.A. he moved back to New York, still hoping to break into the art world. In the meantime he worked as a skilled printer in a photographic color laboratory.

In the spring of 1985, Rahoul fell mysteriously ill. He telephoned one morning and said he had been throwing up; I could hear a male friend in the background. At first doctors thought he had a bad flu, then that it was amoebic dysentery or maybe pneumonia or even tuberculosis. Growing constantly weaker, unable to endure the strong chemicals used in developing color photographs, Rahoul was forced to stop working. His godmother Stella invited him to recuperate in her studio apartment in midtown Manhattan. I visited from Berkeley and found Rahoul very thin, wrapped in a sheet but sporting an Afghan headdress from Stella's hall closet. "New York's a drag when you're sick," Rahoul said. "I'm thinking of going back to the Hindu Kush mountains."

"Oh Ra-hoool," snorted Stella, then in her seventies but elegant as ever. For someone as independent as her, sharing space in a studio apartment was a huge gift of love. From the top of her bookshelf, the last extant Rahoul-being watched with concerned gods' eyes.

The media churned with stories about the mysterious illness spreading among gay men. We held to the hope that Rahoul's weakness was a reaction to the toxic photo chemicals and that all he needed was rest. That summer I went to India to work on my dissertation on storytelling as a form of religious teaching. I was intrigued by the myths, legends, folktales, and personal narratives that I had observed Old Swamiji recounting to visitors who stopped in to seek his counsel. Later, looking through Rahoul's notebooks, I found some of the same stories, almost verbatim, that he had also been inspired to write down on the mountaintop fifteen years earlier.

In New York, Rahoul's energies drained further, and more debilitating symptoms hemmed him in. By the summer, soon after a test for the HIV virus was discovered, he was diagnosed with AIDS. Maya cabled Maw. Drawing on the last of Nani's college fund for the grandchildren, Maw traveled to America on her second trip since 1951.

New Mexico had always been a kind of family base in the United States. This was where Maya and Deven had gone to college, where Rahoul had attended graduate school, and where many family friends still lived. Choosing the profession of our divine and human ancestors, Deven had begun graduate school in architecture in Albuquerque. Maw and Rahoul rented a small house in Albuquerque not far from Deven's home, and after a few weeks, Maya resigned from her job in Berkeley and joined them to help out.

Paw and I remained in India through the fall, sharing worried updates over the phone or whenever I could visit Bombay. Ba set to performing rituals and visiting temples, astrologers, and holy men. I mostly sat on the floor of Old Swamiji's quarters as visitors came and went, and listened with particular attentiveness to his stories that affirmed a serene larger order beyond suffering and loss. Sometimes I found tears rolling toward my chin, but I wiped them with the back of my hand. Surely, a cure would be found any day? How could someone as vitally young and alive as Rahoul not continue living?

In November Paw and I flew together to Albuquerque. We carried many potions, pilgrimage relics, and blessings from Ba. Young Swamiji sent a big laminated close-up of Saptashring Devi's coral-colored face with her enormous goddess eyes to watch over Rahoul. Young Swamiji had also borrowed my tape recorder overnight to record a message. *"Whatever happens, face it fearlessly,"* Young Swamiji advised Rahoul. He went on to sing the "Eight Verses on Nirvana" by the Adi Shankaracharya, whom he had long ago posed as before Rahoul's camera:

Mano-buddhy-ahankāra-chittāni nāham . . .

I am not my mind, my intellect, my thoughts, nor my sense of self,
Not my hearing, taste, smell, nor vision
Not ether nor earth, not fire nor air
I am joyous consciousness, I am Shiva, I am Shiva. . . .

True to his string of fused Gauri-Shankar *rudraksha* beads, Swamiji finished up those eight verses honoring Lord Shiva, "the Benevolent One," and moved on to another eight verses by Adi Shankaracharya addressing the goddess Bhavani, "Giver of Existence."

Na tāto na mātā na bandhurna dātā . . .

No father, no mother, no brother, nor helper
Son, daughter, protector, nor servant
No partner, no skills, no job do I have.
You are my only refuge, only refuge, Bhavani . . .

Rahoul listened from the pillows, eyes huge in his gaunt face.
"I'm so sorry I'm letting you all down," he said. "I didn't mean to be the one who died first."
"You always were precocious," said Maya, holding his hand.
Paw was going through a dry period. He sat at the edge of Rahoul's bed, joking and chatting, then going out to refill his pipe with a fallen face and shaking hands. Maw experimented with recipes that Rahoul might be coaxed to eat despite the thrush on his tongue. Paw and Maw clearly took no pleasure in each other's company, but somehow, for Rahoul, they managed to coexist. Deven visited each day, often bringing his young son. Many of Rahoul's friends arrived from across the country with possible miracle cures—wheat grass, aloe vera juice, shark cartilage pills, maitake mushrooms, herbs like cat's claw and pau d'arco. But Rahoul continued to grow weaker and more disoriented. His curly thick hair thinned and hung flat, developing strands of gray.
Sometimes Rahoul was strong enough to get out of bed, and at night he wandered into the basement, perplexed by why he was there. Sometimes he dreamed that he was well and whole, out dancing, and then he woke up, tried to stand, and fell headlong to the floor. During the day, he could still ask that the stereo be blasted with the latest UB40 album,

and he too could bounce into high spirits, joking and teasing. ("*Elates*: to make one go into high spirits, make proud," reads a mysterious entry in his notebook from 1970, I suspect from a time that he was studying SAT vocabulary.)

"Okay, so this is what I want for my ashes," he told us one afternoon when his energy was good. His old mischief glittered on his emaciated face. "I want some ashes given to Young Swamiji to scatter in Patane on a full moon night. I want some stirred into Maw's compost heap so her flowers will bloom. I want to live on in art too, so please ask Nancy if she'll mix some of my ashes into her paints. And Sam in the Catskills: can you send some of my ashes to him? Oh yeah, and . . ."

I went to Berkeley to find a place to live so I could begin writing my dissertation. In my blithe way as youngest, I was used to Maw and Maya taking primary responsibility. While I was gone, Rahoul started going blind—the worst blow so far. He was failing fast and needed to be moved to the hospital. I caught the next flight I could, and Deven picked me up at the Albuquerque airport. Making our way out of the parking lot, we were delayed in a dense snarl of post-Thanksgiving traffic.

Paw met us by the hospital elevator, pipe in hand. "He's gone," said Paw.

Paw led us back into the room and closed the door. Maw and Maya were with Rahoul. He had died a few minutes earlier. His body lay shrunken under a white sheet. His face was blindfolded with white bandages. For his last struggling hours, kind nurses had covered his already unseeing eyes.

We stood around the narrow bed. Six connected bodies—two parents and four siblings—communed; soon there would be just five. We needed a ritual, and as if to invoke Young Swamiji's presence we thought of his goddess hymns. We put some of the goddess-blessed *kumkum* powder sent by Young Swamiji onto Rahoul's forehead, just above the white bandage. His skin was not yet cold.

"We must tie his big toes together," Paw directed. "It keeps the spirit from wandering."

We got some thread from the nurses down the hall, who had made themselves scarce. Very quietly, without conversation, Paw and Maw stood at the end of the hospital bed, binding Rahoul's limp toes. Rahoul's feet were exactly like Paw's, down to the high arches, the scattering of black hair below the toe joints, and the square shape of the nails. I didn't see Maw reflected in Rahoul's body, but he had once lived inside her as surely as Maya, Deven, and I had.

With a coordinated attentiveness I had never seen between them, our parents Narayan and Didi composed the still body they had made thirty-two years earlier.

: : :

"Let me tell you, death is beautiful!" Young Swamiji exclaimed in 1987 when Maw and I visited him in the jungle and he reported how he had narrowly survived a heart attack. We sat in his bedroom, Maw and I on a carpet against one wall, and Young Swamiji cross-legged on a bed pushed against the other wall. As usual, he was wrapped in a hand-dyed ocher cloth, tied behind his neck, leaving his plump arms bare. At my side, Maw was wearing a yellow sari that marked her partial entrance into his order: not as a full-fledged *sannyasi* renunciate who had left all ties behind, but as a celibate *brahmachari* holy mother. I was the only one not in some sort of robes, though around my neck, I displayed the sparkling crystal *mala* that Young Swamiji had given me in my college years: "Just now, it's for decoration. Later on, when you grow older, you can use the *mala,* if you like," he had said nonchalantly. I had just received my Ph.D. and was briefly visiting India before I moved to Vermont for my first teaching job.

Maw began appearing in yellow after she received formal initiation in 1977 as Ma Dayananda Saraswati. Soon after, she was asked to leave the ashram; just when she had committed everything, her many interests and sociability were judged as not fitting the institutional framework. Feeling betrayed and disenchanted, her settlement from Paw dwindling ever further with inflation, in 1978 Maw moved to a ramshackle mud house without running water in a Kangra Valley village at the base of the Himalayan ranges. The village had also attracted an Indian artists' colony, and the adobe and breathtaking mountain views reminded her of Taos. Maw did not visit Ganeshpuri again, and after Babaji died in 1982, Maya and Jonathan also moved away from the ashram.

Young Swamiji remained an honorary family member. "Baba, death is so nice!" he continued. "Maw, now that I've seen it, I tell you, there is nothing to fear. Nothing! Such a lovely light there was, like the light of the sun and moon together. I was moving ahead through this tunnel of light, but then I came to a door and couldn't enter. I was ready to go, but the Boys and the doctors pulled me back."

Just then the intercom phone rang. Young Swamiji reached over, then leaned forward, so he was balancing on his calves and elbows, receiver cradled to his ear. He looked like a crawling baby frozen in motion. Speak-

ing animated Marathi to whichever of the Boys was on the other end of the
line, he gave instructions on how to receive a delegation of visitors.

Maw raised her hands, balancing an imaginary camera.

"Snap," Maw said. The picture is engraved in my mind: slanted natural light, ocher robes, sandalwood skin, warm earth of the wall behind
him, bright woven oranges and blues of the bedspread. Young Swamiji remains poised, warbling instructions, round and adorable as the butter-baby
Krishna.

Maw's old prediction that someday buses would be chartered to visit
Young Swamiji in the jungle had long since come true. After his first cottage shadowing the ancient foundations was taken over by the Archeological Survey of India, he had been granted the use of more Forest Department land and had built two other mud and thatch cottages on the neatly
groomed property. Tides of people now arrived to bow before Maw's huge
painting of the Goddess in the front room where he sat in audience. The
Boys had their own living space behind the front room. Young Swamiji
withdrew to sleep and to meditate in another cottage farther back, in a qui-
eter corner of the property. Just under his bed, he had excavated a small
underground meditation cave where he worshipped a Bengali stone image
of Kali standing on a prone Shiva, her hair flowing and four arms raised in
gestures of blessing and protection.

On a regular day, dozens of people came through Young Swamiji's audience hall; thousands assembled for full moons and other big festivals, like
one he instituted when the Saptashring goddess visited her Patane sister
goddess and another when Old Swamiji was honored. There wasn't enough
water in the valley, and few facilities to accommodate the mass of visitors, so Young Swamiji decided he must move. In 1989, he relocated to a
property along the road to Aurangabad. Drawing on his engineering background, he designed and built his own red-roofed Kali temple and installed
an image similar to the one he had been worshipping in the privacy of his
underground meditation room. Old Swamiji would probably have felt like
a proud parent seeing the younger *sadhu* settled in his own ashram, Kali
Math, but Old Swamiji had died of a heart attack in 1988.

Maw and I visited Kali Math in the winter of 1990. Young Swamiji received us warmly, as a slightly different staff of Boys rushed about with
walkie-talkies in hand. Swamiji was no longer mostly a peasants' guru;
rather, his guru persona had been remade with the bright gloss of middle-
class and upwardly mobile devotees. His disciples included controversial
politicians, and, before relocating, mysterious attempts had been made on

his life; he now moved amid high security. His new ashram was spotlessly clean and organized, with schedules for chanting, hours for visitors, and a guest house where we stayed. He had come a long way from the young *sadhu* who lived in a small, bare room in the temple and told stories at our family dinner table. Maw and I could see that Swamiji's growing fame demanded an institutional structure and a circle of attendants, but we couldn't help feeling disoriented.

Just a few months later, another heart attack claimed Young Swamiji. He died at forty-nine, the last of the three interconnected holy men to whom Rahoul had introduced us: each as unique a presence—blazing, then lingering—as the sun playing over sea and sky on different Juhu evenings.

::::

"I'm scared of dying," Paw sometimes said glumly, from his armchair in the Juhu apartment where he moved after Nani's house was also torn down to make way for a larger building.

"Did I tell you what Young Swamiji said about death?" was my usual response as I looked up from whatever I was doing while visiting with him—writing letters, transcribing tapes, retyping notes. Keeping busy, I found, was my best shield from the force of Paw's despair.

"I can't remember," Paw always said.

Again, I would repeat Young Swamiji's words as I remembered them—the beauty, the tunnel of light, the door. Paw listened, dazed. Sometimes, Young Swamiji's name inspired Paw to trill, *"It's goo-oo-ood."* At other times, Paw rolled a shoulder, then looked back at the television screen. On the wall behind the television was a gift from Swamiji: a large laminated photograph of Patane Devi, resplendent in a red sari, watching over Paw with goddess eyes.

In 1987, Ba had peacefully slipped away during a midmorning nap. Deven had arrived from the United States with his family the night before, and she had just performed a *puja* with her great-grandson to honor having witnessed four generations of men in the same lineage. If Ba had been able to predict her painless death at a moment of fulfillment, she might have once again reminded us of the many blessings she had received during her meetings with gods, goddesses, and holy men.

Paw was devastated. A year later, he went back to beer. Not a lot, but enough to keep reality blurred and money always tight. The availability of growing numbers of television channels offered him additional anesthesia. He lived alone in a Juhu apartment, facing the television screen and rarely going out. New hangers-on periodically swarmed around him, and his properties continued to disappear: land sold, bank accounts emptied, stocks liquidated. Like his caste ancestors who lost their right hands to a king's pride, Paw's strokes reduced his ability to use that hand and he had taken to asking other people to write out his checks and visit the bank for him.

The strong wish to be free from the tides of Paw's raw moods and murky finances had encouraged me—and, I think, my surviving siblings—to seek out careers in America: Maya as a therapist, Deven as an architect, me as a cultural anthropologist. (Tashi had drifted out of our orbit toward his family of birth, and then into a tragic period of addiction and drug dealing, followed by jail time, more addiction, and eventually death due to cirrhosis of the liver.) We knew, given Paw's lack of health insurance and lifetime of being waited on by women and servants, that his living with any of us in the United States would probably not work out. Nor did he want to move from India. And so, always anxious, often guilty, Maya, Deven, and I each traveled to India when we could to continue the old project of trying to rescue our father. Unless one of us gave up our job, we had no choice but to trust a succession of male servants who looked after his daily needs. We could only hope—and pray—that Paw was somehow protected as he handed over his keys, wallet, bank access, and checks to the latest village migrant.

After my first book came out in 1989—an accessible scholarly book based on my dissertation—Paw gave me his vote of confidence as a writer. When I published a novel a few years later, he never once used the term "lady novelist." "You should write a book called *Ramji and Sons*," Paw urged. "It'll be a great family chronicle."

"What about the daughters?" I always responded, simultaneously touched and annoyed, and aware too that I was flatfootedly ignoring his allusion to Dickens's *Dombey and Sons*.

Paw usually shrugged, as if to say, "Well, that's your business."

After an especially severe stroke in spring 2000, Paw needed more specialized care. Maya traveled to India in search of a responsible relative or a reliable old-age home.

"This is the duty of the children," neighbors and friends censoriously said.

Off in the Himalayan foothills, Maw had continued to flourish: dedicating herself to alternative energy projects and architecture using local materials, sending out astrological predictions, meeting new swamis and lamas, and growing new circles of friends. Worried by Paw's decline, Maw offered to have him come live near her. She reminded us that thanks to a charitable clinic run by her Austrian doctor friend, excellent medical care was available in her village. Then too, with all her local contacts from building projects, she was confident that she could find and train helpers to care for Paw.

"It would spare all of you kids from having to worry," Maw generously insisted.

With enormous difficulty, Maya transported Paw across the subcontinent to live in the house beside Maw, and Deven also flew to India. Together, Maya and Deven sorted through family possessions and moved everything out of the Juhu apartment and up to Kangra. Settled into the house next door to Maw, Paw was forced off beer and attended to around the clock by village men glad to have found local employment. From next door, Maw managed his care, meals, medicines, and finances.

I visited with my husband Ken in the summer of 2001 and found my parents living in one place for the first time in twenty-seven years. When I mentioned this aloud, Maw insisted vehemently that I not use the word "parents." "I don't want to be linked with him," she said. "I resent it deeply that you see me as one of a pair of parents. The person whom I remember as your father disappeared during the years in Juhu. He disintegrated and deleted himself. The person I'm looking after is a wreck who was once Narayan, but it isn't him. Just please don't use that word, okay?"

"But Maw, I can't help it, whatever happened and however absent he was, from my perspective, you're both my parents."

"Do please consider me as a separate individual entity," Maw said, voice choking.

"I do," I assured. "I really do. But——"

The debate over my use of the word "parents" continues, even in Maw's comments on this manuscript. Even as I can grasp some of the pain and disappointment of their connection, I can't seem to shed the convention of pairing the two people whose genes and stories twist through me. (Chandaphui's astrologer in Ahmedabad observes, "Your parents did not have a connection of outer, worldly happiness; their connection was for their own inner growth.")

I had brought my mother and my father each a copy of Stephen Mitchell's new English translation of the *Bhagavad Gita*. Paw was still saying that he was scared of death, and the *Bhagavad Gita* assures us that, with death, a body is cast off like a set of old clothes. The shining, imperishable soul remains unruffled through the transition. Paw had no doubt been exposed to these verses even more often than I had, but I hoped that they might have fresh force in a new translation.

Maw paused from loading rice into a black-painted metal dish intended for the solar cooker she had designed using mud, rice husk, old wool, blackened tin cans, and a single sheet of glass. She put on her glasses and leafed through the book. "This is beautiful but doesn't fully get the flavor of the Sanskrit," she announced.

"Since when are you an expert on Sanskrit?" I asked, annoyed.

"I've chanted chapters from the edition that breaks down each word," Maw countered. "Even after I left the ashram I've continued to study these things alone."

In the house next door, Paw shrugged. *"Bhagavad Gita, Dolce Vita,"* he said.

I turned off Paw's endless loop of CNN headlines and bossily read aloud portions of the book. Paw indulged me. But when we came to the sections on doing your duty through work, Paw broke in.

"I've always been so jealous of people who enjoy their work," he said, bloodshot brown eyes meeting mine. "I was never interested in engineering, architecture, any of it."

"What would you have been if you'd had a choice?" I asked, stunned by his frankness. For a flickering moment I wondered how I carried Sethji, the person who forced Paw into the prison of a profession he disliked.

Paw thrust out his lower lip. "Who can say? Who knows why I became a drunkard?"

I waited, hoping he would help me understand the self-destruction that almost crushed all of us whose lives were bound to his. But Paw looked over his shoulder, this way, then that, groping for the television control I had appropriated. "Anyway, now it's all in the past," he said, returning to his anesthesia of images.

Paw died peacefully in Kangra on a cold January morning in 2002. I arrived a few days later from Madison, when his body had already been cremated. Women don't usually go near cremation grounds, but knowing of my anthropological interests, the local men who had looked after Paw invited me to observe the ceremony in which they gathered any portions of bone left behind in the heaps of ash. Sun glinted off the snowy peaks as I followed them down toward the cremation hut adjoining a stream and stood at a distance with my camera. The funeral priest directed the men as they filled buckets from the stream, washed out the ashes from the cremation hut, and carefully assembled all remaining solid fragments of the body they had so recently tended.

Deven arrived from Albuquerque to do the son's ritual of submerging these bones in the swift, icy river Ganga in Hardwar. We spent just a night and a day in Hardwar, then drove through the night to be back for a village-wide feast in Paw's honor. When I developed my roll of film document-ing the cycle of rituals, two pictures stood out. Both were from the bright morning when the men had worked in the cremation shed. In the first pic-ture, a band of rainbow streaks into the shed, ending a few feet above the spot where a body would be placed. In the second, a big, seven-sided ball of light hovers just above that last location occupied by Paw's body before it was returned to the elements.

I wonder: should I see in this play of light a reminder of the quick, hu-morous core that remained bright in Paw despite the darkness that he lived inside? Images and practices offering a glimpse of inner radiance were a cen-tral part of growing up among gurus, urugs, and aspiring saints. Handling these photographs, I am amazed.

But how can I be surprised?

:::

Rahoul's diaries came to live with me about fifteen years after he died. They had been stored in the climate-controlled storage area of a painter friend in Taos, and as that friend grew frail, Maw entrusted the diaries to me as potential "family chronicler." The notebooks sat in an unopened cardboard box in a corner of my study for almost three years before I could bear to open the pages and read at any length.

The diaries are not chronological or complete. Rather they are compen-dia of quickly jotted poems, exhortations for self-discipline, painful things to process, mentions of sexual encounters, notes for film scripts, to-do lists, telephone numbers, and line drawings. Most have scores of blank pages. Rahoul's handwriting cuts jaggedly up and down, deep into the paper. Through all the years that the diaries span—from 1969 to 1984—he often returns to visionary and mystical themes.

Opening at random the gray-checked notebook from the year before he died, I found a scribbled rush of words describing Saptashring Devi, the Goddess of the Seven Horned Mountain. I typed this entry, dated July 21, 1984, in all its rawness, with a sense of revealing something precious and hidden, knowing that Rahoul would probably have preferred to shape his words before they met other readers, yet also sensing that his words—more than mine—conjure him in all his spinning creativity.

> She stands tall and bold.
> Statuesque in the evening sky → a power rock pulling celestial interplanetary magnetism toward her.
> This is the eye of the EARTH.
> Looking with a tearful eye at today and with the other into the infinity that dwarfs men.
> Without knowing I worshipped you, struggling but not following. It is in this degenerated life of desire and pain you have shown your form to me.

Through Rahoul's eyes, I see the Goddess on the rock face of the mountain and want to bend my head, palms joined. I feel Rahoul's seriousness, the intensity that lay just behind all the teasing and jokes. I include these words, and the other excerpts from Rahoul's diaries that I've scattered through this book, with a feeling of humble uncertainty. I hope that my mirror writing, facing backward, adequately reflects glimpses of what was once his present, lived forward.

When I decided to write this book, I knew I should warn my family, starting with Maw.

"Maw, I'm thinking of starting a book about growing up with all the gurus and urugs and everything," I said hesitantly during a phone call to India, my morning tea coinciding with her suppertime.

"Oh boy! Here comes *My Family and Other Saints*," she said, immediately remembering the title I had threatened her with years earlier. "I think that's a great idea. Please do it while I'm alive, okay, so I can add my own version?"

"Well, I've been writing some pieces . . ."

Across oceans, continents, expanses of sky, Maw's voice rose an enthusiastic octave higher. "*It's goo-oo-ood!*" she warbled.

"*It's goo-oo-ood*," I trilled back.

We were quoting Young Swamiji. But dancing in the smiles shaped by that high-pitched voice was the person who had stepped up the pace of our family's quests: restless, playful Rahoul.

Rahoul Contractor, 1953–1985, self-portrait.